The Cultural Life of Money

Culture & Conflict

Edited by
Isabel Capeloa Gil and Catherine Nesci

Volume 6

The Cultural Life of Money

Edited by
Isabel Capeloa Gil and Helena Gonçalves da Silva

DE GRUYTER

ISBN 978-3-11-063454-9
e-ISBN (PDF) 978-3-11-042089-0
e-ISBN (EPUB) 978-3-11-042099-9
ISSN 2194-7104

Library of Congress Cataloging-in-Publication Data
A CIP catalog record for this book has been applied for at the Library of Congress.

Bibliographic information published by the Deutsche Nationalbibliothek
The Deutsche Nationalbibliothek lists this publication in the Deutsche Nationalbibliografie;
detailed bibliographic data are available on the Internet at http://dnb.dnb.de.

© 2018 Walter de Gruyter GmbH, Berlin/Boston
This volume is text- and page-identical with the hardback published in 2015.
Cover image: "Two Dollar Bill" by Andy Warhol, circa 1980.
Printing and binding: CPI books GmbH, Leck

♾ Printed on acid-free paper
Printed in Germany

www.degruyter.com

Table of Contents

IV Cognitive Moneyscapes

Coda: The Art of Giving

Isabel Capeloa Gil
Introduction

On the Cultural Life of Money

"It's just money. It's made up of pieces of paper with pictures on it, just so we don't have to kill each other in order to get something to eat." The claim made by banker John Tuld (Jeremy Irons) in the 2011 trading flick *Margin Call* suggests that money and culture go together. In the rather simple explanation provided by investment banker Tuld, money is nothing but a material icon invested with symbolic power that both structures and is structured by the cultural-economic system of capitalism. The sentence holds a clear and essentialist ring, insinuating an inextricable link between capitalism and the regulatory dimension of normative culture and thereby equating capitalism to the structure that prevents the relapse of mankind into *homo homini lupus* and the violent drive that leads men to act as hungry wolves before other men. Nevertheless, this simplistic connection of capitalism and culture also obscures a narrative affirming that instead of curbing violence, the system itself triggers aggression. In either case, in Tuld's assertion, money, materialized as a piece of paper with iconic value, becomes indistinguishable from the system of culture. The film is thus enlightening for the questions that guide this book.

The Cultural Life of Money aims to understand the manifold ways in which money signifies, produces meaning and impacts on human experience. As the values and the experiences of euro-modernity expanding out across the globe fall under the auspices of the strictures of capitalism, cultural life seems to be deeply entangled with the system of money. One factor the current global financial crisis has taught us, scholars in the humanities and social sciences, is that any understanding of the current state of affairs requires researching the deep entanglement of money and cultural systems and without this informed discussion the flaws will never be mended. This comes across both in the conjuncture ruling over the production of value in economic systems and in the way money shapes social relations and affects discursive practices. As the *Margin Call* quote indicates, money's material life is utterly dependent on its structures of representation. We thus also need to discuss the vocabulary underpinning the rhetoric and then interpret its narratives, be they of crisis, austerity, growth, welfare, neo-liberalism or socialism, in order to understand the cultural life of money and become able to start imagining alternative scenarios.

1 How money shapes cultural theory

In turn, this explains why cultural theory has paid so much attention to the relationship between money and culture. The shift from an idealistic theory of culture as a normative model for intellectual improvement and fostering "sweetness and light," in Matthew Arnold's renowned formula (Arnold 1961), to a perception of culture as lived experience as conveyed by early ethnography[1] served the purposes of a material turn that was to objectify both artifacts and individuals, thus contributing to shape a disciplinary system of knowledge based on the inequality of cultures. While Nietzsche and Freud perceived the work of culture as a mode of repressing the violent drives lurking in the psyche, Marxism envisaged culture as a regulator of the challenges brought about by nature. In Marxist materialism, what gives rise to culture, Terry Eagleton argues, is not the struggle for meaning but need (Eagleton 2000:108). Culture is then shaped by the action of human labor upon nature, defined basically by the investment of bodily force in transforming the conditions of existence. Hence, the force of labor determines human existence, but is itself exploited by the mediation of capital. Money thus intervenes in the action of culture enacted through labor by adding a system of ownership to the structure of exchange mediated by an abstract icon. As Marx writes in the third of his *Economic and Philosophical Manuscripts* (1844) on "The Power of Money": "Money is the procurer between man's need and the object, between his life and his means of life. But that which mediates my life for me, also mediates the existence of other people for me. For me it is the other person." (Marx 3: 322) The theory about the dissolving and alienating power of capital lies at the root of the Marxist critique of political economy. In this discursive economy, money becomes an abstract icon that supports social inequalities and substantiates the domination of one human being by another. Beyond its contribution to overcoming the radical violence that lies at the core of human interaction in unequal natural conditions, money builds a new inequality into the very fabric of culture.

Like Marx, Georg Simmel also traces radical shifts in culture back to the dissolving power of money by underlining the embedding of violence and fascination in the work of money. In *The Philosophy of Money* (1900) [*Philosophie des Geldes*],[2] Simmel portrays the historical and social genealogy of money culture

---

1 See here Tylor (1874), who, in the introduction to *Primitive Culture*, defined culture as "that complex whole which includes knowledge, belief, art, morals, law, custom, and any other capabilities and habits acquired by man as a member of society" (Tylor 2010: 1).

2 See also the earlier studies in "The Psychology of Money" (1889), published initially as "Zur Psychologie des Geldes," *Jahrbuch für Gesetzgebung, Verwaltung und Volkswirtschaft* 13 (1889),

and identifies its embedding in the structure of desire. The debasement of coinage, the introduction of paper money as value backed by simple trust in a government and its national mint, along with the abolition of the gold standard, each represent stages in a progressive refiguration of money from a material mediator for barter and trade into a valueless icon legitimized by symbolic trust. This raises the question of how to represent value when the material denominator clashes with the perceived social evaluation thereof. Simmel's study also discloses the irrationality that underpins the obsession with the accumulation of capital and how this affects the construction of a commodity culture marked by mania. Money culture thereby becomes responsible for a substantial transformation in the perception of culture, namely, the shift from culture as a subjective endeavor based on the advancement of moral knowledge and on technological mastery into an overtly objective culture marked by the emancipation of material objects and their empowerment vis-à-vis disempowered human subjects.[3] This shift involves a contradictory logic as the empowerment of objective culture rests upon the dissolution of the object-like dimension of money into both symbolical and psychological value.

Marx and Simmel drew attention to two major traits of money culture, the first is its contextual dimension or the lack of essentiality in the determination of value, which thus becomes utterly dependent on the social and cultural conditions that surround its use; the second stems from its psychological impact and the irrationality of choice that, because people have a tendency to miscalculate probabilities, ultimately defines the general volatility of the system (Ferguson 2008: 344). As usage of money depends on the fine line between rational choice and irrational hoarding, the system structured upon such recourse to capital proves inherently unstable through its dependence on the unpredictability of human behavior. The psychological hold that, as Elisabeth Bronfen contends, renders money both an alluring fetish and destructive icon in late modern capitalist culture promotes an unlikely alliance between its dreamlike quality and

---

1251–1264; and "Money in Modern Culture" (1896), published as "Das Geld in der modernen Kultur" in *Zeitschrift des Oberschlesischen Berg und Hüttenmännischen Vereins* 35 (1896), 319–324. **3** The emancipation of common objects in aesthetic philosophies around 1900, as in the writings of Arts and Crafts thinker William Morris went hand in hand with a radical critique of material culture. See William Morris, "Art and Its Producers" (1888) or "The Arts and Crafts of Today" (1889). A representative example of the opposite may be found in Hugo von Hofmannsthal's essay "Gabriele d'Annunzio" (1893). Simmel's critique of objective culture is at the root of his critique of the tragedy of culture in "Der Begriff und die Tragödie der Kultur" (1911/12) (Simmel 2000); and "Die Krisis der Kultur" (1916, in Simmel 1999).

the violent collateral damage caused by hazardous investments on the real life of citizens (Bronfen 2008: 65).

As the recent debate surrounding the miscalculations of Harvard economists Carmen Reinhardt and Kenneth Rogoff regarding the impact of austerity policies on debt-ridden economies has demonstrated, spread sheets and numbers do not exist as a pure reality beyond the murky conditions of contextual existence[4] and data sets require articulation from the misty realm of culture. Indeed, the movement to scientify economics, which grew with the establishment of classical economic theories, the drive to distinguish the complex and murky realm of the subjective social sciences and the humanities from the clear, rational, and arguably objective territory of numbers has increasingly become subject to dispute following the rise of the culture paradigm. As the recent austerity crisis has shown, mathematical models are not easily imparted on a cultural reality.[5] This is certainly no novelty, as theoretical physicists like Albert Einstein and Werner Heisenberg[6] had already noted that mathematical language was no different from the symbolical conventions of natural language. Einstein believed numbers to be as much a cultural product and subject to wild motions of interpretation, as the word or any other sign, when he stated that "As far as the laws of mathematics refer to reality, they are not certain; and as far as they are certain, they do not refer to reality" (Einstein 1921:124).[7] More recent ventures into totalizing explanations of the world from the perspective of economics such as the popular book written by the University of Chicago economist Steven Levitt and *New York Times* writer Stephen Dubner, *Freakonomics, A Rogue Economist Explores the Hidden Side of Everything* (2005), also end up unconvincing when applying economic theory to explain fraud in the classroom or demonstrating how sumo wrestlers cheat. Levitt's and Dubner's claim is merely a symptom of the dissemination of economic discourse and its increasing demand to explain other fields of the imagination. The naturalization of the economy in public discourse occurs on several levels, and threatens to essentialize a discursive practice and render it real, objective and mandatory.

---

4 See Reinhardt and Rogoff (2010: 573). On the criticism thereof, see the paper "Does High Public Debt Consistently Stifle Economic Growth? A Critique of Reinhardt and Rogoff" by Herndon et al. (2013) that sets out the coding errors in Reinhatdt's and Rogoff's study.

5 On the culturalization of the austerity debate, see Blyth 2013.

6 See Heisenberg (2003: 36).

7 "Insofern sich die Sätze der Mathematik auf die Wirklichkeit beziehen, sind sie nicht sicher, und insofern sie sicher sind, beziehen sie sich nicht auf die Wirklichkeit." The quote is taken from a speech entitled "Geometrie und Erfahrung" and given at the Königliche Preussische Akademie der Wissenschaften in Berlin in 1921.

The first level occurs with the gluing of money culture to essential nature. As the opening quote from *Margin Call* resoundingly explains, were it not for money, humans would attack each other like wolves. The social construct of money thus gets naturalized into a basic need of human lived experience. This evolutionary drive is not unbeknownst to classical economic theory. Thorstein Veblen applied a similar neo-Darwinist line in an article published in the *Quarterly Journal of Economics*, in 1898, asking "Why is Economics not an Evolutionary Science?" and clearly favored an evolutionary approach on the grounds that markets displayed adaptive behaviors similar to those of humans. The evolutionary drive is also echoed in Joseph Schumpeter's theory of creative destruction as the gales of capitalism and its system of boom and bust are equated with the natural cycles of life. Like the genes for human subjects, consumer goods, new markets and new modes of industrial production also provide the organic tissue that rule the life of capitalism.[8]

Wryly, in 2008, the year Lehman Brothers collapsed, historian Niall Ferguson published *The Ascent of Money*, a historical account of the lives of capitalism that aims to portray the cultural life of money as a new space of natural war. According to Ferguson, "financial history is essentially the result of institutional mutation and natural selection" (Ferguson 2008: 350), a raw space of unheeded competition ruled by an evolutionary process that requires occasional outbursts of destruction. Because "every shock to the financial system must result in casualties" (2008: 357), the space of money is the space of raw competition and war. Instead of struggling to "tame the beast," we instead rather need to understand the "origin of financial species" (2008: 358) and look at the financial markets as

---

[8] In a passage from *Socialism, Capitalism and Democracy*, Schumpeter argues that both industrial capitalism and finance are subject to an evolutionary process: "This evolutionary character [...] is not merely due to the fact that economic life goes on in a social and natural environment that changes and by its change alters the data of economic action; this fact is important and these changes (wars, revolutions and so on) often condition industrial change, but they are not its prime movers. Nor is this quasi-evolutionary character due to quasi-autonomic increases in population and capital or to the vagaries of monetary systems of which exactly the same holds true. The fundamental impulse that sets and keeps the capitalist engine in motion comes from the new consumers' goods, the new methods of production or transportation, the new markets, the new forms of industrial organization that the capitalist enterprise creates [...]. The opening up of new markets, foreign or domestic, and the organizational development from the craft shop and factory to such concerns as US Steel illustrate the same process of industrial mutation – if I may use the biological term – that incessantly revolutionizes the economic structure *from within*, incessantly destroying the old one, incessantly creating a new one. This process of Creative Destruction is the essential fact about capitalism" (Schumpeter 1987: 82–84).

mirrors of a mankind who, in Ferguson's dire analysis, is ruled by basic instincts for blood and destruction.

In this evolutionary rhetoric, the culture of money undergoes transformation into primal nature, a savage space that excludes the intervention of normative action, determined solely by the invisible hand of self-interest. This picture forecloses on the very scope for ethical intervention in capitalism. A shrewd denunciation of the natural competitive nexus of capitalism comes across in Naomi Klein's attack on "disaster capitalism," a radical spin-off that thrives on hazard, natural catastrophe and social upheavals for a highly profitable return on investment (Klein 2007). A sort of capitalism that does indeed thrive on the misfortune of others. In this view, money fosters a culture of violence and certainly does not further the good life.

This process of naturalization also occurs on a discursive level. Angela McRobbie (1994), Fredric Jameson (1991), George Yúdice (2003) and Lawrence Grossberg (2010) have denounced the takeover of the cultural by economic rhetoric that at times has turned culture into mere expedient (Yúdice 2003), a tool to promote global market expansion, while others such as Doreen Massey, Stuart Hall and the signatories of the Kilburn Manifesto (2012) have condemned the colonizing of the imagination by the rhetoric of money. From childrearing to elderly care, from leisure to academia, society seems to have been reduced to "human capital," to an "economy of care," to the "knowledge economy." The vocabulary of money has reclassified roles, identities and relationships, thereby renaming experience and transforming the imagination.

2 Symbolization and fiduciary culture

The productive vocabulary of the economy has also affected the production of knowledge in the humanities and in cultural studies in particular. Traditionally, the relationship has been one of mistrust. In Antiquity, Plato criticized the sophists not only because they took money in exchange for useful words, but also because he saw in the intellectual practice of sophistry an exchange of meaning bordering on the commodity exchange of monetary transactions. Pauline theology is often quoted as the origin of the intellectual abhorrence of money but, in fact, what Paul criticizes in the epistle to Timothy is the excessive love of money which then becomes "the root of all evil" (1 Timothy 6:10). These two brief examples already address some important issues at the root of the, at times, star-crossed relationship between money and the world of culture. Both Einstein's mistrust of numbers and Plato's critique reflect on how at the heart of the relationship between money, economics, language and the world of cultural creation at large lies the issue of symbolization.

Etymology provides insight into the problem. In fact, the Greek etymon *séme* means both word and coin. Marc Shell, in his seminal book *Language, Money and Thought* (1982), shows how deep the relationship between the institution of money as a measure of exchange is linked with cultural issues, from the attribution of a face value to a piece of metal, in the case of the coin, to the brawls and discussions surrounding the introduction of paper money, which was perceived as a virtualization of value, and perhaps not such a different mechanism to that nowadays considered for Linden dollars in the Second Life web platform or for the Bitcoin.

Writers have for long dealt with the representation of money and economic affairs. Not only because many of them, like Edgar Allan Poe and Charles Baudelaire, were afflicted with economic problems, but also because money culture was diagnosed as being at the root of the very structure of symbolization and representation. Aristophanes's *Lysistrata*, for instance, a play about the war of the sexes, also presents a caricature of what happens to *oikonomia*, the tending of the household, when women refuse to manage their homes and families. Literature not only imagines and creates worlds, but also works to suture the gaps in the organization of the social. By drawing on the imagination to come to terms with crises and thus responding to the aporias of historical and ideological reality, the literary is not only a source of understanding of the cultural life of money, but has also contributed to shaping it. One economic paradigm shift was acutely discussed by Shakespeare in *The Merchant of Venice*, a play that sought to come to terms with the changing economic systems of the Renaissance. Furthermore, in part II of *Faust*, particularly in the so-called "Paper Money Scene" (Act I, scene IV), Goethe gave vent to contemporary anxiety over inflation due to the debasement of coinage and the circulation of paper money introduced during the French Revolution. Mephistopheles's introduction of paper money discloses the production of meaning by the systematic use of meaningless signs (*Faust* 2, lines 6085–6174). On a more symbolical note, the structural work of money culture can even be observed in the Prologue in Heaven, in the pact between both God and Mephisto, as well as later between Mephisto and Faust, with Faust's soul as barter icon.

In addition, the fictionality of literature also denounces the fiction of money. As Fernando Pessoa argued in the *conte philosophique* "The Anarchist Banker" (2006: 72), money is the most important social fiction of all. The fiction about the fiction becomes a double negative with an ambivalent reach. Arguably, by vent of its imaginative work, literature works to draw readers to believe in the financial fiction and so much so that they actually forget its fictionality, while simultaneously denouncing money's fictional and dissolving role.

The belief in the narrative of money resonates with its overwhelming performative value as fiduciary fiction supports an economy of meaning that acts on the social and produces change. In point of fact, the performative core has also productively marked the metaphorical repository of economic discourse. This is a pattern traceable back to Xenophon, who in the *Oeconomicus* compared a harmonious choric dance to a well-managed home (*oikos*) and hence to the managerial nexus of society (Oe 8, 21). The Greek historian stressed how harmonious movement endowed the surrounding environment and the setting where the dance took place with beauty and order. Movement hence acquires a demiurgical quality sustaining what Giorgio Agamben calls the "managerial paradigm" (*paradigma gestionale*) (Agamben 2009: 33), or the model of the well-managed space/house/city. In the twentieth century, Frankfurt School theorist Siegfried Kracauer went back to the topic of dance to formulate his critique of capitalist society. In an article published in the *Frankfurter Zeitung* in 1927, he took the Tiller Girls, an English girl troupe from Manchester, which had swept Europe and the US as a storm, as the epitome of the phantom-like dimension of capitalism. In *The Mass Ornament*, Kracauer viewed the synchronic movements of the girls' legs at once as an abstract ornament, a superficial figure, and an unconscious allegory of the tendencies of a particular era and of an economic system that worked to dissolve agency in the cash nexus of mass production. The Tiller Girls' alienated movements represent the principle of capitalist production. The waves and geometrical figures thus created, not only simulate a false organicism, but also mimic taylorization, so that, ultimately, the girl's legs correspond to the hands in the factory (Kracauer 1995: 79). Written before the depression, Kracauer's essay is certainly a product of Weimar culture's critique of capitalism's false organicism and its normative patterns. Although ideologically apart, Kracauer is not so far off from Joseph Schumpeter's cycle theory. What distinguishes the capitalist narrative is precisely its strong, and for Kracauer, annihilating and eventless story.

The changing role of money is then based on cultural perceptions, on acts of value: first, on a cultural-political act that refers to recognizing the status of the institution supporting the currency and affording it value; then, on the acceptance of the currency by those amongst whom it circulates and, finally, on the trust in its face value. Money thus becomes a system of representation underlying discursive practices and shaping both the material way we live as well as the ways in which we make sense of the world.

The active language exchange between the world of the economy and the metaphors we live by is unavoidable in the study of culture and its implication in the politics of articulation between discourse, representation and the manifold economies of meaning they produce. When Pierre Bourdieu speaks of "social, symbolic and cultural capital" (Bourdieu 1986), Lewis Mumford refers to the "linguistic economy of abundance" (1967), Stephen Greenblatt discusses "cultural negotiation," Samuel Weber speaks about the "cult of capitalism" (in the essay opening this volume) and Adorno coins the term "cultural industry," not only does the symbolic exchange between money, language and thought once again become clear, but what these and many other culturally-pervasive terms point out is the fact that the economy is also a practice of discourse that frames the way societies are discursively organized, how they reflect upon their structure and values, which constrain the ways individuals are perceived, see themselves, and deal with others.

Furthermore, despite the consistent efforts to denounce the interpretative subjectivity of discourse in the humanities extending to any affairs pertaining to management and economy, it has become increasingly evident that the skills, the knowledge and, why not, the values cultivated within the complex realm of the non-exact sciences are pivotal both to the ever necessary stress on management ethics, as well as to a convincing mediation of trust in the system. In the end, as recent crises have made clear, more than numbers, it takes ethical values and interpretative, hermeneutical skills to make sense of the quagmire of runaway capitalism.

How much hermeneutical skills were, in fact, urgently needed in the financial world was demonstrated as early as 2001 by journalist Bethany McLean in the pages of *Fortune magazine*. In the March 2001 issue of *Fortune*, McLean, who holds a B.A. in English Literature and worked as an investment banker for Goldman Sachs in the 1990s, published the first article to question Enron's inflated stock price. In this piece, entitled "Is Enron Overpriced?," McLean questioned the "virtuoso performance," the numbers which seemed "impenetrable to outsiders" and resumed the company's performance to the statement that "In the end, it boils down to a question of faith." When she was questioned about the reasons that had led her to warn of Enron's problems, she replied "When you come out of a liberal arts background, you want to know why something is the way it is." And she added "In accounting, there is no reason why. There is no fundamental truth underlying it."

A disclaimer is perhaps here in order. To argue that money and culture go together is not a critique of the science of economics, but rather a claim for a politics of articulation that sees in the economic and financial system we inhabit a culturally-based dimension grounded on the contradictory dimension of money as both material icon and symbol with changing value. Elena Esposito's *The Future of Futures* (2011) is a striking analysis of the paradoxical nexus involved in the deep play between culture, money cultures and the science of economics. And yet, it is deeply entangled in the contradictory logic of the system. While arguing that money works "because it represents a social relation, or because it is a social relation consisting of obligations and claims among the participants in the economy" (Esposito 2011: 51), Esposito claims that money in a modern economy is subsumed into value itself, that is, it has no value but for the worth that others grant it. The Simmelian line is clearly visible here even if the trick of the argument only emerges once time is placed into the equation, a point that also represents the nodal point of Samuel Weber's chapter in this book. Despite the fact that it is so utterly without value, despite the fact that neither the commodity nor the currency have a worth per se, Esposito argues that:

> Because it is abstract and indeterminate, its value remains, even if one waits before spending it. It remains available even when one defers the decision in view of other situations, other partners or different conditions. The meaning and function of money lies in this temporal delay, in the possibility that is offered by money for using time to increase decision and choice options. (Esposito 2011: 62)

The abstract dimension of money renders it an object that is utterly subsumed into its outside. Rhetorically, the face value of money has no identity. Just as a coin or a banknote carry a face that is not the object's own, the value of money is always dependent on the perception of others – be it the market or a certain community. It is an object "utterly without value" (Simmel 2010: 365) that is subsumed into the abstract notion of value itself. In this equation, time does not provide for the materialization of financial worth, it may quite obviously prove the opposite. However, the importance of time lies in the fact that it determines a conjuncture framing the cultural life of money that incorporates the process and the context whereby capital shapes social and cultural life and is in turn defined by the mode of existence within a certain lived cultural environment. The cultural life of money then refers to the process whereby a material icon invested with the symbolical power to rule social exchange, ultimately becomes a discursive practice structuring social and political relations and an explanatory narrative that mediates the way societies produce meaning.

3 Structuring the cultural life of money

This book aims to understand the manifold ways in which money signifies, produces meaning and impacts human experience. No matter how outrageous this claim may be to purists, what the current crisis has taught us is that for once we do need to know just why some things are the way they are. With an interdisciplinary insight spanning a wide range of fields ranging from macro-economic theory and management to theology, philosophy, history, cultural theory and cultural studies, literature, linguistics, communication sciences, cultural management, and film studies, this book discusses the power of art and literature to ask why our economic system is structured the way it is, how it frames the way we make sense of the world and the kind of bartering that structures the relation between culture and money. Over the past decade, the growth of humanities-based cultural economic studies,[9] which have sought to discuss how culture simultaneously shapes and is shaped by the economy (Throsby 2001, Taylor 2004, Grossberg 2010), stems not only from the overwhelming perception that as the song goes "money makes the world go round," but also from the felt need to understand the complex networks of exchange that pervade the web of culture. Moreover, this academic trend is also influenced by the need of the humanities and social sciences to reclaim the economy of culture both as an intellectual project and as lived experience. In this equation, culture is not simply a brand to address yet another externality of the economy, but a project of collective living and individual transformation that acts both on the social and the cultural.

Over the past few years, the world has staggered from one financial crisis to another. Hopping from the sub-prime bubble to the 2008 crash and banking crisis, and from the European debt crisis and the austerity mantra to the ultimate declaration of city bankruptcy in Detroit, the neat disciplinary separation of economics and culture has been consistently challenged. To understand the current state of affairs, we need to understand the cultural life of money, the conjuncture that rules the production of value in economic systems, how money shapes social relations and affects discursive practices. Only thus, by discussing the vocabulary, by understanding the rhetoric and interpreting the narratives, be it of crisis, austerity, growth, welfare, neo-liberalism or socialism, may we otherwise begin imagining the cultural life of money. As Doreen Massey contends:

> We should be thinking of the economy not in terms of natural force and intervention but in terms of a whole variety of social relations that need some kind of coordination. Each form of social relation has its own characteristics and implications, and thus appropriateness to different parts of the economy and society. Above all, we need to bring the "economic" back into society and into political contention, not just as debates about economic policy, but questioning also the very way we think about the economy in the first place. (Massey 2013: 16)

---

9 See below the chapters by Goggin, Santos and Abrantes for a further mapping of cultural economic studies.

The aim to put culture back at the center of the economy that grounds this collection of essays began in 2009, as the waves of the 2008 market crash were rocking the foundations of the global financial system and a research project was triggered by a conference hosted by the Research Centre for Communication and Culture at the Faculty of Human Sciences of the Catholic University in Lisbon, titled 'The Cultural Life of Money'. Its main intent was to bring together interdisciplinary contributions that would tackle diverse economies of meaning underpinning the constraints and the possibilities of money culture. A strategic grant from the National Foundation for Science and Technology (FCT) enabled the coming together of a remarkable group of scholars to discuss the predicaments of the cultural life of money over two days.[10]

As then argued, though this conference was not primordially motivated by the crisis discourse surrounding capitalism, it would unavoidably be dealing with it. Clearly, conjunctures find a way into the shaping of research interests and hence, though the reasons behind this venture did not directly emerge out of an instrumental perspective, the fact of the matter is that the sense of discomfort generated by changing social conditions and the lived reality of the narratives of crisis in Portugal and Europe have certainly contributed to further the visceral relevance of this theme.

The 2008 crash and the ensuing sovereign debt crisis plaguing European economies have inspired popular culture to address the facts and the fiction of money culture. The stream of trading flicks of the *Wall Street* saga type has increased[11] and was joined by *Margin Call* (dir. J.C. Chandor 2011), *Limitless* (dir. Neil Burger 2011), *Bailout: The Age of Greed* (dir. Uwe Boll 2013), *Too Big to Fail* (dir. Curtis Hanson 2011) and *The Wolf of Wall Street* (dir. Martin Scorsese 2013). At the same time, denunciatory documentaries have also mushroomed as the tragedy of money gained momentum.[12] The glitter and the tragedy of the ownership of money, the irrational mania that according to Simmel renders humans comparable to hamsters (Simmel 1997: 235), are powerful drivers of representation and have pervaded high and low culture, philosophical and literary reflections and popular entertainment alike.

The Cultural Life of Money brings together a scholarly collection of essays discussing the role played by money and the economy in the self-fashioning of soci-

---

10 Special thanks are due to Madalena Torres and Board Member Mr. Joaquim Goes at BES without whose support the event would not have been possible. A special word of thanks is due for the opening up of the BESArt Collection and providing a special visit for all event participants.
11 The 1987 film had a sequel, *Wall Street. Money Never Sleeps*, in 2010.
12 See *Enron. The Smartest Guys in the Room* (dir. Alex Gibney 2005), *Capitalism: A Love Story* (dir. Michael Moore 2009) or *Inside Job* (dir. Charles Ferguson 2010).

eties and individuals. The studies focus on money as a signifier drawing meaning from context, as a discursive practice that structures social relations and a narrative that is backed by the trust in the economic-cultural system of capitalism. The first section, entitled "Philosophies of Money," brings together four contributions that substantiate seminal academic discourses in the cultural study of money. While Samuel Weber addresses the nexus that foregrounds the pervasiveness of a certain theological economy and its remnants in the current debate surrounding the sovereign debt crisis in Southern Europe, economist João César das Neves resorts to the earliest treatises of economics to demonstrate the resilience of a discourse of crisis, of desire and catastrophe, cheating and condemnation that ultimately responds to the sole stable indicator in the long process of capitalism: human behavior. However, despite the common genealogical approach, Weber and Neves could not formulate their concerns from more disparate positions as the former underlines stability to challenge naturalcy while the latter emphasizes change to conclude for normalcy. From political philosophy, economic history and cultural theory we come to cognitive narratology as Ansgar Nünning insightfully discusses how metaphors shape the way we think about reality and work to naturalize it, contributing to imagine the world in normative and non-normative ways and ultimately determining distinct money cultures.

Samuel Weber's "Money is Time. Thoughts on Credit and Crisis" draws on Benjamin Franklin's letter of advice to a young tradesman as the starting point for a judicious argument on the nexus articulating money, time and credit and the theological economy substantiating belief in capitalism. As an (in)valuable sign, money presupposes a temporal process to be invested with meaning that in this economy necessarily means a return on investment. In an uncanny doubling, the future of money is epitomized in different futures. Thus, this theological investment in a time to be, the structural delay at work in capitalism, brings it close to the logic of religious salvation and its investment in an afterlife of plenitude, which in the material conditions of finance means profit. This "'way to riches' via 'the way to the market' ultimately expresses the effort of capitalism to make good on the redemptive promise of Christianity." Here, Benjaminian Weber seems to solve the aporia denounced by the other Benjamin, Walter, who in the fragment "Capitalism as religion" (1921) argued that capitalism is indeed a guilt-inducing cult that does not aim at salvation but rather damns believers to eternal blame (Benjamin 1991: VI, 100). Clearly, like the two Benjamins, Marx and Weber have both later conveyed how the connection between capitalism and religion has been consistently influential in modern philosophical thinking on the economy. Nevertheless, arguments that ground the religious turn in the current wave of capitalism even though harking back to past rhetoric do indeed present different and more coeval challenges while also reflecting distinct theological strands of Christianity. As Hannah Rosin wrote in a 2009 article for *The Atlantic Monthly*, the prosperity Gospel that lies at the root of a certain protestant ethic[13] joined hands with a gambling, speculative wager on the casino economy in order to create the American brand of financial capitalism, which always bets on the unheard blessing of the next wager even despite the obvious failure to pay-off in the meanwhile (Rosin 2009). This particular strand of evangelical capitalism has strayed beyond the American borders and is arguably at work in the environment of the European sovereign debt crisis.

In "Money: From Midas to Madoff," economist João César das Neves undertakes a genealogy of the theory of economics and points out the ambiguity that lies at the core of money, whose value(less) dimension is increased by an inbred speculative volition. Resorting to Aristotle, César das Neves distinguishes two different dimensions in the cultural life of money: the *oikonomikê*, pertaining to a natural-way of wealth production, and the *chrematistikê*, the unnatural kind of wealth accumulation. King Midas and Bernard Madoff represent two figurations of this inescapable duality that lies at the core of a money culture, which certain neo-classical economic theories dauntingly naturalize.

Why do money narratives, metaphors and images play such an important role in the self-identification of societies and individuals? In "Metaphors We Pay For, or: Metaphors of the 'Financial Crisis' Shaping the Cultural Life of Money," Ansgar Nünning argues that metaphors act as cognitive mediators instilling a way of world-seeing that conditions the ways in which we produce meaning. Nünning examines various metaphors of crisis in order to understand the crucial role they play in the political and economic discourse of exception. Metaphors "not only serve as means of structuring, narrativizing and naturalizing cultural transformations, they are also important sense- and indeed world-making devices." Providing an insightful analysis of key money culture metaphors – such as "time is money," "business is a game" or "money is the lifeblood of the economy" – the article demonstrates that these metaphors "naturalize" financial crises and are strategically deployed so as to instill politically and ideologically charged narratives.

In his *Philosophy of Money*, Georg Simmel claimed that there was a strange pleasure in the ownership or in the anticipation of the ownership of money,

---

13 This is of course the Weberian take on the link between capitalism and protestant ethics, a point made in his 1905 work *The Protestant Ethic and the Spirit of Capitalism*. More recently, Jackson Lears distinguishes two different figurations of the American dream, one the Protestant myth of the self-made man, a hard-working character that thrives through labor, whereas the second figuration is that of a "speculative confidence man," as Lears calls him, who prefers "risky ventures in real estate," and a more "fluid, mobile democracy" (Lears 2003: 2–3).

which he compared to aesthetic pleasure in that it permitted consciousness a free play and the incorporation of all possibilities of wealth without any connection to reality. The symbolic exchange between money and aesthetic pleasure as well as, on a more material note, the value of and the role played by art investment in the contemporary financial world is discussed in the second part of the book, "The Arts and Finance."

In "Death and Diamonds: Art and Finance," Joyce Goggin discusses the riveting relation between art and the financial world. Despite the split ways which according to highbrow academic discourse distinguished the path of aesthetics from that of finance in late eighteenth century, a latent practice of unconfessed seduction was taking place between the two spheres as Hoggarth's example tellingly reveals. In fact, Goggin draws on the apparently insoluble aporia between the valuelessness of art and the use-value of money to suggest that in the end it is money, and what others have called its dissolving Midas-like effect transforming everything it touches, that ultimately colonizes the very definition of the aesthetic. As with Damien Hirst's diamond skull, originality and aesthetic value have indeed been subsumed, under the industrial mode of production, into re-producibility and marketability. So much so, that even death is rendered the alluring trope of a new aesthetics.

The question of counterfeiting is at the center of Márcio Seligmann Silva's tackling of art's ability to produce meaning otherwise. In "Art and Its Potentialities," he takes an in-depth look at Baudelaire's famous prose poem "La fausse monnaie," arguing for art's economic potential in the reshaping of the subject before the overwhelming virtualization of the real that lies at the root of speculative capitalism. Following a logic that Walter Benjamin theorized in his essay on mechanical reproducibility in late modernity, art renegotiates the shift from cult value to exhibition, by enacting a re-turn of its cultic dimension and paying virtual tribute to the new divinity of the market.

Alfred Opitz's† chapter, "The Magic Triangle: Considerations on Money, Art and S***," tackles the role of the abject in the contemporary art system. Opitz traces the origins of the obsession with bodily discharges to a time long before the Whitney Museum, in 1993, brought the work of artists Andrés Serrano, Louise Bourgeois or even Joseph Beuys together under the heading "Abject Art Movement." From a systemic perspective, the author inspects the negotiations between the non-symbolic represented by excrement, the aesthetic and the art market, suggesting that the magic triangle seeks to respond to the basic anthropological drive to equate the transcendence of the symbolic with the basic, dirtiness of human existence.

Titled 'Literature and Money Matters', the next section brings together a set of articles reflecting on how literature matters for fiduciary culture and deals with the gales of capitalist crises. Drawing on Marx, Simmel and Walter Benjamin, the authors address the long cascade that, sweeping from modernity into postmodernity, engagingly discloses the emergence of a cultural discourse of crisis that is deeply entangled with the work of capitalism. From Thomas Mann and Brazilian Aluísio Azevedo to Martin Amis and Juli Zeh, the novels discussed in these chapters present an imaginary cartography of economic evil while using the singularity of literary aesthetics to convey modern literature's seismic ability to make sense of the pitfalls of valueless money and its impact on lived experience.

Paulo de Medeiros opens the section with an essay on counterfeits in modernist fiction and postmodernist art to conclude that the narrative of Euro modernity has blurred the limits between actuality and spectrality thus revealing the counterfeit as a reality without existence while disclosing real money's phantom-like dimension. Medeiros refers to postmodern art and modernist prose fiction to shed light on counterfeiting as a representational strategy for dealing with the challenges of capitalism. Counterfeit money could not be a more fitting postmodernist pun on the blurring of boundaries, on the radical critique of fixed ontologies and on the postmodern drive to essentialize fake and raise it to the euphoric status of the new real. Modernist prose, nonetheless, seismically diagnosed the hollow signification of an economic system that was to become the other face of the project of euro-modernity. Baudelaire's play on false money, as Pessoa's ambivalent equating of the virtuous individual with the confidence man, represent the anxieties before a system that is perceived as unreal, while simultaneously revealing the two-sides of self-interest that support the structure of money culture.

The collusion between the creative uselessness of art and the normative institutionalization of bourgeois modernity is the topic of Teresa Seruya's and Helena Gonçalves Silva's discussion of Thomas Mann's *Buddenbrooks* and Martin Amis's *Money*. The grand family saga *Buddenbrooks* seismically speaks to the contradictions of capitalist modernity. It addresses the tension between artistic *ennui*, the strenuousness of labor and the commodification of literature, with which writers were struggling to come to terms with. Almost a century apart, Mann's and Amis's novels tellingly narrate the aporias of the relationship between culture and money, questioning in fact the very possibility of a stable cultural life of money, which is more often than not figured as a pathological relation, marked by miserliness or hoarding, greed or waste. Money seems to provoke a primordial disruption in the characters in a regression to a state of irrationality. Indeed, in the oxymoron of modernity as Vivaldo Santos's discussion of Brazilian writer Aluísio Azevedo suggests, the mirror the usage of money raises to the modern subject destroys the very promise of civilized modernity. Then again, through boredom or violence, as Filomena Viana Guarda contends in her discussion of Juli Zeh's novel about the Third Balkan War, the structure of capitalism cuts across the tissue of enlightened culture. What literature suggests with these examples is the latent enmity between the order of capital and the order of culture. In a reversion of sorts, money is now emplaced as the savage violent nature that literature's regulatory creativity works to curfew.

But why do we spend money? And why do we believe in the value of money? Thus far, the arguments have clearly made the case for a conjuncture, for culture rather than nature. The fourth part of the collection of essays, however, brings a new note into the argumentative stream. In the section entitled "Cognitive Moneyscapes," three articles come to terms with the cognitive angle in the cultural life of money. Ana Margarida Abrantes's essay, "Cognitive Science and How We Think About Money," argues that money is a representation established and maintained by social cognition. Mapping the potential scope of the emerging field of neuroeconomics, Abrantes defends the neurobiological foundations of economic behavior. Though contending that what the mind does is structured by a collective synergy, defined as culture, Abrantes places the naturalization of economic discourse back at the center of intellectual concerns. Furthermore, although the psychological argument about what drives individuals to spend money, risk losing it, develop an overwhelming desire for money hoarding, or believe in a system that is structured to fail systematically, is not a novelty – Simmel for one placed it at the center of his philosophy of money – , what the cognitive approach provides is a new (or recycled) evolutionary approach to money culture as it looks to the brain as a source of understanding for the large scale challenges to the economy.

Vera Nünning furthers the argument in her discussion of the novel *Kept*, which she considers as a "thought experiment" about the ways in which literary narratological strategies provide insight into why money matters in our societies. Albeit virtually, as all fiction does, the novel by D. J. Taylor stages exemplary money usage, images and practices that promote either normative or transgressive behavior (robbery) and by so doing strengthen the laws that rule the social order. However, Nünning concludes that while fictions of money, considered as literary thought experiments, do not allow for conclusive deductions, they certainly do suggest the possibility of imagining the world otherwise.

This is precisely the driver behind the tri-dimensional platform *Second Life*, the possibility of imagining a second life, otherwise. Cátia Ferreira's study looks into the ways in which *Second Life* creates a moneyscape that is strucutured by the logics and modes of value production of capitalism while simultaneously introducing the possibility of an alternative virtual economy. This new *produsage* stems from the digital use of content by first-life residents and affords for the emergence of an alternative social dimension where money has the potential to matter differently. The growth of this virtual economic system takes the abstraction of money to entirely different heights and its impact on the real economy is yet another stage in the material decoupling of money.

And is not the ultimate decoupling that of the gift? The closing chapter in *The Cultural Life of Money* is dedicated to philanthropy. Emílio Rui Vilar, former president of the Gulbenkian Foundation, maps the western roots of the philanthropic project and makes a case for philanthropy as a strategy of social and individual responsibility towards society. Philanthropy rises above the strict moral imperative to become a recurring action in the daily strengthening of the social contract. The article ends on a felicitous note: "It is a common belief that money cannot buy happiness, but the money of a few, if well spent, can surely contribute to the happiness of many." In our current predicaments, this is not yet the solution, but it is certainly worth the try.

Works cited

Agamben, Giorgio (2009) *Il regno e la gloria. Per una genealogia teologica dell'economia e del governo* (Milan: Neri Pozza).

Arnold, Matthew (1961) *Culture and Anarchy* (Cambridge: Cambridge University Press).

Benjamin, Walter (1991) *Gesammelte Werke*, vol. VI, ed. Hermann Schweppenhäuser (Frankfurt am Main: Suhrkamp Verlag).

Bennett, Tony, Lawrence Grossberg, and Meaghan Morris (eds) (2005) *New Keywords. A Revised Vocabulary of Culture and Society* (Oxford: Blackwell).

Blyth, Mark (2013) *Austerity: The History of a Dangerous Idea* (Oxford: Oxford University Press).

Bourdieu, Pierre (1986) "The Forms of Capital," in *Handbook of Theory and Research for the Sociology of Education*, ed. J. Richardson (New York: Greenwood), 241–258.

Bronfen, Elisabeth (2008) "The violence of money *Revista de Comunicação e Cultura* 6, 53–66.

Eagleton, Terry (2000) *The Idea of Culture* (Oxford: Blackwell).

Einstein, Albert (1921) *Geometrie und Erfahrung* (Berlin: Springer/Preussische Akademie der Wissenschaften).

Esposito, Elena (2011) *The Future of Futures. The Time of Money in Financing and Society* (Northampton: Edward Elgar).

Ferguson, Niall (2008) *The Ascent of Money* (London: Allen Lane).

Frisby, David and Mike Featherstone (eds) (1997) *Simmel on Culture* (London: Sage).

Gil, Isabel Capeloa (2013) "The Risk Doctrine. On Money Uncertainty and Literature," in *Literatur als Wagnis/Literature as Risk*, ed. Monika Schmitz-Emans (Berlin, New York: De Gruyter), 267–289.

Goethe, Johann Wolfgang (1962) *Faust*, trans. Walter Kaufmann (New York: Anchor Books).

Grossberg, Lawrence (2010) *Cultural Studies in the Future Tense* (Durham: Duke University Press).

Herndon, Thomas, Michael Ash and Robert Pollin (April 2013) "Does High Public Debt Consistently Stifle Economic Growth? A Critique of Reinhardt and Rogoff." <http://www.peri.umass.edu/fileadmin/pdf/working_papers/working_papers_301–350/WP322.pdf> (accessed 8 October 2014).

Heisenberg, Werner (2003) *Quantentheorie und Philosophie* (Stuttgart: Berlin).

Jameson, Fredric (1991) *Postmodernism, or, The Cultural Logic of Late Capitalism* (Durham: Duke University Press).

Klein, Naomi (2007) *The Shock Doctrine: The Rise of Disaster Capitalism* (New York: Picador).

Kracauer, Siegfried (1995) *Mass Ornament: Weimar Essays*, trans., ed. and introd. Thomas Y. Levin (Cambridge, Mass.: Harvard UP).

Lears, Jackson (2003) *Something Like Nothing. Luck in America* (New York: Viking).

Levitt, Stephen and Stephen Dubner (2005) *Freakonomics. A Rogue Economist Explores the Hidden Side of Everything* (New York: William Morrow).

Marx, Karl (2001) *Economic and Philosophic Manuscripts of 1844*, trans. Karen Mulligan (New York: Prometheus Books).

Massey, Doreen (2013) "Vocabularies of the Economy in *After neoliberalism ? The Kilburn Manifest,* by Stuart Hall, Doreen Massey and Michael Rustin, *Soundings. A Journal of Politics and Culture*, 1–17. <http://www.lwbooks.co.uk/journals/soundings/pdfs/Vocab ularies%20of%20the%20economy.pdf> (accessed 12 December 2013).

McRobbie, Angela (1994) *Postmodernism and Popular Culture* (London: Routledge).

Mumford, Lewis (1967) *The Myth of the Machine. Technics and Human Development* (New York: Mariner Books).

Pessoa, Fernando (2006) *Prosa publicada em vida*, ed. Richard Zenith (Lisboa: Assírio e Alvim).

Reinhart, Carmen M. and Kenneth S. Rogoff (2010) "Growth in a Time of Debt," *American Economic Review* 100.2, 573–578.

Rosin, Hannah (2009) "Did Christianity Cause the Crash?," *The Atlantic*, December 2009. <http://www.theatlantic.com/magazine/archive/2009/12/did-christianity-cause-the-crash/307764/> (accessed 8 August 2013).

Schumpeter, Joseph (2010) *Capitalism Socialism and Democracy* (New York: Martino Fine Books).

Shell, Marc (1993) *Money Language and Thought* (Baltimore and London: The Johns Hopkins University Press).

Simmel, Georg (1999) *Der Krieg und die geistigen Entscheidungen. Grundfragen der Soziologie. Vom Wesen des historischen Verstehen. Der Konflikt der Modernen Kultur Lebensanschauung*, in *Gesamtausgabe*, vol. XVI, ed. Gregor Fitzi and Otthein Rammstedt (Frankfurt am Main: Suhrkamp).

Simmel, Georg (2009 [1900]) *Philosophie des Geldes* (Köln: Anaconda).

Taylor, Mark C. (2004) *Confidence Games. Money and Markets in a World Without Redemption* (Chicago: University of Chicago Press). (1999) *The New Jerusalem Bible* (Standard Edition) (New York: Doubleday).

Throsby, David (2001) *Economics and Culture* (Cambridge, UK, and NY: Cambridge University Press).

Tylor, E.B. (2010 [1871]) *Primitive Culture Researches into the Development of Mythology, Philosophy, Religion, Art, and Custom* (Cambridge: Cambridge University Press).

Veblen, Thorstein (1898) "Why is Economics not an Evolutionary Science?," *Quarterly Journal of Economics* 12, 373–397. <http://socserv2.mcmaster.ca/~econ/ugcm/3ll3/veblen/econe vol.txt> (accessed 8 October 2013).

Yúdice, George (2003) *The Expendiency of Culture: Uses of Culture in the Global Era* (Durham: Duke University Press).

I Philosophies of Money

Samuel Weber
Money is Time:
Thoughts on Credit and Crisis

1

Although the precise origin of the phrase "Time is Money" is difficult to determine, it was Benjamin Franklin who popularized the phrase in his "Advice to
a Young Tradesman, Written by an Old One" (21 July 1748).[1] What has been
less well remembered than the phrase itself, however, is the word he used in introducing it: the advice that this "old" Tradesman gave to his "young" interloc-
utor began with an admonition to "remember"– indeed, with a series of such ad-
monitions. The first was to "Remember that Time is Money." Both the title of his
essay, defining it as "advice" given by an "old" tradesman to a "young" one, and
the admonition to remember – repeated six times at the start of the essay – suggest that a certain experience of "time" was already informing Franklin's letter
even before it began with its famous formulation, equating it with money. For
time is already at work in Franklin's title, distinguishing the "Young Tradesman"
from the "Old One." And a certain experience of time already shaped the manner
in which Benjamin Franklin introduces each of the bits of advice he gives to the
Young Tradesman. He begins each admonition by urging his reader to "remember" what he is about to say – a gesture that qualifies his advice as something
that was perhaps once known, but that with the passage of time could easily
have been forgotten.

Even before he begins by identifying time with money, time is, at it were,
lurking in the background and calling the shots, both as the condition of the experience that the older man is about to share with the younger one – as the condition of knowledge – but also as that which brings with it the possibility of such
experience and knowledge being forgotten or ignored.

Franklin's manner of giving advice thus suggests that time has a double face
and a contradictory function. It can be both productive and destructive; it can

---

1 Franklin's letter was the object of a detailed commentary in Max Weber's study of *The Protestant Ethic and the Spirit of Capitalism*. The following essay can be considered as a supple-
mentary consideration of Franklin's text, following the suggestive fragment of Walter Benjamin
on "Capitalism as Religion" (Benjamin 1996: 288 – 291), in which Benjamin argued that through
its internal structure capitalism is not merely promoted by Protestantism but is the heir to
Christianity as such.

both take away and bring back. It is the dual, and indeed contradictory (if not dialectical) potential of time that sets the scene for the advice that Franklin will give to the young Tradesman. Its essence or upshot will consist in the admonition, made explicit at the end of the letter, not to allow time to go to "waste." Time, which in a certain sense itself establishes the possibility of waste, should not itself be wasted. For to waste time is to waste money, and, as Franklin concludes, "The Way to Wealth, if you so desire it, is as plain as the Way to Market [...] waste neither Time nor Money, but make the best Use of both." (Franklin 1748)

To not waste time, to diminish its destructive character and to augment its productive potential, is here equated with the accumulation of wealth: to be wealthy is thus in a certain sense to overcome the destructiveness of time. But if the "way to wealth [...] is as plain as the way to market," then the adage for which this essay of Franklin's will be remembered, "Time is Money," tells only half the story. For if wealth is acquired through the way to the market, it is not only time that is money, but money, as that which opens the way to the market, which is also and necessarily time. More precisely, money, like the market itself, presupposes a temporal process. Money, like buying and selling, takes time. For the exchange of goods is never simply instantaneous. Exchange is a process that takes time, even where money is not yet involved, as with the bartering of goods. Once, however, money has entered the picture, the temporality of the process of exchange grows ever more manifest. And since the exchange of goods for money is part of a process of circulation that at some point entails the reconversion of money into goods, money also takes time, is involved in time and indeed, can also be converted into time. But it is not just the fact that money takes time, or that it can buy time – for instance, time free from work or the time of an extended life span – that justifies the inversion of Franklin's adage.

Rather, it is the fact that money, which, as a medium of circulation, is already oriented toward the future, necessarily entails some sort of credit, in regard to which the temporal dimension is constitutive and irreducible. Money necessarily entails credit because its "value" is never simply intrinsic to its simple being, to the fact of its mere possession; its value realizes itself in the future, when it will be put to use as a means or medium of exchange. It is thus no accident that Franklin's second "reminder" to the Young Tradesman concerns credit and its relation to money: "Remember, that credit is money. If a man lets his money lie in my hands after it is due, he gives me the interest, or as much I can make of it during that time. This amounts to a considerable sum, where a man has good and large credit [...]." (Franklin 1748)

Time is money not just in the sense of being the medium of circulation and the measure of value, but also because of a very peculiar quality of money, which allows it to mimic a characteristic otherwise associated with living beings: that of self-production and reproduction. This constitutes Franklin's third reminder to the young tradesman:

> Remember, that money is of a prolific, generating nature. Money can beget money, and its offspring can beget more, and so on. Five shillings turned is six, turned again it is seven and three-pence, and so on till it become an hundred pounds. The more there is of it, the more it produces every turning, so that the profits rise quicker and quicker [...]. (Franklin 1748)

I interrupt Ben Franklin's portrayal of money in mid-sentence, at a crucial, indeed as we shall see below, at a critical turning point. But before we proceed, let us just take note of how money is portrayed here as a special kind of living entity: one capable of reproducing and augmenting itself apparently without end or limit: "The more there is of it, the more it produces every turning, so that the profits rise quicker and quicker..." Sounds familiar? Well, the continuation and completion of the sentence my citation has interrupted sounds not just familiar, but uncannily so. This is how Franklin concludes his encomium to money and thereby completes what Grammarians might call a run-on sentence: "[...] so that profits rise quicker and quicker, he that kills a breeding sow, destroys all her offspring to the thousandth generation. He that murders a crown, destroys all that it might have produced." (Franklin 1748)

Money, thus described, appears as an uncanny double not just of living beings but of the deity: with living beings it shares their reproducibility, but with the deity it shares the lack of limit – i.e. a certain immortality. However, this is not the way Franklin expresses the idea. Rather, in a single, long, run-on sentence, he "turns" from the unlimited self-reproduction as the growth of "profits" to death as the result of willful killing: "He that kills a breeding sow" robs her forever of the ability to reproduce, and the same with anyone who "murders a crown [...]." (Franklin 1748) The "crown" in question is of course, not the monarch but the designation of a currency unit. However, the naming of currency units after the symbol of political sovereignty suggests an analogy between the survival of the monarchy and the ability of money to reproduce and multiply. This analogy distinguishes both money and monarchy from the limited life span of individual living beings.

Thus, Franklin's identification of time with money, of money with profit, and of profit with wealth, assumes a very particular connotation: the possibility of overcoming the finitude and mortality that otherwise limits the time of living beings qua individuals, through the unlimited reproducibility associated with profit-producing wealth. What proves important here is the fact that reproducibility, as Franklin describes it with respect to money, entails not just reproduction but expanded reproduction. The circulation of money as credit yields interest: it returns not just the same but rather more of the same, the same as more of itself.

When Franklin therefore asserts – reasserts, since he did not invent the proverb, but merely recalled it – that "time is money," he turns time into a sub-species of the Self; he transforms it from a medium of alterability into a medium of self-fulfillment and self-aggrandizement, a medium through which the self-same – the private individual – reproduces and expands itself as "profit": as that which "moves forward" – a major buzzword today, whether in political, commercial or ethical discourses – in the effort to maximize itself. Credit, as the generator of profit, is thus situated squarely within what might be called an "economy of the self" understood as both private and as individual, which is to say: ultimately in-divisible and homogeneous.

Nevertheless, if time is money, it is only because money, in its turn, is also time – and this poses a problem for interpretations such as that of Franklin. For time is ambiguous. It appears as the condition of an Economy of Self-fulfillment, but it is also the medium that condemns the Self to disappear, at least qua private individual. And this perspective of the private individual informs all of Franklin's discourse. It is a perspective that reflects the heritage of the Reformation in all of its ambivalence. This ambivalence can be retraced to the convergence and confusion of the categories of the "individual" and the "singular". The "singular individual" constitutes the distinctively "Protestant" dimension of the Reformation, which transfers the Good News of the Gospels from the rites administered collectively by a universal church to the faith experienced by the private individual. "Faith alone" and not "good works" is declared to be the path to grace and salvation. But this "aloneness" of both faith and its bearer or vehicle, the single individual, remains situated within the horizon of sin, guilt and redemption. And it is this horizon, common both to the Reformation and to the Catholic Tradition it seeks to reform, that subordinates the moment of what might be described as differential singularity – which is radically relational and heterogeneous – to that of an appropriative individualism that insists on the ultimate homogeneity and indivisibility of "man". As fallen, sinful and guilty, the individual is mortal and finite; but as redeemable that same individual can become immortal and participate in the infinitude of the divine. In his Leviathan, Hobbes quotes St. Paul to this effect (I. Cor. 15. 21, 22): "For since by man came death, by man came also the resurrection of the dead."

To be sure, the resurrection of the dead will not of course take place as such on this earth. But something analogous to an earthly resurrection can be imagined, and it is precisely the production of profit through credit, the production of value through capital, the production of money through the circulation of money. This circulation is not simply the "good works" of man: it involves the "faith" that Luther insisted was the sole path to grace. But it is faith in the potential of debt to redeem the mortal consequences of sinful guilt. In this perspective, Calvinism could regard success in business and the accumulation of worldly wealth as a sign of election. Although Calvin thereby rehabilitates a certain kind of "good works" as having redemptive value, the ensuing fascination with credit as producer of profit locates the production of wealth, and hence of grace, in the sphere of "circulation" rather than in that of "production" or of work per se.

Thus, the emphasis can easily be shifted from the production of goods – what today is referred to as the "real economy" – to the circulation of financial objects, such as derivatives, credit and interest swaps etc., speculating on time and the future – referred to as the "virtual economy" – that tends to become the standard of value in so-called advanced capitalist societies. However, although this tendency is still far from dominant in the eighteenth century, the contemporary effort to separate "real" from "virtual" economies (in German this will come to be known as the distinction between "schaffendem" and "raffendem" capital) is already called into question by Benjamin Franklin's emphasis on the interrelatedness of credit and work, i.e. of circulation and production. The religious traditions condemning certain forms of usury are modified by Franklin's advice to use credit wisely as a path to wealth. And, as already mentioned, his description of the ability of money to proliferate and grow tends to invest it with a form of life that allows it to appear as a secular correlative of Grace, rather than as the work of the Devil. Conversely, Franklin's surprisingly ungrammatical invocation of "he who kills the breeding Sow" (today more likely to be called the "cash cow"), and who thereby "destroys all her Offspring to the thousandth Generation," uses the same vitalist analogy to justify the use of credit. In short, for Franklin the refusal to use money to make money through credit and debt is tantamount to a crime against life itself, defined as the ability of individuals to reproduce and to regenerate themselves and thereby to overcome their finitude. Conversely, without exploitation of the profit-producing capacity of money in a capitalist economy, time reverts to its state in a fallen and sinful nature, which it no longer redeems by serving as a medium of accumulation and aggrandizement through exchange. In sum, without the generation of profit, time remains the medium not of self-fulfillment and preservation, but of death and degeneration.

That this economic-theological alternative is seen by Franklin as rife with political implications is underscored by the linking of the murder of the breeding sow to regicide through his allusion to the "Crown." Just as the monarch figures the ability of the nation to survive beyond the life-spans of its individual members, so the "crown" that produces more of its own figures represents the capacity of money to transcend the mortality of its human agents.

The basis of this association, condensed in the "murder of the crown," is the conviction that the speculative use of money can purge time of its destructive effects on individuals by transforming it into a medium of redemption. Luther's maxim *sola fide* has been transformed into *solo credito*. However close these two words may seem – faith and credit – they nevertheless are also significantly different from one another. The shift from faith to credit brings redemption down to earth, and hence, into time: which is to say, into a time considered as a medium that is homogeneous, and therefore measurable and calculable: chronological time. In his fifth and last call to remember, Franklin emphasizes the link between the calculability of time and its relationship to the profitable use of credit:

> Remember this saying, *That the good Paymaster is Lord of another Man's Purse.* He that is known to pay punctually and exactly to the Time he promises, may at any Time, and on any occasion, raise all the Money his Friends can spare. This is sometimes of great Use; Therefore never keep borrow'd Money an Hour beyond the Time you promis'd, lest a Disappointment shut up your Friends' Purse forever. (Franklin 1748)

This importance of punctuality in the repayment of debts brings into the open a second shift with respect to the Lutheran *sola fide*. The debtor (or creditor) may be a private individual, separate from others, but he is not isolated. Money relations, which are also market-relations, require the interaction of individuals who are distinct from one another but also interdependent; to be alone with money and credit no longer means to be isolated with God. But neither does it signify equality with the other. In fact, through punctuality – a certain control over time – the debtor appears in the image of his Creator and gains control over his creditor: "[T]he *good Paymaster is Lord of another Man's Purse.*" The relation between debtor and creditor is still determined in terms of mastery and lordship, but it is the debtor who is now in the position of mastery, not the creditor.[2]

And yet it is important to remember that this analogy is possible only because both creditor and debtor have a common purpose: to harness the creative power attributed – accredited – to money in order through its use to generate and appropriate more of it: the one by borrowing, the other by lending. The borrower especially has to appear trustworthy, for he is constantly under scrutiny by the lender, and, Franklin emphasizes, "Creditors are a kind of People, that have

---

2 In contemporary discussions of US-Chinese economic relations, there seems to be little consensus about which of the two nations – the creditor nation (China) or the debtor (US) – is more dependent on the other.

the sharpest Eyes and Ears, as well as the best Memories in the World." (Franklin 1748). In response to such scrutiny, it is above all required that the debtor not confuse possession – his present state – with ownership, which belongs to the future:

> Beware of thinking all your own what you possess, and of living accordingly. 'Tis a mistake that many People who have Credit fall into. To prevent this keep an exact Account for some Time of both your Expences and your Incomes [...] you will discover how wonderfully small trifling Expences mount up to large Sums [...]. (Franklin 1748)

The trap of credit operates through the lure of present possession, and it can be avoided only by the power of calculation to overcome time.

If time is money, and credit also money, then time – homogeneous, calculable, appropriable – is also credit, but only where it becomes the medium of calculation and redemption. This redemption entails not just the repayment of principle, but also of interest. It is not yet salvation, but it anticipates it through the surplus it involves, which, as we have seen, for Franklin as for many others involves a surplus of life over the living – which is to say, over the mortality of the living being in its singularity.

In this perspective it can be seen that the motto that adorns the money of the United States – "In God We Trust" – may be distinctive, but it is by no means entirely idiosyncratic. For if it is the state that serves as primary guarantee of its money, the ability of the state to provide that guarantee presupposes a control over time that ultimately appeals to a certain "faith" or "trust". In this fiduciary sense, both state and money are secular heirs to the redemptive function formerly attributed to the Church, and following the Reformation, reattributed to the faith of the private individual. What, however, remains consistent and unchanged in this shift is the promise of redemption – from sinful guilt through faith, and from deliberate debt through credit.

In this respect, credit is not just, as Franklin thought, one particular form of money, but rather its essence. This is because money is intrinsically temporal and temporality, despite its calculability, uncertain. Money is intrinsically temporal because it must circulate; but what is uncertain is that the circulation will turn a full circle and provide a "return" on "investment" – which is to say, that it will serve not just as a means of exchange and of circulation, but also of reproduction and appropriation. In a capitalist system, the goal of private appropriation defines the horizon of economic activity. And this in turn requires a certain faith or trust in the calculability of the future. Or rather, in the ability of financial circulation to overcome the uncertainty of the future by coming full circle and producing a "return".

It is this point of view – that of the private appropriation of profit – that allows Franklin to define credit as a form of money. However, if Franklin takes this point of view for granted, later economists, such as Rudolf Hilferding, emphasize the difference between the two. In his 1910 study of *Finance Capital*, Hilferding distinguishes credit from money. Credit, he argues, involves a merely "private" relationship, a "promise" or "promissory note" to pay at some later date, whereas "money" is guaranteed "publicly," by society or the state.

Although Hilferding's distinction between publicly-backed "money" and privately-backed "credit money" overlooks the fact that there can be publicly backed credit as well: Government bonds – US Treasury short term bonds, for instance, which at the moment of this writing are in great demand, and are therefore offering practically zero interest – it nevertheless raises two very significant issues. The first concerns the relation of time to the categories of "public" and "private." Time is more easily taken for granted when processes – in particular, financial processes–seem predictable, transparent and calculable. In the case of money – which is really a form of public credit – this is what creates the appearance of a certain timelessness, as distinct from private credit – transactions between banks, for instance, and borrowers. That this distinction is not tenable, however, becomes manifest in periods of extreme inflation or deflation, when the nominal value of money may remain the same, but when its real value – its "buying power – can change daily if not hourly. Money can thus be "redeemed" at its nominal worth at any time – and in this sense its value seems impervious to time – but its real value may in the meantime have declined or augmented drastically. The fact that the nominal value of money stays the same, while its real value changes radically, indicates that money is not a thing whose properties are fixed independently of time but are rather determined by a process that, like every process, requires time in order to proceed. The ostensible stability of money with respect to "credit money" is the result of its apparent subordination to human volition and control: one can decide when to use money as a means of payment or investment, and so it seems that money allows one a certain control over time considered as the medium of incalculable change and alterability. But although this aleatory dimension of time can be taken for granted more easily with respect to money than with respect to credit, this should not blind us to the fact that both, money no less than credit – and indeed no less than capital itself – are inscribed in a process of exchange that renders them intrinsically temporal in their very being, which is never simply self-contained in the present moment.

The apparent difference between money and credit has therefore more to do with the tacit assumption that volition and self-consciousness can, when identified with the public sphere – above all, that of the state – in certain circumstances at least, overcome the uncertainty of time, rather than with the intrinsically aleatory structure of money or credit as such. This is also why there is something shocking in the recent spectacle of a country like Iceland on the verge of bankruptcy. That this evaluation is, however, not free of ethnocentrism is demonstrated by the fact that one is far less shocked or reluctant to speak of "failed states" when the states concerned are located in the Southern hemisphere, rather than in the Northern hemisphere.

Nevertheless, if this demonstrates that the difference between "private" and "public" or "social" in financial matters is not absolute, it does not mean that the differences between the two can be simply ignored. Obviously there is a distinction between buying on credit and paying in full at the time of purchase, just as there is a distinction between public (or "social") and private credit and debt. When Hilferding emphasizes that credit involves a "private guarantee" as distinguished from the "social guarantee" that underwrites the nominal value of money, he implies at least two things about the exchange process. First, that it is designed to turn a full circle: it is quite literally "circulation" and not just an arbitrary movement of substitution through exchange. In short, it must not be forgotten that we are dealing with a "limited" economy of appropriation and not a "general" one, to use terms popularized by Georges Bataille.[3] And second, that this circularity depends on the credibility of redemption: the belief or confidence in the "promise" involved in "promissory notes," the credibility involved in all "letters of credit." For credit to be creditable, its redeemability must inspire confidence. During the 2008 credit crisis, for instance, "letters of credit" which are used in international transactions were increasingly refused or rejected by prospective creditors or sellers, with the result that international commerce began shrinking rapidly.[4] The reason for this, according to Nobel Prize-winning economist and newspaper columnist Paul Krugman, was simply that no confidence was being extended any more by private lenders to private borrowers: "What lies behind the credit squeeze is the combination of reduced

---

3 See Jacques Derrida's dis-seminal essay on this subject: "De l'économie restreinte à l'économie générale" (Derrida 1967: 369–407). In this early essay, Derrida sought to envisage a notion of "sovereignty" and of "general economy" that would exceed the metaphysics of presence as resumed in the Hegelian dialectic. Later, with the emergence of the notion of *singularity*, he will abandon this attempt.

4 "Hardly a day goes by without news of some further disaster wreaked by the freezing up of credit. As I was writing this, for example, reports were coming in of the collapse of letters of credit, the key financing method for world trade. Suddenly, buyers of imports, especially in developing countries, can't carry through on their deals, and ships are standing idle: the Baltic Dry Index, a widely used measure of shipping costs, has fallen 89 percent this year," Paul Krugman wrote (2008).

trust in and decimated capital at financial institutions" (Krugman 2008). These "financial institutions" are of course dedicated – as are all other economic institutions in a capitalist economy – to the appropriation of profit and its "maximization." To be sure, the notion of "maximization" may be interpreted in different ways. The main distinction organizing those different interpretations is once again related to the interpretation of time: they are either "short-term," "mid-term," or "long-term." A long-term perspective places the emphasis not just on generating profit for the individual enterprise, but on securing the system of exchange on which all such enterprises depend. A short-term perspective, in contrast – and this is what has become dominant in the last decades – will tend to ignore those systemic conditions of exchange and focus only on the generation of the greatest amount of profit in the shortest possible time-span. Even today, this carries over into the behavior of banks and speculators; banks receive subsidies designed to facilitate lending. However, without constraints they often deploy these funds either to buy other, weaker banks and thus strengthen their competitive position and hence their ability to generate profit through market-control, or to gamble on risky speculative ventures since the money they are risking has become readily accessible (a consequence of the "too big to fail" policy of the current US regime). The question is whether there is not a tendency of the capitalist system itself to prioritize the short-term over the longer-term perspective, especially when the rewards of short-term gains – "bonuses" – become the primary factor in determining company policies.

For as Benjamin Franklin emphasized over two centuries ago, it is not enough that the debt be repaid, in full and on time. It must be repaid with interest, with "offspring," so that its value has increased over time. Time, instead of consuming living beings, seems thus to be organized so as to allow them to increase their being, insofar at least as this being is identified with their property, their wealth, their holdings. A newly revived saying, stemming from J. M. Keynes, sums up the attitude that informs such a conception of time: "In the long term, we are all dead." With this remark, Keynes sought to parry conservative condemnation of government deficit spending as destructive in the long run. But today it can also serve to reinforce the carpe-diem attitude that provides a justification for subordinating longer-term investment to shorter-term profit taking. Where the long-term is acknowledged today is mainly in ecologically motivated discourses. The rise of the words "sustainable" or "renewable" provide an indicator of the mind-set at work in such matters. The longer-term is important insofar as it can offer "sustenance" or "renewal" of what is already on hand. In such an attitude there is both the recognition of individual mortality, and the desire to transcend it – generally, however, not so much through the survival of supra-individual, collective traditions, but through the intensification of individual appropriation. Financial speculation depending on calculation of future market-values can create the appearance of a power that seems to transcend the temporal mortality and finitude that is inseparable from the bodily existence of living individuals. At the same time, such speculation often tends to confirm the inescapability of the "ultimate crash," whether of individuals or of the system itself. A recent example is "short-selling," in which speculators sell stocks in order to drive prices down, and then buy them "back" shortly thereafter at a lower price; this is then repeated and is probably at least partly responsible for the extreme volatility shown by global stock markets in the past months.[5] But the figure of Bernard Madoff condenses all of these ambivalences. On the one hand, aided by the introduction of computerized trading, due mainly to the computational skills of his brother, Peter, Bernie appeared to many as a time-transcending figure, one whom Elie Wiesel, one of his victims, described as a "god." On the other hand, Madoff was presumably intelligent enough to know that it was only a matter of time before he would be exposed: the question of course was how much time. However, it is difficult not to suspect a strong self-destructive acknowledgement of mortality in the same person who appeared to transcend it. "The God that failed" was here not the God of Communism denounced by Arthur Koestler, but the God that personified that quintessence of present-day computerized finance capitalism. Important, however, is that in both cases, it was still a God that failed. Theology continues to inform economics as it did the revolutionary ideology that sought to destroy and replace it.

Precisely because it decorporalizes material goods by speculating on their future exchange-value, "investment" appears to attain a "spiritual" status that seemingly transcends the limitations of mere matter and material bodies. It can appear to itself as a generator of wealth in a manner that is somewhat reminiscent of the creation of life through the divine logos. Nevertheless, future returns on present investment – or in the case of credit vehicles, on private promises – retain a degree of uncertainty. For the promise of "redemption" is simply never immune to temporal changes. It must always reengage, in one form or another, with the temporal process of exchange.

Franklin takes stock of this in the "advice" he extends to the "young tradesman". He does not and cannot promise the Young Tradesman immortality, nor can he show him the path to Grace, but he can indicate "the Way to Wealth" which, as he puts it, "is as plain as the Way to Market. It depends chiefly on

---

5 On 20 September 2008, the US SEC in conjunction with the UK Financial Services Authority issued a short-term ban on the short selling of financial stocks. But an extension of this ban to the stock market at large has at the time of this writing not yet been implemented despite increasing calls for such action.

two Words, INDUSTRY and FRUGALITY; i.e. Waste neither Time nor Money, but make the best use of both" (Franklin 1748).

The two words that Franklin uses suggest how the destructive effects of time are to be mitigated. First through work, and second through the avoidance of "waste" (i.e. "frugality"). Industry and frugality, work and economy, both entail teleological activities, and indeed the two mean almost the same thing. "Waste" is to be avoided through an organization of work by a volition that knows what it wants and how best to attain it. "Industry" entails energy, discipline and focus. Both "industry" and "frugality" presuppose a notion of work that is thoroughly teleological. For it is this self-conscious and volitional teleology that, for Marx, like Aristotle before him, distinguishes human work from the merely goal-directed behavior of bees, as Marx notes in *Capital:* "A spider conducts operations that resemble those of a weaver, and a bee would put many a human architect to shame by the construction of its honeycomb cells. But what distinguishes the worst architect from the best of bees is that the architect builds the cell in his mind before he constructs it in wax." (Marx 1977: 284)

The difference between human labor and the no less complex goal-directed actions of bees resides in the fact that with humans the purpose of the activity is represented by consciousness prior to the activity itself. The implication of this a priori consciousness is that laboring human beings, in contrast to animals or insects, know what they are attempting to accomplish before they begin working. This in turn suggests that consciousness can transcend temporal and spatial separation insofar as this renders the future representable, and as such also presentable, i.e. realizable through work. Considered in this way, namely as deliberate and volitional, work appears to be an activity that transcends time, at least insofar as the latter is considered a medium of separation. For what work in this sense does is not just to modify the materials on which it operates, but to alter them so that they ultimately conform to a pre-existing plan, an idea, a representation. In other words, time and space are thereby transformed from a medium of alterability and, for living beings, of decomposition no less than of growth, into a medium of actualization, a medium that allows the "self-same" to be realized as the product of work.

Certainly, in commodity-production, objects are produced not directly to satisfy the needs of their producers, but rather those of their consumers through a process of exchange. But consumption remains an indispensable goal of commodity-production, even if mediated by exchange. Consumption may thus be deferred through the separation of producer and consumer and through the introduction of sellers and buyers. But the ultimate horizon of the work process remains that of a volitional and conscious teleology. It is this volitional and self-conscious teleology that allows work to appear to retain a certain redemptive value despite the Reformation attack on "good works" as the path to grace. For the "grace" provided by work is that of an end-product that fulfills the plan of the producer: a product that remains the same over time and space. A product that in this sense "survives" the ravages of time – even when conceived as a throwaway from the outset.

Work thus provides a model of the self as a conscious process fulfilling itself in time and space. Productive labor in this sense is the secular heir of divine creativity. But since the producer inhabits a "fallen" world, that analogy must be mediated by the process of exchange. For it is only the "other" of the producer who can obtain the grace of self-fulfillment through consumption – and through credit, the economic-theological heir of sinful guilt.

Franklin's "way to riches" via "the way to the market" ultimately expresses the effort of capitalism to make good on the redemptive promise of Christianity. If Carl Schmitt argued that all the notions of the modern theory of the state are theological in origin – and by that he means Catholic – then the reality of post-Reformation capitalist modernity is that the economization that Schmitt so feared and fought against is ultimately nothing more or less than the attempt of such political theology to bridge the gap that separates the state of the world from the City of God. If the principle of the latter, according to the Schmitt of *Roman Catholicism and Political Form*, is the principle of "representation," then the principle of modern capitalism as its heir is that of a certain "speculation" in which what may be described as de-presentation mirrors and transfigures the (nation-) state of the fallen world. Walter Benjamin retraced the genealogy of this process in his study of the *Origin of the German Mourning Play* [*Ursprung des deutschen Trauerspiels*]. His account culminated in his reworking of the category of "allegory." Allegory is a form of negative representation, signifying the "non-being of what it represents." Benjamin was well aware of the relationship between allegory and money, even if alluding to it only briefly in his study: "Whatever it touched, its Midas-hand turned into something significant. Transformations of all sorts were its element; and their schematism was allegory. The less this passion is confined to the Baroque period, the more it is able to reveal the Baroque dimension in later phenomena." (Benjamin 1991: I, 403)

It proves worthwhile here to recall that the Baroque Mourning Play and its use of allegory originated in what Benjamin called the Counter-Reformation, embracing not just Catholicism but all organized religion and indeed, all forms of organization as such. Faced with the radically subversive antinomianism of the Lutheran doctrine of *sola fide* – which Benjamin, implicitly following Max Weber, clearly distinguishes from its Calvinist version – , all organized politics and religion saw themselves forced to justify the redemptive dimension of those "good works" that Luther had so radically called into question. The thrust of that Lutheran antinomianism – also the origin of the Kantian "antinomies," of which "the antinomies of the allegorical" were perhaps the earliest expression – was to insist on the irreducibility of the singular against the universalist pretentions of the Church and its derived political institutions. It is this insistence on singularity that challenged all established authority, which justified itself through appeals to a generality that could no longer be taken for granted.

At the end of his treatise, Benjamin cites an anecdote drawn from the life of Saint Theresa that illustrates the ambiguous situation of the singular believer, and of the Church, at the time of the Reformation. Characteristically, Benjamin describes the scene but then leaves its interpretation largely up to the reader:

> Saint Theresa has a hallucination in which she sees how the Madonna places roses on her bed; she recounts this to her confessor. "I don't see any," he replies. To which she responds: "The Madonna brought them for me." In this sense, the ostentatiously acknowledged subjectivity becomes a formal guarantee [*zum förmlichen Garanten*] of the miracle, because it announces the divine action itself. (Benjamin 1991: I, 408)

If, for Carl Schmitt, whose shadow haunts this scene, the religious "miracle" is the forerunner of modern political sovereignty, in his view based on the power of the sovereign to make a "decision" that is utterly singular, paradigmatically that of suspending the constitution by declaring a state of exception – for Benjamin such a decision can hardly decide anything at all, and indeed can never fully take place. For how is the Sovereign to save the polity if his situation, as a fallen individual, remains inscribed in the very creation that, qua singular, demands salvation? For Benjamin, the Sovereign is therefore not "saved" by the "principle of representation" but rather undone by it, in the form of allegory.[6]

What is left is the experience of the mystic, the "hallucination" which she "shares" with her confessor, although only negatively, precisely by confirming that he cannot participate in it: "I don't see anything" he replies. Nor can he. For the Good News that for the Christian mystic here takes the form of a hallucination, the image of the roses placed on the bed by the Madonna, is no longer destined for the representative of the Universal (Catholic) Church, nor for any representative at all, it is but for the wholly private and solitary individual, alone with her faith in God, sola fides. The private vision of the mystic thus an-

---

6 In Benjamin's "political anthropology," the Sovereign therefore necessarily becomes a Tyrant, the tyrant a martyr, and out of the martyrdom of sovereignty emerges the new and decisive political figure, the *plotter*. But the plotter no longer saves: he consummates the fall of a world without grace. Examples – not cited by Benjamin – are Iago and Loge. Other more recent examples, this time drawn from "real" politics and not literature, can be left to the reader's imagination.

ticipates the belief in the sanctity of private property that will inform the economic-theology of capitalism.

For the way that leads from the vision of Saint Theresa to the scenes of modern consumer and finance capitalism is both long and yet, as Benjamin Franklin suggests, also "plain" for all to see. All that is needed is faith: *sola fide*. But faith in what?

For the United States, at least, the answer is clear enough: The faith required is faith in the promise that to spend is to "save," and to save is to be saved. Since this may not be entirely clear – especially to those not wholly familiar with American English – let me explain it with an anecdote. In 1973, which was the year of the first oil crisis, following the Israeli victory in the Yom Kippur war, the Japanese automobile maker, Datsun – forerunner of today's Nissan Motors – launched an advertising campaign in the U.S. using the slogan, "Datsun Saves!" What was meant was that Datsun's cars required less fuel to run, and hence "saved" money, especially at the then current price of gas. However, the slogan hit a raw nerve and for two interrelated reasons. First, the word "save" was and remains the master-word of American advertising discourse. As such, the word dominates the world of consumption in the United States. In order to understand its peculiar significance, it is helpful to recall that of all industrialized countries, the United States is the one whose private citizens actually "save" the least: they have less money deposited in savings accounts with guaranteed, if low, annual interest rates. So when the word "save" returns, as it were, as the chief "buzzword" of American advertising, it is as the antithesis of what the word means in "official" English (if that exists anywhere). It does not mean putting money aside so as to have a reserve for difficult times. It means rather the contrary: spending money, and not just spending money, but spending money that you often – generally – do not have.

What may be called the American religion of consumption is built therefore on two primary articles of faith. The first is that the more you spend, the more you save. The second is the more you "save" in this way, the more you are "saved": that is, lifted out of your ordinary, everyday, vulnerable and ultimately mortal existence and placed in a sphere of ownership that for many is the secular correlative of divine redemption. The more the individual seems to possess – forgetting Franklin's warning, that to possess is not necessarily to own – the more that individual appears to approach the goal of autonomy, through which the individual seems to acquire something of the omnipotence of the single and exclusive, life- and world-creating God.

It is these two articles of faith that endow credit with creative power, and then raise the indebted to the status of the sinful who are however to be redeemed. The greater the debt, the greater the redemption. The more you borrow, the more you are "saved". This religion bears the mark of the dominant Protestant "ethic" that informs American capitalism: the original sin of humankind, which condemns it to suffering, work and ultimately to death, can be redeemed not by "Good Works" but by "faith alone"; or rather, not quite by faith alone, but by faith in action. The action required, however, is not that of producing Good Works, but that of consuming them, whereby the process of consuming – of buying on credit – becomes the true path to grace and to salvation.

As anyone knows who has spent any time at all in the United States, the ubiquitous advertising of most commodities – and especially of more expensive ones, such as automobiles – tends to formulate the cost not in terms of actual prices, but in terms of monthly credit payments. This did not start with home mortgages – the "subprime" mortgage crisis marked simply the culmination of a process that had begun long before. Buying on credit was already prevalent in the nineteenth century even while its mass use only began with the spread of credit cards following the Second World War. In 1952, the ratio of private debt to income in the United States was 52 %. In 2006, it had grown to 126 %.[7]

Up until fairly recently, there was little concern – either popular or among professional economists – about growing private and public indebtedness in the United States. There are many reasons for this, of course, but one of them is probably less obvious and hence less discussed. It has to do with what Walter Benjamin describes as the "antinomy" that characterizes Baroque allegory – which is its response to the radical antinomianism of Luther. Since from this perspective the redemption of sinful, fallen, mortal beings can no longer be entrusted to Good Works (the Catholic mass, for instance, or confession), the increase in debt (and guilt) paradoxically can serve as the condition of "redemption," both by confirming the guilty debt of the individual, and by promising the redemption of that debt and guilt. Since however this redemption never takes place on Earth, but only with the End of Time, the manifestation of the possibility of salvation becomes paradoxically not just the accumulation of wealth (the Calvinist response), but also the accumulation of debt – or rather, in a strange synthesis, the accumulation of indebted possession, of expropriable property, of ownership that is not really one's own.

This is a tendency that Benjamin describes in his fragment, "Capitalism as Religion": "Capitalism is presumably the first case of a cult that is aimed not at expiation, but at culpabilization (*verschuldend*). An enormously guilty conscience (*Schuldbewusstsein*) that does not know where to find expiation resorts

---

7 http://www.rapidtrends.com/blog/private-debt-is-much-higher-now-than-during-the-great-depression/.

to the cult, not in order through it to expiate its guilt, but to render it universal
[...]." (Benjamin 1991: VI, 100) The precise manifestation of this attempt to uni-
versalize guilt and debt is one very fundamental factor behind what today is
known as "globalization". What the present crisis reveals, among other things,
is how much not just the United States but the world's economies depend on
the "cult" of deficit consumption that has increasingly driven the American market since the Second World War.

Why save, when credit alone – *sola fide* – is the only and clear path to salvation? The American obsession with "saving" the world – the tradition of so-
called "manifest destiny," today reformulated as the mission of American
world leadership – is only one particularly fateful projection of the Puritan
sense of profound and pervasive guilt, to which American history, with its gen-
ocidal treatment of native Americans and its exploitation of African-American
slave labor, has so often paid all too real tribute.

Consumption "saves" and consumption requires credit. This is, to be sure,
particularly evident in the United States, and it is no accident that the worldwide
economic crisis that we are currently undergoing should have started in the United States. But the fact that this crisis so quickly engulfed the world's economies,
belying the popular thesis of the "decoupling" of those economies from American economic and political hegemony, indicates that, as Horace wrote and Marx,
among many others echoed: *tua res agitur*, ("it is your cause"). Conditions that
once were characteristic of and to some extent limited to the American experience are today increasingly imposing themselves worldwide and it is therefore
important to analyze the different local situations that have permitted this impo-
sition to take place, and within the realm of the possible, try to modify them.

Let me then conclude with some thoughts on the conditions that may have
rendered possible the widespread appeal of the American model of what I have
been calling "theological economy." If, as Benjamin suggested, Capitalism is itself a Religion and not just the result of one; if qua religion its strength lies in the
fact that it responds to questions and problems that previously only organized
religions effectively addressed; and if moreover the religion that capitalism follows in the wake of is Christianity, by developing the sense of universal culpabilization and indebtedness to include the deity itself, which today conceals itself behind individualist avatars, such as the "star" and the "state" – it is
because the idea of inexpiable guilt and debt produce a "cult" – an organized
and repetitive practice – of consumption that allows credit and debt to appear
as the constituents of saving grace. In this perspective, it is significant that
the responses of governments, first to the credit crisis and now to the full-
blown recession that has overtaken the so-called "real" economy, involve the
augmentation of debt, only this time public debt rather than private debt: public

debt designed to "save" private enterprise, private banking, private finance from self-destruction by rehabilitating the credibility of credit. Marx had already remarked on the fact that British English distinguished between the Royal Treasury and the National Debt. What we now are seeing, however, is the State Treasury – the various National and Supra-National banks – attempting to come to the rescue of the private banks and corporations: the nationalization of private debt.

Under given circumstances, such public, governmental spending is surely necessary and inevitable, but it is important to see how it constitutes an attempt to restore credibility to a system of credit that has largely been discredited.

This discredit, I believe, derives from a system of credit that ultimately seeks to transcend its own limits through a "return" that seeks to be without limit and without end. It is this "return" – the capitalist form of profit as redemption – that must be rethought. Furthermore, this holds true not just because it involves a return that over the past decades has increasingly been appropriated by private individuals or groups, to the increasing exclusion of the vast majority of others who make up society. This year, before the crisis really began to develop, the upper 1 % of the population in the United States had gained possession of 28 % of the country's wealth – more than in 1929 at the end of the "roaring twenties." During the same period, despite the spread of economic "development" to vast regions of the world, the gap between possessors and dispossessed, between rich and poor, has increased over the past two decades worldwide, both within countries and between them. The growth in worldwide violence seems closely related to such tendencies, whether concerning former fishermen whose traditional livelihoods were destroyed by shipping routes turning into pirates preying on that shipping, or whether it concerns Islamic fundamentalists who, as in Iran or in Pakistan, seek to address needs of the population that are largely ignored by the existing state and by civil society. Rejection of "Western" and "modern" values by ever larger populations in the world are just some of the more obvious and disturbing results of the same system of "economic theology" that has produced the current crisis.

What ultimately informs this system, driving it and also, I suspect, constituting much of its worldwide appeal, is the accreditation of a system directed ultimately at defining reality in terms of the private appropriation of wealth and power, a system that in turn is informed by the notion of a literally in-divisible and autonomous in-dividual as its constituent and defining subject. "Freedom," in the American lexicon at least, is first and foremost, freedom of the "individual" to do as he or she pleases as long as it does not limit the freedom of other individuals. The "other" is thereby reduced to just another "individual," another "self," another potential property-owner and proprietor – which means, of course, that the other is reduced to just more of the same. Salvation, like damnation, is hereby construed as essentially the property and destiny of autonomous individuals, and individuals are construed as being what they are prior to and independently of their relations with others. This, I submit, is ultimately the basis of the expected "return" on investment that is expected to round off and close the circulation of commodities, the circulation of credit and consumption, in which debt comes a full circle in order to magically produce a greater, more aggrandized self. Deficit spending thus emerges as the not so secret mechanism of self-fashioning.

The notion of the individual, as individual property-owner, individual debtor and lender, is as deeply rooted in the Abrahamic tradition as Adam and Eve, as Cain and Abel. But it is heightened by the fact that the Creator God takes the form of a human individual in order to "save" mankind from its sins and to bring it the Good News of Eternal Life. With the Reformation that message is shifted from the manifest external world with its Church and its sacraments, to the more interior, more individual faith that was felt to bind the individual to God. But the individual is never simply undivided: it is also and above all singular: unique not in the sense of being self-contained, but in the sense of being incommensurably linked to what it is not: to other beings, whether human, living or inanimate; to other times and to other places. It is this incommensurability that "indebts" the individual to a singularity that is irreducibly heterogeneous, that comes from elsewhere and is on its way elsewhere, however much it may try to fashion a self that would stay the same over time and place.

But there is also a truth at work in this system of self-fulfillment as self-consumption. It resides in the fact that the debts of the singular – as distinct from individual – are irredeemable, if by redemption is meant a return to the same. This is perhaps the other meaning of the phrase that inverts Franklin's adage by asserting not just that "time is money" but that "money is time." For money, the means and medium of private appropriation, of rendering the different commensurable – money is always inscribed in a time that carries circulation beyond every attempt to close its movement in a circle. This is why one of the most powerful factors in precipitating the current crisis has been the effort to overcome the deleterious effects of time through calculation, and more recently through highly computerized calculation, which has produced a focus on the short-term: the short-term maximization of investment at the expense of the economy itself.

However, this also explains why the current crisis may help to reimpose a sense of time as something more than the short-term perspective of short selling and leveraged buyouts has allowed many to believe. Whether it will call into question the basic articles of faith that have allowed "redemption" to be defined in terms of the self-identical individual rather than of the heteronymous singular – time alone will tell.

2

The previous text was written at the time of the 2008 crisis, which had been provoked by the collapse of the "subprime mortgage" real estate "bubble": at the time of this writing, September 2011, a new crisis has emerged, different from the first but by no means unrelated to it. It is the crisis of what is called "sovereign debt": the indebtedness of nation-states. This began in 2008 with the default of the three major Icelandic private banks, which in the meanwhile caused the "sovereign debt" of Iceland to mount from 28 % of GDP in 2007 to 90 % of GDP today. This was the worst financial crisis of a national government since the Argentinean economic crisis of 1999 – 2002, which peaked with the freezing of all bank accounts in the country for twelve months, allowing for only minor sums to be withdrawn each week and at the end of 2001 leading to widespread public protests and confrontations between police and demonstrators.

But the Icelandic crisis was different since it was no longer in a part of the world that could be considered to belong to the "developing" world, as opposed to the "developed" economies, centered in Europe and North America. Still, it did not yet emanate directly from the functioning of the central government but rather from the private sector.

Starting, however, in late 2009, fears of a sovereign debt crisis concerning European states began to emerge, concerning Ireland, Portugal, Greece and Spain. This, in turn, has called into question the stability of the entire Euro Zone, including several of its central members, such as Italy and France. The crisis in credit has now extended from the private sector to the public sector, as the term, "sovereign debt" clearly indicates. And this correspondingly begins to clarify the distinction between "private" and "public" as it affects credit and credibility. For the so-called "sovereignty" on which nation-states are predicated is increasingly revealed to be anything but absolute. Here, two aspects in the traditional notion and history of "sovereignty" have to be distinguished: its temporal aspect and its spatial dimension. Temporally, as Kantorowicz has argued (Kantorowicz 1997), the notion of national sovereignty developed after the 1648 Peace of Westphalia as the heir to the "*corpus mysticum*," the social body of the church with its attendant administrative structure. This latter notion – contrasted with the corpus natural – "would come to be transferred to political entities, the body politic."[8] This meant that although the human beings in whom the authority and power of that body was incarnated – the King – remained mortal, the authority itself could be considered to be immortal, or at least to transcend the finite span of individual lives. Yet this temporal dimension of sovereignty was simultaneously qualified by a spatial limitation. For the scope of the sovereign power was defined and delimited by territorial borders. This was the most evident distinction between nation-states and the Universal Church, which claimed global validity, corresponding to the belief in a monotheistic Creator-God. The "supremacy" attached to the political authority of the nation-state was thus spatially limited, while at the same time claiming to be temporally unlimited.

This tension between the temporal and spatial claims of supreme authority that constitute the political sovereignty of the nation-state has of course had effects that are anything but merely theoretical: disputes over borders, efforts to extend territory, attempts to establish spheres of influence and control beyond a state's territorial borders and more generally, the relations between the nation-state and other nation-states and the entities and institutions that lie outside of its territory – all of these have produced the conflicts continuing throughout the history of nation-states.

The problem of "sovereign debt" reveals another dimension to this tension. It shows how the distinction between domestic and foreign, between inside and outside of a given territory, has become increasingly blurred as the development of communication technologies radically relativized the distinctions between space and time. The "market" of creditors – those who purchase government bonds and obligations – functions to a large degree independently of territorial boundaries.

What, however, does characterize this market – and this takes us back to the arguments developed in the previous text – is what I have described as the logic of a profitable "return." If money is loaned, bonds are purchased, and more generally debt itself has become a privileged object of speculation – as in Credit Default Swaps (CDS) – then what has remained constant is that all of this financial speculation is done with a single purpose: that of turning a profit, of producing a return. The return, however, can include and be based on default – that is on non-return, as in the CDS – where money is paid out if and when a bond-issuer defaults on its obligations and cannot pay back the debts incurred. Defaults are thus turned into a profitable object of speculation.

Whereas such speculation was however up to a point largely confined to the private sector, the novelty of the Sovereign Debt Crisis stems from its extension to

---

8 http://plato.stanford.edu/entries/sovereignty/ (accessed 9 October 2014).

the public sphere. The financial markets are now able to speculate on the default not just of banks or of other financial institutions, but of entire nation-states, such as Greece, Portugal, Spain, Italy, Ireland and France. This nevertheless reaches to the heart of the very structure that enables market relations to function.

What after all is a market? Here is a contemporary definition from *Wikipedia*[9]:

> A market is any one of a variety of systems, institutions, procedures, social relations and infrastructures whereby parties engage in exchange. While parties may exchange goods and services by barter, most markets rely on sellers offering their goods or services (including labor) in exchange for money from buyers. It can be said that a market is the process in which the prices of goods and services are established.

However complicated the reality of modern "markets" is, compared to this simple and rudimentary description, one thing remains constant: the motivation of market participants in a capitalist society derives from getting the best possible return on their "investment": the lowest possible price for the buyer, the most profitable price for the seller. Yet, to the extent that the market involves not just the exchange of goods between physical individuals, but the exchange of objects that can be highly abstract between very different types of buyers and sellers – say a financial investment firm such as Goldman Sachs and an individual, retirement fund or even nation-state – the question of credibility becomes increasingly important and difficult to assure. The subprime mortgage crisis involved the "packaging" of "toxic" mortgages so that their "toxicity" could no longer be easily recognized by the buyer. And since this was often done with the express intention of the seller enriching itself at the expense of the buyer, but without the latter's knowledge, the question of credibility became all the more urgent.

In the 2008 crisis, the function of governmental regulators was already severely compromised: the SEC and other agencies did not do an effective job, and indeed, given that many of their members had been or would be involved in the very institutions they were supposed to regulate, their regulatory power was largely called into question. The same could indeed be attributed to the highest level of government, when finance ministers and advisors all came from the very institutions that again they were supposed to regulate in the public interest.

This increasing disproportion of power between private and public sectors, together with a policy of increased "deregulation," which declared "government is part of the problem, not the solution," left little room for any effective advocacy or enforcement of public interests as opposed to private interests.

---

9 http://en.wikipedia.org/wiki/Market_(economics) (accessed 3 February 2015).

The very bases of political "sovereignty" were thus severely undermined, not from without ("War on Terror") but also and perhaps above all from within, by the prevalence of the interest in private enrichment over the minimal conditions necessary for social institutions – including markets – to function.

This has finally come to a head with the "Sovereign Debt" crisis, which manifests the direct dependency of state institutions, supposed to ensure the minimal degree of social cohesion and order necessary for any sort of interchange to take place, upon "the market" as the embodiment of the private interest requiring a profitable return on investment. Thus, countries such as Greece, whose credit ratings are downgraded by the same privately-owned and organized rating agencies that facilitated the subprime mortgage deception, have to pay exorbitant rates of interest to borrow money, which makes the likelihood of their default an inevitability.

Hence, today we are witnessing not just the triumph of the Private over the Public interest, but also the undermining of the social conditions in which private entities interact with one another: both within countries and between them. As a result, the tendency – and danger – is that the privatization of public policies produces a state of mind holding the "debtor" morally responsible for the upcoming default: debt converges with guilt, with the impending threat of retribution serving to highlight the salvation of the virtuous.

In short, the perspective of the autonomous subject serves as a justification for the destruction or subordination of whole societies, if not of social life itself. And this leaves only force – military force – as the last available guarantee of social interaction and arbiter of conflict.

The only alternative is one that develops a practice of debt that is not regulated by a notion of "redemption" as either salvation of the Self or its financial correlative, a profitable return on investment. The relation of finite living beings to time and space must be acknowledged as one of a debt that cannot be repaid, but that can open the way to a future no longer dominated by the dictates of redemption. "Debt forgiveness" must become a term designating something other than the abdication of public interest before private enrichment. The conditions of social interaction must be allowed to transcend the horizon of private appropriation. The alternative is a crisis not just in "sovereign debt," but in the very conditions of earthly life as such.

Works cited

Benjamin, Walter (1991) *Gesammelte Werke,* vol. I & VI, ed. Hermann Schweppenhäuser (Frankfurt am Main: Suhrkamp Verlag).

Benjamin, Walter (1996) *Selected Writings I* (Cambridge, Mass.: Harvard University Press).

Derrida, Jacques (1978) *L'Ecriture et la différence* (Paris: Editions du Seuil).

Franklin, Benjamin (1748) "Advice to a Young Tradesman," *The Papers of Benjamin Franklin*, vol. 3, 1745–1750 (The Packard Institute of Humanities). <http://franklin papers.org/franklin/framedVolumes.jsp> (accessed 9 January 2014).

Hilferding, Rudolf (1910) *Das Finanzkapital. Eine Studie über die jüngste Entwicklung des Kapitalismus* (Vienna: Verlag der Wiener Volksbuchhandlung).

Kantorowicz, Ernst H. (1957) *The King's Two Bodies. A Study in Medieval Political Theology* (Princeton, N.J.: Princeton University Press).

Krugman, Paul (2008) "What To Do," *The New York Review of Books*, 18 December 2008. <http://www.nybooks.com/articles/22151> (accessed 9 January 2014).

Marx, Karl (1977) *Capital: A Critique of Political Economy,* introd. Ernest Mandel, trans. Ben Fowkes, vol. 1 (New York: Vintage Books).

Philpott, Dan (Summer 2014 Edition) "Sovereignty," *The Stanford Encyclopedia of Philosophy*, ed. Edward N. Zalta. Forthcoming URL: <http://plato.stanford.edu/archives/sum2014/en tries/sovereignty/> (accessed 9 October 2014).

Ansgar Nünning
Metaphors We Pay For, or: Metaphors of the 'Financial Crisis' Shaping the Cultural Life of Money

1 Deploying metaphors to describe financial crises: Introducing the topic, goals and outline of the chapter[1]

In an article published in *The Wall Street Journal* (27 September 2008) tellingly entitled "In Financial Crisis, Metaphors Fly Like Bad Analogies", Michael M. Phillips provides some interesting examples as to how the real financial crisis has generated a plethora of metaphors of crisis and money, some of which are indeed "bad analogies" or unwittingly funny catachreses. After putting forward several examples, the author goes on to ask "Why the rush to deploy metaphor to describe the Wall Street crisis?", providing an initial answer by quoting John D. Casnig, founder of 'the Metaphor Observatory': "Metaphor is used when we can't understand something in its own context". Although one can readily agree with this explanation, it does not provide much in the way of enlightenment concerning either the metaphorical implications and mini-narrations of metaphors of crisis, or the functions they serve to fulfil.

Taking these observations about the common propensity to talk about the financial crisis in metaphoric terms as its cue and point of departure, this essay explores both the role that crisis metaphors play in shaping the cultural life of money and the functions that these metaphors fulfil as figurative knowledge and mini-narrations. The central hypothesis of this essay may be summed up in one sentence: the cultural life of money is largely shaped and determined

1 The present article is partly based on a translated version of an earlier article published in German, devoted to sketching out a narratology of crisis (cf. Nünning 2007), on a recent article in which I have tried to further explore the metaphor (and mini-narrative) of crisis (Nünning 2009) and on a forthcoming essay dealing with the same topic and trying to gauge the uses of cognitive metaphor theory for the study of culture (see Nünning 2011/forthcoming). I am very grateful to the colleagues I have thanked in the articles mentioned above and to the participants of the CECC-conference from which the present volume has emerged for valuable suggestions. Special thanks to my research assistants Ilke Krumholz and Simon Cooke, who translated the German article on which this much revised essay is based, for their valuable suggestions and support.

by metaphors as well as by the mini-narrations and narrative kernels they entail. We argue that the metaphors used when talking about money markets in general and the financial crisis in particular not only structure that perceived and experienced in our everyday realities, but that these metaphors also provide the categories by which we conceptualize and structure abstract cultural phenomena like money and money markets, and wide-ranging changes like the financial crisis that has held such a firm grip on the media and our lives since at least September 2008. The focus falls on questions about how societies collectively deal with and account for the cultural transformations brought about by the financial crisis, and just what role metaphors play in these processes. Arguably "the metaphors we pay for", to adapt (and misquote) Lakoff and Johnson's felicitous formulation "the metaphorical concepts we live by", provide one of the keys to understanding the topic at hand, i.e. "The Cultural Life of Money", and even more so to coming to grips with the role of metaphors in shaping the cultural life of money. More specifically, the crisis metaphor has arguably served to spare the fates of quite a few banks.

Using these preliminary examples and observations as a point of departure, this article argues that metaphors not only structure what we perceive and experience in our everyday realities (cf. Lakoff & Johnson 1980), but that crisis metaphors also provide the categories in terms of which we conceptualize and structure the domains known as the money markets and the world of finance and correspondingly determining the cultural life of money in subtle ways. We focus on questions about how societies collectively deal with and account for crucial changes such as the 'financial crisis', and what role metaphors play in these processes. We argue that in order to come to terms with the role metaphors play in shaping the cultural life of money, we would be wise to begin by looking at the discursive and metaphorical strategies deployed in efforts to describe and to cope with the 'financial crisis' because they not only serve as means of structuring, narrativizing and naturalizing what has happened in the world of finance, but they are also, as we seek to demonstrate, important sense- and indeed world-making devices. Moreover, the article aims to look more closely at the actual cultural, economic and political work that metaphors do and attempts to convey how "no metaphor comes without ideological freight" (Eubanks 1999: 437). On the contrary, metaphors are not only "the understanding of something in one conceptual domain [...] by conceptual projection from something in a different conceptual domain" (Turner/Fauconnier 1999: 403), they also serve as subtle economic and political tools that are heavily imbued with cognitive, emotional, and ideological connotations.

Following some preliminary considerations on how crises in general and the current financial crisis in particular are treated in the media society (section 1) the first of the two main sections deals with the development of the building blocks of a metaphorology (and narratology) of crisis with the help of some key concepts from narrative theory and from metaphor theory (section 2). This attempt to outline the main features of a metaphorology of crisis is concluded by a short overview on the functions which metaphors (and plots) of crises fulfil (section 3). We then argue that in order to come to terms with the role played by metaphors in shaping the cultural life of money, it might be useful to begin by looking at the discursive, literary, and cognitive strategies deployed in the attempt to cope with disastrous changes because these not only serve as means of structuring, narrativizing and naturalizing cultural transformations, they also represent important sense- and indeed world-making devices.

2 Why money metaphors matter: Metaphors of crisis as figurative knowledge, mini-narrations and ways of shaping the cultural life of money

One might as well begin with the question of why metaphors matter when attempting to come to terms with the cultural life of money? The most obvious answer would probably be that discourses about money and the world of finance seem to be teeming with metaphors. As both countless reports on the recent, or ongoing, financial crisis (crises?) in newspapers and the wide range of common money metaphors listed on the website www.Metaphorology.com serve to demonstrate, money and the world of finance belong to those domains that people commonly write and talk about in figurative language.

The main reason for this widespread tendency to talk about crucial events and transformations in the world of the economy and finance in metaphoric terms is not hard to determine. Resorting to metaphors proves to be a means of conceptualizing that which defies direct observation and experience. As with those other abstract political entities that tend to be conceptualized metaphorically, for example history, government, and the state, both money itself and the crucial changes taking place in money markets are phenomena of considerable abstractness, complexity and elusiveness and anything but clearly delineated in people's experience as well as not at all easy to conceptualize or to come to terms with.

Moreover, talking about the ups and downs of the money market in metaphoric terms is a way of telling a story about, and making sense of, a domain the complexity of which the vast majority of people fails to understand. Philip Eubanks has argued that metaphors project "mininarrations" (Eubanks 1999:

437), and other theorists have also acknowledged the cognitive and knowledge-creating potential of metaphors. In the preface to his seminal encyclopedia of philosophical metaphors, the editor Ralf Konersmann answers the question of what metaphors actually are by providing a somewhat unusual functional definition: "Metaphors are narratives that mask themselves as a single word"[2] (Konersmann 2008: 17). The subtitle "figurative knowledge" ("Figuratives Wissen") of the preface, which is actually a highly interesting essay on the nature and functions of metaphors, sheds light on another key aspect of metaphors: the felicitous phrase "figurative knowledge" emphasizes how metaphors do indeed generate knowledge, albeit of this figurative kind.

It is through the production of narrative kernels, emotionally and ideologically charged plots, and figurative knowledge that both money metaphors and the metaphor of crisis, as drawn on by most commentators in their attempts to make sense of the crucial events and changes occurring in the globalized money markets, shape not only culture and theories, but also our worldviews and the cultural life of money. In what has become one of the classics of metaphor studies, *Metaphors We Live By*, George Lakoff and Mark Johnson observe that "the people who get to impose their metaphors on the culture get to define what we consider to be true [...]" (Lakoff/Johnson 1980: 160). Anyone who doubts that they are right has only to recall George W. Bush's haranguing about 'weapons of mass destruction in Iraq', which turned out to be weapons of the mind and mere metaphors but which nonetheless got 'to define what we' – or at least a large part of the American people – 'considered to be true' and themselves turning into verbal weapons of mass-destruction. This serves to show that metaphors prove a powerful way of world-making, affecting our thinking and sometimes even determining what actually happens.

The same holds true for the ways in which we talk about money and try to make sense of the mysterious and apparently random complexities of the world of finance. As with many of the other crises the media confront us with almost daily in what seems the age of crises and catastrophes, the recent financial crisis was largely conceptualized in metaphoric terms. This arguably has far-reaching consequences given how metaphors shape the ways we think and feel about what is happening: Whoever manages to get to impose their crisis metaphors on the elusive events and changes occurring in the world of finance gets to define what people consider true. Nowhere is the world-making function of metaphors more palpable than in media discourses able to turn just about any event, situation or cultural change into a severe crisis where not an actual catastrophe.

---

2 "Metaphern sind Erzählungen, die sich als Einzelwort maskieren."

The metaphor of crisis prevailing in accounts and descriptions of the upheavals of the money markets provides a fascinating case-study of how metaphors not only serve to shape prevailing views of crucial changes that have occurred in money markets worldwide since 2008, metaphors are also simultaneously shaped by the cultures from which they originate. On the one hand, metaphors project structures and emotions onto cultural or financial phenomena, which otherwise defy direct observation and thus serve to make sense of them. In doing so, they play a central role in shaping common views of the domains they purport merely to describe. On the other hand, metaphors also get shaped by everyday cultural notions. As Zoltán Kövecses has convincingly shown in a number of publications (1999, 2000, 2002, 2005), metaphors not only reflect prevailing cultural models, they also shape or even constitute cultural models. By focussing on this reciprocal relationship between the metaphor of crisis and our culture in general and the cultural life of money in particular, this article explores both the implications of the metaphor and the functions that the metaphor of crisis serves to fulfil within culture, arguing that metaphors and the mini-narratives they entail largely determine the cultural life of money and financial crises. One might go so far as to argue that metaphors not only shape the forms and fantasies surrounding the cultural life of money, they may even influence financial facts as the course of the financial crises since 2008 arguably serves to demonstrate.

Given the sheer number of today's crises and the ubiquity of crisis metaphors in our contemporary media culture, it comes as no surprise that the media themselves have taken up the topic of metaphors of the crisis. In the aforementioned article "In Financial Crisis, Metaphors Fly Like Bad Analogies", Michael M. Philips provides a wide range of interesting examples of how the real financial crisis has generated plenty of metaphors of crisis and illness, some of which are indeed "bad analogies" or unwittingly funny catachreses. What the examples serve to show, however, is that the discourses of crisis generate ever more metaphors, most of which have the body and illness as the main source domains. Cases in point include "the patient's arteries are clogged, and he'll get a heart attack unless we do something", "the image from prognosis to prescription", 'tainted medicine', and credit being "the lifeblood of the economy".

Though the ubiquity and pervasive importance of crisis metaphors in contemporary media culture may be hard to deny or ignore, it may be less obvious that the word 'crisis' is at all a metaphor, let alone a case in point as far as metaphors being 'narratives that mask as a single word' are concerned. However, this is exactly what the metaphor of 'crisis' is, as we have tried to demonstrate elsewhere (see Nünning 2007, 2009). Describing the financial turmoil as a 'crisis' or as "putting even healthy businesses at risk" (Willman 2008) serves to structure how we understand them, while also projecting "mininarrations" (Eubanks 1999: 437) onto them. As we aim to demonstrate, the metaphor of crisis provides an ideologically charged plot and explanation of the events that have occurred on the money markets rather than neutral descriptions thereof. It is arguably "the metaphorical concepts we live by", to use Lakoff and Johnson's (1980: 22) felicitous formulation, or, in this case, the metaphors we have to pay for for years on end, that provide the key to understanding the topic at hand, i.e. the cultural life of money. Should one accept the Lakoff and Johnson (*Ibid.*, 106) view "that most of our conceptual system is metaphorically structured", then one might even go so far as to argue that metaphors and narratives are the most powerful tools we have for making sense of cultural transformations, endowed as they are with the power of reason and the power of evaluation (cf. Lakoff/Turner 1989: 65).

3 Metaphors of money and the 'Financial Crisis': Metaphorological and narratological observations

In order to put some more flesh on the skeleton above, let us take a look at some of the most common money metaphors in order to get to grips with the question as to just where metaphors, money and its cultural life meet. We commonly accept that metaphors abound in everyday ways of talking about money itself, i.e. money as a target domain is typically referred to in figurative terms. But money also serves as a source domain or vehicle to describe other domains. The following brief list gives a highly selective overview of some common money metaphors:

> Time is money.
> Business is a game.
> Our share of the pie is shrinking (wealth is a piece of the pie).
> Money has no smell. (*pecunia non olet*)
> Money is the lifeblood of the economy.

The very popular metaphor of 'time is money', which maps money onto the target domain of time, "suggests that any time spent on anything other than making money is making one poorer – a very stressful perspective" (www.Metaphorology.com). As soon as this common money metaphor is reversed ('money is time.'), a very different metaphor emerges that has quite liberating implications:

"it reminds us that money can be used to buy time for almost any purpose. With enough of it, we can quit doing most of the things we don't want to do, to free up our hours and days for what we are passionate about." (*Ibid.*) Whereas the common metaphor 'time is money' implies that any time invested [*Sic*] in activities that do not result in more or less immediate monetary payback is not time well spent [*Sic*], a mere switch in the metaphor's order bears far-reaching cultural and emotional effects, changing the ways we think about money and time.

Variations on the last metaphor in the above list, i.e. "Money is the lifeblood of the economy" have recently been applied over and over again, leading to all those bailouts designed to avoid financial meltdown, which is, of course, yet another metaphor, and one that comes with very alarming emotional undertones and ideological freight at that. What most of the metaphors deployed to describe the financial crisis have in common is that they conjure up a very disquieting atmosphere amidst appalling scenarios. Causing an atmosphere of anxiety and fear, the crisis metaphor itself implies that the money market upheavals are themselves a matter of life and death. The same holds true for other metaphors deployed in the context of the financial crisis, with the metaphors of "financial 'tsunami'" and bailouts helping "save everyone from the rising financial flood waters" (Phillips 2008) representing just two of the countless cases in point.

Cognitive metaphor theory sheds light on the narrative structure and the discursive construction of crises, illuminating the various implications of the 'financial crisis' metaphor. Should the term 'crisis' be transferred to the world of finance, we need to above all remember that we are dealing only with a metaphor: As a brief look into the history of the concept reveals, the term crisis originates from the vocabulary and semantics of ancient medical science (cf. Winau), as Alexander Demandt points out in his seminal book *Metaphors for History* [*Metaphern für Geschichte*]: "Originally it meant 'decision' and in antiquity this quite unmetaphorical meaning was already applied to history" (Demandt 1978: 27). However, the modern concept of crisis is not determined by this original meaning but by its derivative medical application: "In the writings of Hippocrates and Galen, *krisis* describes the point of time during a course of disease at which the fate of a patient, whether he recovers or dies, is determined" (*Ibid.*).

This organology-related background is preserved in the modern discourse of crises in both history in general and economic and financial history in particular: "Wherever a crisis is identified, a patient can be discovered as well; be it in reality or in the mind of the person speaking of the 'crisis'" (*Ibid.*). Thus, speaking of a banking crisis or a financial crisis is equivalent to the diagnosis of disease, with the banks or the money markets being the patient whose life is at stake. The metaphor of the financial crisis, however, does not merely evoke images of disease, of a patient, and of healing; rather, the metaphorics also project both a diagnosis and a certain story or plot pattern onto the situation.

Cognitive metaphor theory conceptualizes what is involved in such a complex process of metaphoric projection in terms of 'blending' or 'conceptual integration'.[3] Foregrounding the mapping process and exploring how the source domain is mapped onto the target domain, cognitive approaches characterize metaphoric blending processes as a 'mechanism of creativity' (Turner/Fauconnier 1999): "Image-schematic projection creates a new virtual realm, the blend, which is no longer subordinate to either the source (vehicle) or the tenor (target) but instead creates an emergent structure that exists neither in the source nor the target domains" (Fludernik/Freeman/Freeman 1999: 387). This model does not only consider how people draw on their pre-existing conceptual and cultural knowledge when they use or process metaphors, but also demonstrates how metaphoric projection is anything but a one-sided, uni-directional affair. On the contrary, what is involved is a process of mutual integration of two distinct conceptual domains.

In the present case, both the personal sphere of illness and the economic and financial sphere of crucial changes in the money markets are projected onto this blended space, which, while bringing together the salient features of the two knowledge domains involved, "exactly resembles none of them" (*Ibid.*, 393): "This selective borrowing, or rather, projection, is not merely compositional – instead, there is new meaning in the blend that is not a composition of meanings that can be found in the inputs" (Turner/Fauconnier 1999: 398). By creating conceptual blends between the personal domain of illness and the public sphere of economics, crisis metaphors profoundly affect the way in which economic and financial changes are perceived and understood. They thereby suggest that the essential character of such changes is that of a dangerous illness in the respective system. Moreover, the choice of the metaphor largely determines the human understanding of, and reactions to, the situation or transformation designated as a crisis.

Once a certain situation is metaphorically marked as a 'financial crisis', this kind of definition or diagnosis of a situation simultaneously implies and activates certain frameworks and narrative schemata. To begin with, 'crisis' in general and 'financial crisis' in particular implies great anxiety and insecurity, a

---

3 It is, of course, beyond the scope of the present essay to present a detailed account of cognitive metaphor theory or of conceptual integration network theory. For a brief introduction, see Fludernik/Freeman/Freeman (1999, 387–392) and Turner/Fauconnier; for comprehensive accounts, see Fauconnier (1994; 1997), Fauconnier/Turner (1998), Turner (1996), and Kövecses (2000, 2002, 2005, 2006).

dangerous threat potentially affecting lots of people. In the case of a crisis, the climax and turning point in a dangerous development is either reached or imminent. As the English saying, "We must bring things to a crisis", nicely puts it, a crisis always also represents a moment of decision-making. Thus, labeling an event as a 'crisis' not only provides a specific definition for the respective situation, but also evokes certain narrative schemata, development patterns, and plots. On the one hand, describing a situation as a 'crisis' is also always a diagnosis from which certain therapeutic perspectives and action scenarios for future development derive. On the other hand, the schemata activated interpret the possible courses of events lying ahead in some specific way.

Who and what is sought after in a situation like a 'financial crisis' is apparent according to the respective culturally available crisis plots, because when talking about a 'crisis' specific actions and developmental patterns get simultaneously invoked. Depending on the social realm of action (e.g. the economy, politics, international relations), there may be different crises but the fundamental scheme remains the same, both from a narratological perspective and from the point of view of metaphor theory: What is required in a crisis is active crisis managers (i.e. according to the original literal meaning, physicians but figuratively speaking, politicians, management boards, 'financial experts', etc.), crisis management plans, and purposeful actions (in short: successful crisis management). Speaking about a crisis always evokes conventionalized schemata and plot patterns sketching out the future course of action. For this reason, diagnosing a financial crisis always already represents more than a specific definition of the situation in question and, in retrospect, oftentimes appears a self-fulfilling prophecy.

In order to get to grips with the question of why metaphors matter when we try to understand their important role for affecting the cultural life of money, we should, heuristically, bear in mind the fact that common media talk about a financial crisis actually remains just a metaphor and that this metaphor does not just represent or embellish the world of the money markets but also fulfils extensive structuring, narrativizing and constructive functions – just as metaphors do in general. The medical vehicle 'crisis' provides particular elements or 'slots' characterizing the special features of crisis plots. For a start, two central members of the cast are of importance: a patient or crisis-ridden organism; and a physician or observer, who diagnoses the disease from a "privileged control-room" (cf. Hielscher 2001: 319). In the case of financial crises, the patient whose life is at stake is, of course, the banks or the countries (recently especially Greece and Ireland) that are in dire financial straits and in great need of being saved. Politicians and experts of all sorts have usurped the role of the physicians who have not only diagnosed the disease but who have also made far-reaching decisions about what they consider the best therapy or treatment, prescribing the appropriate corresponding medication and remedies.

This already serves to show that the metaphor of 'financial crisis' implies a number of other aspects that include the following (and making no claim to be comprehensive): disease symptoms, or aspects of the crisis condition; an anamnesis, i.e. inquiry into the medical case history of the disease (according to the patient); the diagnosis, i.e. the detection or evaluation of the kind and quality of the disease as well as the condition of the patient, which is based on precise monitoring and examination; the therapy, i.e. the identification of every possible remedy and method of treatment; and the therapist, namely somebody who administers the therapy (he or she may be, but does not necessarily have to be, the same person as the physician or the privileged observer). In addition, the metaphor 'crisis' always evokes a number of culturally determined connotations and associations with the main such facets including: alarm, anxiety, danger, threat, disturbance, fear and concern, and a search for remedies.

The fact that the metaphor of crisis already largely pre-structures the target domain of the world of finance, and that it furthermore implies a general developmental scheme with regard to the narrative pattern that potentially forms the basis of every crisis scenario, is therefore crucial to a metaphorology and narratology of crisis (see Nünning 2009). Cognitive metaphor theory demonstrates that metaphors not only structure the way in which we understand cultural phenomena and processes, they also project "mininarrations" (Eubanks, 437) onto the respective tenor or target domain. As soon as we speak about 'crisis', a course-of-disease scheme is invoked: "There is an identifiable beginning, which is to be understood as a cause and which starts a development which leads to a reasonable ending; disturbances of this structure provoke an extensive awareness of danger" (Bullivant/Spies 2001: 17).

Moreover, by projecting a crisis plot upon the dramatic changes and events that we have witnessed in the money markets since 2008, the metaphorical concept of 'financial crisis' serves to narrativize and naturalize them. The projection of crisis-plots may be understood as an interpretive strategy or cognitive process of the sort that has become known as 'naturalization', which makes complex economic or historical phenomena intelligible in terms of culturally accepted frames. To interpret cultural or economic transformations in terms of such culturally bound plots involves a way of naturalizing changes by attributing to them a function in some larger pattern supplied by accepted cultural models. Culler clarifies what 'naturalization' means in this context: "to naturalize a text is to bring it into relation with a type of discourse or model, which is already, in some sense, natural or legible" (Culler 1975: 138). This kind of metaphoric naturalization is so greatly ingrained into our everyday cognitive strategies applied in dealing with and accounting for cultural changes that, in all probability, we are neither conscious nor hardly, if ever, notice it.

Consequently, speaking about or diagnosing a banking crisis or financial crisis includes not only defining the action-roles identified above but, as a result of the systematic logic and underlying mini-narration of the metaphor, also linking past, present and future in a comprehensive plot. With regard to the past, the diagnosis of a financial crisis implies a negative, more or less teleological development towards a critical stage. By contrast, the present in a crisis-diagnosis is perceived and interpreted as a decisive moment and as a realm of possibilities. With regard to the future this results in a spectrum of different possibilities and potential development structures, which range from the extremes of death and dissolution of the organism in question, on the one hand, to recovery and overcoming the crisis on the other. The age-old similes for particular peoples and states are typical examples of this. Organic crisis metaphors were frequently used to describe the Fall of Rome: sickly Rome lying on the deathbed (cf. Demandt 1978: 80). In the present financial crisis, banks and whole countries have been lying on their deathbeds, with 'Lehmann Brothers' and many others actually 'passing away', while some luckier ones were saved by previously unheard of bailouts the gigantic size of which makes many minds boggle.

Apart from the already mentioned action-roles and fundamental images, the metaphoric origin of the rhetoric of crisis draws attention to further aspects which are of interest for coming to terms with the crucial role that metaphors have played for the cultural, and economic, life of money in the recent financial crises. This includes the question of the causes or the initiators of the crisis, the question of concepts and solutions, the question of selecting crisis managers and actors to find a solution for the crisis, as well as the question of the crisis-experience of the respective protagonists, not to mention the cultural crisis-awareness of an era. The respective demeanor or attitude towards a crisis ranges from resignation and melancholy on the one hand, to euphoria on the other: "The experience of a crisis can lead to the resolute refusal of accepting the impending loss and provoke the impulse to seriously defend the endangered goods; however, the experience of a factual commotion of what was valid so far can also be turned into an argument for the necessity of its downfall" (Bullivant/Spies 2001: 15 – 16).

It is obvious that due to the range of implications that the metaphor of crisis offers, different attitudes towards financial crises produce entirely different plots. Speaking of 'the' crisis plot would therefore be highly questionable. Rather, by means of the metaphoric language of crisis, a broad spectrum of possible development structures is evoked, according to which the option which actually occurs depends on the skills of the protagonist in crisis management. The spectrum of possibilities range from the extreme of recovery or even improvement, to versions of sitting it out and twiddling one's thumbs in the middle (which usually leads to an aggravation and worsening of the crisis), right to the other extreme of death and destruction, which befall not only individuals, but also empires (witness the Roman Empire), banks and potentially even countries as the result of a crisis.

As the above metaphorological and narratological analysis of metaphors of money and the financial crisis serves to show, such metaphors, by virtue of their more or less coherent entailments, provide a systematic way of talking about and making sense of the economic upheavals that have recently occurred on money markets worldwide. Lakoff and Johnson (ch. 2) have emphasized what they call the "systematicity of metaphorical concepts" (Lakoff, Johnson 1980: 7) and have spelled out its implications: "The very systematicity that allows us to comprehend one aspect of a concept in terms of another [...] will necessarily hide other aspects of the concept. In allowing us to focus on one aspect of a concept [...], a metaphorical concept can keep us from focusing on other aspects of the concept that are inconsistent with that metaphor" (*Ibid.* 10). Metaphors "form coherent systems in terms of which we conceptualize our experience" (*Ibid.*, 41) – and the mysterious world of finance, one might add. Highlighting certain aspects of complex economic and financial processes while hiding or even repressing others, metaphorical concepts like the 'financial crisis' serve as both sense-making devices and as "'strategies of containment' whereby they are able to project the illusion that their readings are somehow complete and self-sufficient" (Jameson 1983: 10).

4 The metaphors of 'Financial Crisis' as diagnosis, discourse-strategy, and licensing story: Functions of crisis-metaphors and crisis-plots

In closing, the question presents itself as to what functions might be fulfilled by the metaphor, narrative, and rhetoric of the 'financial crisis' that has so ubiquitously and even inflationarily been used in politics and the media. Rather than just taking the dominant rhetoric of world-wide financial crises implied in the metaphors at face value or even mistaking such tropes for a simple reflection of economic or financial reality, one might look more closely at the functions that such money metaphors fulfil. Several functions are identifiable, although many of them are syncretized in specific texts and media.

First of all, the widespread manner of speaking of someone or something as being plunged 'deep into crisis' is aimed at generating interest and "page-turner excitement" (Bebermeyer 1981: 352), especially in the media. A further general function seen is that of drawing on crisis-plots as a means of making sense and coherence: situations perceived as 'crises' are those "which are virtually urged to be narrated, for the production of coherent, sense-making and identity-providing stories, models, and attempts at arrangement, which bring coherence, sense- and identity to produce" (Hielscher 2001: 314). Renate Bebermeyer has concisely sketched out further fundamental functions from the perspective of linguistics:

> The original academic terminus crisis has two simultaneous functions to fulfil, one of which is structural, deriving from its availability as a readymade building-block for the quick production of ever new composites. Besides its building-block capacity, the 'crisis'-concept has a second, double-sided task: on the one hand, it is called on as a demonstrative and at the same time expression-varying substitute word for its compositional derivates; on the other, it offers, free from the grip of its compositional role, a general and generalised, negatively loaded catchword summary of all developments and changes calling forth unrest and angst (Bebermeyer 1981: 354).

As the intense debates about financial crises have conveyed, in politics in particular, crisis-metaphorics have long been part of the rhetorical basics of polemics against other parties and those who think differently. For politicians "crisis is [...] – depending on need – confirmation and alibi, both are offered one from the most different of motivations; one profits massively from the crisis-pound" (*Ibid.*, 349). The reasons for this are clear: "Some politicians need pessimism, 'the world of growing crises and dangers' and therefore also the vocabulary of catastrophe, in order to effectively place themselves and their strategies in the light; the current journalistic compulsion to overuse and sensationalism – a report needs a media-justifying (big) format to be heard – does the rest." (*Ibid.*, 355) The implicit message launched by the steely crisis managers and media pros is thus: "A danger named is a danger banished" (cf. *Ibid.*, 356)[4].

Moreover, by reducing the complexities, contingency, and elusiveness of the chaotic facts, the metaphors of financial crisis impose form upon a chaotic reality. Another function is therefore to impart a relatively clear and orderly structure and plot to amorphous and highly complex economic, financial and political phenomena and processes, thus serving as unifying and ordering devices. What deserves to be emphasized is that the structure which metaphorical mappings allow us to impart to a given domain "is not there independent of the metaphor" (Lakoff/Turner 1980: 64). Metaphoric projections represent coherent organizations of complex phenomena in terms of 'natural' (or naturalized) categories like illness: metaphors are "structured clearly enough and with

---

4 "Gefahr benannt – Gefahr gebannt."

enough of the right kind of internal structure to do the job of defining other concepts" (Lakoff/Johnson 1980: 118). Despite their inevitably reductive character, the metaphors of financial crisis can fulfil heuristic or cognitive functions in that they represent a particular diagnosis of a situation (cf. Grunwald/Pfister 2007). As conceptual tools, metaphors generally resemble models. Imposing form and structure upon an untidy, contingent, and chaotic reality, metaphors, like crises, serve as models for thought that, as conceptual fictions, people and whole cultures live by (cf. Lakoff/Johnson 1980).

Equating the functions of metaphors entirely with those of models, however, ignores creative usages of metaphors in the representation of cultural objects or economic transformations. In contrast to models, which represent structural relations, metaphors impose structures and "often do creative work" (Turner 1987: 19). As the above analysis conveys (see section 3), the ubiquitous metaphors surrounding the 'financial crisis' serve to demonstrate that metaphors not only create individual target domain slots but also determine the way in which a given target domain is perceived and understood in the first place. The second reason metaphors are more than just conceptual or cognitive models derives from the importance of evoking emotion within the metaphorical process, as Paul Ricœur (1978: 143) and Zoltán Kövecses (2000), among other metaphor theorists, have convincingly shown. Of far greater interest to the cultural historian than the functions metaphors share with models are those metaphoric functions that shed light on the ideological, normative and political implications of metaphors as popular as crisis.

In addition to their power to impose structure, metaphors of financial crises also serve as important means of conditioning emotional responses, fostering as they do reactions of fear, shock and stress. This emotional function becomes particularly obvious in the case of such financial crisis metaphors as 'the lifeblood of the economy' because they imply a sense of collective threat and arguably the dominant affective component in this metaphor type. Such financial crisis metaphors not only help to generate emotions, they also rhetorically assert the need for effective crisis-management. Since these emotional entailments serve to foster the widespread willingness to subscribe to gigantic bailouts payable by future generations, metaphors of financial crises are arguably not only 'metaphors we live by' but also metaphors that we have to pay for.

Another function of the financial crisis metaphors consists of providing contemporaries with simplified but relatively coherent frameworks for interpreting recent economic and financial developments as well as the political decisions taken within the framework of crisis management. As mental models, metaphoric fictions provide powerful tools for making sense of complex situations and economic changes. By actually commenting upon the economic events that they purport merely to reflect or to report, financial crisis metaphors serve as a means for explaining complex financial processes. The structure and logic inherent in the crisis-metaphor, for instance, not only greatly reduces the complexity of the target domain phenomena but also transforms a chaotic series of events into a simple story or a crisis-plot (see section 3 above). With regard to how "metaphors can be made into mininarrations" (Eubanks 1999: 437), the metaphor of crisis represents a perfect case in point.

As with many others metaphors, financial crisis metaphors also fulfil important normative functions given how they authorize and propagate ideologically charged diagnoses and interpretations of the situations they otherwise purport merely to describe. By providing a diagnosis, they project particular norms and values onto the target domain. Although as a rule one cannot extract a very sophisticated economic theory from any of the crisis and money metaphors examined above, they tend to leave no doubt as to what the desirable form of action or reaction should be: effective crisis-management. In other words, financial crisis metaphors are never deployed for merely descriptive purposes but rather in a prescriptive way, subtly propagating normative views rather than providing neutral descriptions. Drawing on values deeply embedded in culture, metaphors of crises not only project features and structural relations from the various source domains onto the respective target domains and cultural transformations, they also imply how the entities of the two domains are to be evaluated within the new blend resulting from this conceptual integration (cf. Lakoff/Turner 1989: 65).

Therefore, crisis metaphors correspondingly often serve as political arguments in how the form of the diagnosis usually already implies the best political remedy. As the politically motivated applications of crisis metaphors in the recent discussions about the global financial and economic crises have illustrated time and again, the often fierce debates about the pros and cons of the various bailouts were carried out at least as much in metaphorical as in literal terms even while many of the political protagonists are unlikely to be aware of the metaphorical nature of crisis discourses. Though 'crisis' is, of course, also an economic concept, the actual applications of the term in the media and the surrounding discourses show that the metaphoric implications, more often than not, gain the upper hand.

Other salient examples here are the host of crisis and money metaphors that have been deployed in articles in *The Financial Times* and many other newspapers about the volatile stock-markets in and since 2008. In contrast to other more covert uses of crisis metaphors, the metaphoric nature of the medicinal discourse of crisis is foregrounded as soon as other metaphors belonging to the same metaphoric field are applied, i.e. to what Weinrich and others have felicitously called

Bildfeld. A typical case in point is an article published in *The Financial Times* (11 October 2008) entitled "Fear Prevents Patient from Responding to Treatment": "The patient is not responding. Liquidity infusions, co-ordinated rate cuts, state-sponsored bank bail-outs – nothing seems to be working. The London market is in cardiac arrest" (Hume 2008). Opposition politicians can, of course, raise the question of whether "the right medicine is being given in the right dose at the right time" (Bowers, 2008). Even though politicians, business leaders, and economists may agree on the diagnosis, the metaphorical implications of 'crisis' provide no guarantee that any agreement on remedies can be expected.

As these examples show, metaphors of money and financial crises fulfil legitimizing or licensing functions because they provide rationalizations and justifications for whatever diagnosis and therapy the 'crisis-managers' come up with. Forging emotional and functional links between such manifestly unlike phenomena as the world of banking and finance and the realm of illness, the financial crisis metaphor serves as an important means of legitimizing whatever desperate measures the government proposes. As the example quoted above serves to illustrate, even desperate remedies are in order in efforts to cure a sick patient's disease because exceptional times such as the global banking crisis require exceptional remedies. Though people tend to agree that even someone like President Obama cannot cure a sick world economy alone, he has been depicted as the powerful doctor who "must mend a sick world economy" (Wolf 2009). The prevailing diagnoses of global economic crisis seem to legitimize just about any desperate and tough remedy, the more so as long as everybody agrees that 'the patient is still in intensive care' or even 'in cardiac arrest', that there is great danger of contagion or infection, and that the financial turmoil has begun to put even formerly healthy businesses at risk. In short: the legitimizing or licensing functions of the metaphor implies that crises call for immediate crisis intervention by experienced crisis managers, even radical attempts at first aid are no longer questioned, and if prolonged therapy seems unavoidable, this is also readily accepted on having achieved agreement on suitable remedies.

In doing so, metaphors not only provide highly simplified accounts of complex cultural changes, they implicitly also project what Eubanks aptly calls "licensing stories" (Eubanks 1999: 424): "[F]or us to regard any mapping as apt, it must comport with our licensing stories – our repertoire of ideologically inflected narratives, short and long, individual and cultural, that organize our sense of how the world works and how the world should work." (*Ibid.*, 426) In the light of the Eubanks hypotheses about what motivates metaphoric mappings, it is probably no coincidence that crisis metaphors currently prove the most popular of all of the tropes applied to describing the state of affairs prevailing. This may largely be attributed to the fact that the licensing stories associated with fatal illness ensure that the measures proposed are generally regarded as especially apt, reflecting as they have done a broad cultural, ethical, and normative consensus: "That is to say, our world-making stories give us the license – provide the requisite justification – needed to regard possible metaphoric mappings as sound." (*Ibid.*, 426–427) The licensing stories implied in the metaphors of financial crises not only provide historical or economic mini-narrations about the 'natural' origin and genesis of the problematic situation, they have also served to license and legitimize the phantasmagoric bailouts for any number of banks, and more recently European countries, that exceed our imagination.

Lastly, and arguably most importantly, metaphors of crises are central to the formation and maintenance of collective identities because they provide simple and coherent accounts of complex developments and because the mini-narrations entailed in these metaphors have important propagandistic and ideological implications, nurturing a culture's dominant fictions. Financial crisis metaphors, for instance, arguably tend to serve as subtle ideological handmaidens of capitalism, because they glorify the world of the money-markets that the crisis-manager set out to save. Metaphors thus help to nurture that culturally sanctioned system of ideas, beliefs, presuppositions, and convictions that constitutes sets of beliefs, hierarchies of norms and values or "system of ideological fictions" like capitalism.[5] The images and stories projected by financial metaphors are thus instrumental to what one might call the imaginative forging of the fictions of late-capitalism.

5 Metaphors and the cultural imagination, or: Metaphors shaping the cultural life of crises and of money

In short: metaphors of money and financial crises serve to narrativize and naturalize complex cultural, economic and political transformations, projecting ideologically charged plots onto the developments they purport merely to represent or to illustrate. In doing so, they arguably do creative work in serving to define how the cultural transformations associated with the current economic and financial problems are understood by contemporaries, familiarizing people with complex processes that are largely beyond their ken or understanding. Generating a whole network

---

5 Cf. Said (1978/1995: 321), who calls Orientalism a "system of ideological fictions" and who equates that phrase with such terms as "a body of ideas, beliefs, clichés, or learning" (*Ibid.*, 205), "systems of thought", "discourses of power", and with Blake's famous "mind-forg'd manacles" (*Ibid.*, 328).

of ideological implications and normative entailments, the metaphoric mappings involved in the metaphor of 'financial crisis' also play "a central role in the construction of social and political reality" (Lakoff/Johnson 1980: 159). Since metaphors have "the power to define reality" (Ibid., 157), they even constitute a license for policy change and political and economic action (cf. Ibid., 156).

Although the narratology and metaphorology sketched out for the financial crisis can certainly not offer a cure to either the banks or countries afflicted by the various financial crises or the medial production of crises, they do nevertheless promise a little healing or relief in how they provide some rays of light that allow one to see better through the crisis-fog spewed out by the media. Narratological and metaphorological analysis of the metaphors surrounding the financial crisis guides our attention, on the one hand, to the narrative structure and plots that those metaphors entail. On the other hand, analysis of the metaphorical origin and implications of the metaphorical concept of crisis sheds light on the action-roles and plots of the mini-narratives implicit to every diagnosis of crisis.

In conclusion, I would like to provide a brief assessment of the value that a cognitive and cultural analysis of metaphors such as 'financial crisis' or 'lifeblood of the economy' may have for the study of the relationship between metaphors, the cultural life of money, and the history of mentalities. As the above analysis has hopefully shown, crisis and money metaphors may profitably be understood as narrative kernels or mini-narrations that consist of a single word and that shed light on the cultural discourses from which they originate. On the one hand, the metaphors of crisis underscore the hypothesis that metaphors indeed shape both culture and the cultural life of money, turning our contemporary media society into a veritable culture of crises and crisis-managers. On the other hand, the example of the financial crisis also demonstrates that metaphors are themselves shaped by culture in that the ubiquitous discourses and metaphors of crisis reflect the penchant for exaggeration and sensationalism so characteristic of contemporary media-culture. The widespread media manner of speaking about banks, companies, and even entire countries and economies as being plunged 'deep into crisis', suitably dramatic as it is, targets generating interest, excitement, urgency, and the illusion of great importance, underscoring the newsworthiness of whatever the respective story may be about.

What I hope to have demonstrated is that a cultural and historical analysis of metaphors may hold great value to the study of culture, and for gaining insight into the ways in which metaphors affect the cultural life of both crises and money. A reconsidered notion of metaphors which takes into consideration their cultural implications and historical contexts can indeed "help to explain the cultural motivations of metaphoric mappings" (Eubanks 1999:421) and to "develop a richer account of conceptual metaphor as a cultural phenomenon"

(420). In contrast to the primarily synchronic and ahistorical account of conceptual metaphors which has so far predominated in cognitive metaphor theory (cf. Lakoff/Johnson 1980; Lakoff/Turner 1989), a historicized and cultural approach to metaphors throws new light on "how [...] metaphors operate concretely in the communicative world", revealing "not just mental processes but also something of our culture" (Eubanks 1999: 421). As Ana Margarida Abrantes' contribution, as well as other articles in this volume, also proves, money metaphors are very much a cultural and historical phenomenon as they are inflected by the cultural, economic, and political discourses of the period from which they originate, determining just how we think and feel about money.

As long as the patient, be it an important bank or a European country in need of financial support, "is still in intensive care" (Willman 2008), politicians will continue to convince us that 'exceptional times require exceptional remedies', as former British prime minister Gordon Brown and many of his colleagues often claimed as the banking and financial crises unfolded. In so doing, they have made very effective recourse to both the logical entailments and the emotional and ideological implications of metaphors of crisis that have become so ubiquitous in the countless reports and commentaries on the various crises that the money markets and governments have attempted to cope with since 2008. The 'financial crisis' metaphors examined above have not only served to shape the cultural life of money in many ways, they have also turned into metaphors that we will have to pay for in the years to come.

Works cited

Bebermeyer, Renate (1981) "'Krise' in der Krise. Eine Vokabel im Sog ihrer Komposita und auf dem Weg zum leeren Schlagwort," *Muttersprache. Zeitschrift zur Pflege und Erforschung der deutschen Sprache* 91, 345–359.

Bowers, David (2008) "Bad Medicine," *The Financial Times* (3 December 2008).

Bullivant, Keith and Bernhard Spies (2001) "Vorwort," in *Literarisches Krisenbewußtsein. Ein Perzeptions- und Produktionsmuster im 20. Jahrhundert*, ed. Keith Bullivant and Bernhard Spies (Munich: iudicum), 7–18.

Culler, Jonathan (1975) *Structuralist Poetics: Structuralism, Linguistics and the Study of Literature* (London: Routledge & Kegan Paul).

Demandt, Alexander (1978) *Metaphern für Geschichte: Sprachbilder und Gleichnisse im historisch-politischen Denken* (Munich: Beck).

Eubanks, Philip (1999) "The Story of Conceptual Metaphor: What Motivates Metaphoric Mappings?," *Poetics Today* 20.3, 419–442.

Fauconnier, Gilles (1994), UK: *Mental Spaces: Aspects of Meaning Construction in Natural Language* (Cambridge, UK: Cambridge University Press).

Fauconnier, Gilles (1997) *Mappings in Thought and Language* (Cambridge, UK: Cambridge University Press).

Fauconnier, Gilles and Mark Turner (1998) "Conceptual Integration Networks," *Cognitive Science* 22, 133–187.

Fludernik, Monika, Donald C. Freeman and Margaret H. Freeman (1999) "Metaphor and Beyond: An Introduction," *Poetics Today* 20.3, 383–396.

Grabes, Herbert, Ansgar Nünning and Sibylle Baumbach (eds) (2009) *Metaphors Shaping Culture and Theory. REAL – Yearbook of Research in English and American Literature* 25 (Tübingen: Narr 2009).

Grunwald, Henning and Manfred Pfister (eds) (2007) *Krisis! Krisenszenarien, Diagnosen und Diskursstrategien* (Munich: Fink).

Grunwald, Henning and Manfred Pfister (2007a) "Krisis! Krisenszenarien, Diagnosen und Diskursstrategien," in Grunwald and Pfister 7–20.

Hielscher, Martin (2001) "Kritik der Krise. Erzählerische Strategien der jüngsten Gegenwartsliteratur und ihre Vorläufer," in *Literarisches Krisenbewußtsein. Ein Perzeptions- und Produktionsmuster im 20. Jahrhundert*, ed. Keith Bullivant and Bernhard Spies (Munich: iudicum), 314–334.

Hume, Neil (2008) "Fear Prevents Patient from Responding to Treatment," *The Financial Times* (11 October 2008).

Jameson, Fredric (1983) *The Political Unconscious: Narrative as a Socially Symbolic Act* (London: Methuen [1981]).

Kövecses, Zoltán (1999) "Does Metaphor Reflect or Constitute Cultural Models?," in: *Metaphor in Cognitive Linguistics*, ed. Raymond W. Gibbs and Gerald J. Steen (Amsterdam: John Benjamins), 167–188.

Kövecses, Zoltán (2000) *Metaphor and Emotion. Language, Culture, and Body in Human Feeling* (Cambridge, UK, and NY: Cambridge University Press).

Kövecses, Zoltán (2002) *Metaphor. A Practical Introduction* (Oxford: Oxford University Press).

Kövecses, Zoltán (2005) *Metaphor in Culture. Universality and Variation* (Cambridge, UK: Cambridge University Press).

Kövecses, Zoltán (2006) *Language, Mind, and Culture. A Practical Introduction* (Oxford: Oxford University Press).

Konersmann, Ralf (ed) (2008) *Wörterbuch der philosophischen Metaphern* (Darmstadt: Wissenschaftliche Buchgesellschaft).

Konersmann, Ralf (2008a) "Vorwort: Figuratives Wissen," *Wörterbuch der philosophischen Metaphern*, in Konersmann 7–21.

Lakoff, George and Mark Johnson (1980) *Metaphors We Live By* (Chicago and London: University of Chicago Press).

Lakoff, George and Mark Turner (1989) *More than Cool Reason: A Field Guide to Poetic Metaphor* (Chicago and London: University of Chicago Press).

Nünning, Ansgar (2007) "Narratologie der Krise: Wie aus einer Situation ein Plot und eine Krise (konstruiert) warden," in Grunwald and Pfister 48–71.

Nünning, Ansgar (2009) "Steps Towards a Metaphorology (and Narratology) of Crises: On The Functions of Metaphors as Figurative Knowledge and Mininarrations," in Grabes et al. 229–262.

Nünning, Ansgar (2010) "Making Events – Making Stories – Making Worlds: Ways of Worldmaking from a Narratological Point of View," in [Vera] Nünning et al. 191–214.

Nünning, Ansgar (2011) "Towards a Metaphorology of Crises, or: The Uses of Cognitive Metaphor Theory for the Study of Culture," in *Cognition and Culture*, ed. Ana Margarida Abrantes and Peter Hanenberg (Bern: Peter Lang).

Nünning, Ansgar, Herbert Grabes and Sibylle Baumbach (2009) "Metaphors as Ways of Worldmaking, or: Where Metaphors and Culture Meet," in Grabes et al. XI-XXVIII.

Nünning, Vera, Ansgar Nünning and Birgit Neumann (eds) (2010), *Cultural Ways of Worldmaking: Media and Narratives* (Berlin, New York: De Gruyter).

Phillips, Michael M. (2008) "In Financial Crisis, Metaphors Fly Like Bad Analogies," *The Wall Street Journal* (27 September 2008).

Ricœur, Paul (1978) "The Metaphorical Process as Cognition, Imagination, and Feeling," *Critical Inquiry* 5.1, 143–159.

Said, Edward (1995) *Orientalism: Western Conceptions of the Orient* (Harmondsworth: Penguin [1978]).

Turner, Mark (1987) *Death is the Mother of Beauty: Mind, Metaphor, Criticism* (Chicago and London: University of Chicago Press).

Turner, Mark (1996) *The Literary Mind* (Oxford: Oxford University Press).

Turner, Mark and Gilles Fauconnier (1999) "A Mechanism of Creativity," *Poetics Today* 20.3, 397–418.

Willman, John, (2008) "CBI Urges Action on Cash Flow," *The Financial Times* (23 November 2008).

Winau, Rolf (2007) "Krise (in) der Medizin: Die Entwicklung des medizinischen Krisenbegriffs und das ärztliche Selbstverständnis," in Grunwald et al. 41–47.

Wolf, Martin (2009) "Why Obama must mend a sick world economy," *The Financial Times* (20 January 2009).

www.metaphorology.com

João César das Neves
Money: From Midas to Madoff

The cultural life of money may be approached from many viewpoints. This essay tries briefly to use only one of those, that of the economic theory of money. This choice is based not on any claim of its special importance or relevance, but merely on personal limitations. I have no way of making any contribution outside of this field (and not really sure there is one to make in it). As Economics holds many connections with other cultural fields, this limitation may somewhat be reduced by the choice of reference authors. In particular, we must note that the first economist to state a theory of money was Aristotle, a figure who spans far beyond Economics and clearly also one of the most influential authors in the field as may easily be proven.[1] This theory is found in two main texts: Book I of *Politics* and Book V of *Nicomachean Ethics*. Much may be gained from capturing the cultural life of money. Some of the features open up some important clues about the cultural life of money.

1 The body of money

We may start with the definition of money proposed by Aristotle, which extends widely in his statement of its usage. In fact, money is defined according to its own function:

> All commodities exchanged must be able to be compared in some way. It is to meet this requirement that men have introduced money; money constitutes in a manner a middle term, for it is a measure of all things. (NE 1133a.19)
>
> Money then serves as a measure which makes things commensurable and so reduces them to equality. (NE 1133b.15)
>
> This leads us to the very nature of money, being as it is related to custom, to the social role which defines the concept:
>
> Money is called nomisma (customary currency), because it does not exist by nature but by custom (nomos), and can be altered and rendered useless at will. (NE 1133a. 28–31)

From this analysis further analysis on the function of money ensues:

---

[1] Joseph Schumpeter, in his masterly *History of Economic Analysis* states: "Whatever may be its shortcomings, this theory, though never unchallenged, prevailed substantially to the end of the nineteen century and even beyond. It is the basis of the bulk of all analytic work in the field of money" (Schumpeter 1954: 63).

> For the natural necessaries are not in every case readily portable; hence, for the purpose of barter, men made a mutual compact to give and accept some substance of such sort, as being itself a useful commodity, was easy to handle in use for general life, iron for instance, silver and other metals, at a first stage defined merely by size and weight, but finally also by impressing on it a stamp in order that this might relieve them of having to measure it. (P 1257a. 34–40)

This theory, based on functions and usages, in itself helps us understand the dramatic evolution in the "body of money," the physical or non-physical substance into which money is incorporated. This, furthermore, represents a crucial aspect to determining the cultural life of money. Anything that performs such functions serves as money.

Money started out as a valuable good. In particular, the primitive currencies, now called "commodity money," were economic products applied as standards for transactions. Then, from the Classical Era onwards metal currencies emerged as coins. These, in turn, evolved into paper-money and onwards into electronic money. Today, 90 % of the currencies in circulation hold no physical existence, being mere bank-dependent computer registers.

Another question related to the body of money stems from the evolution in currency denominations in effect in each country. Table 1 shows a few interesting cases of countries that have shared the same currency for some part of their histories. In the nineteenth century, Portugal had the same currency as two of its colonies, Brazil and Angola. Today, Portugal shares a common currency with Germany. For this reason, the four countries have a relationship in currency terms. It is interesting to note how much they diverged from their common fixed point.

With the euro, Portugal has a currency which is 200,000 times that of 1910, the real. This was achieved by means of two jumps, one in 1911, to the escudo, and one in 1999 to the euro. Although apparently very violent, these transformations are far lower than those witnessed in the other three countries.

In Brazil, the real, which again became the national currency in 1994, is 2,750,000 million million (2.75×10^{18}) times the original real. In Angola, this relationship is much less pronounced as the present quanza is only 1.25 million million (1.25×10^{12}) the 1910 real. This number is similar to the evolution in Germany where the euro is 19.6 million million (1.96×10^{13}) times the legal tender in effect at the beginning of the twentieth century, the goldmark.

Table 1: Evolution of monetary unit

Country/Currency	date of change	Jump
Portugal		
Real		1
Escudo	1911	1000
Euro	1999	200
Brazil		
Real		1
Cruzeiro	1942	1000
Cruzeiro novo	1967	1000
Cruzado	1986	1000
Cruzado novo	1989	1000
Cruzeiro	1990	1
Cruzeiro real	1993	1000
Real	1994	2750
Angola		
Real		1
Escudo	1914	1000
Angular	1928	1.25
Escudo angolano	1958	1
Kwanza	1977	1
novo kwanza	1990	1000
kwanza reajustado	1995	1000000
Kwanza	1999	1
Germany		
Goldmark	1873	1
Papiermark	1914	1E+12
Reichsmark	1924	10
Deutschmark	1948	1
Euro	1999	1.95583

The conclusion inevitably drawn from this brief consideration of all these evolutions in the body of money is that money, in itself, does not exist. The history of economics transformed money from a very valuable good (commodity money) into a good of dubious value (metal money), into one of no intrinsic value (paper), and then into something which holds no physical existence (electronic money). Today, the bank based, fiduciary money we spend performs the same invisible role as gold did in previous societies.

This all enables us to challenge a popular conception represented in the statement by the famous bank robber, Willie Sutton. He reportedly said "Why do people rob banks? Because that's where the money is" (Sutton 1976).

Today, although the banks are still where the money resides, it is pointless robbing them as there is no physical money to steal.

2 Money fever

A second important facet to the cultural history of money is its effect on people. In order to analyze this facet, we may return to Aristotle.

> Indeed wealth is often assumed to consist of a quantity of money, because money is the thing with which business and trade are employed. But, on other occasions, on the contrary, it is thought that money is nonsense, and entirely a convention, by nature nothing, because when those using it have changed the currency it is worth nothing, and because it is of no use for any of the necessities of life and a man well supplied with money may often be destitute of these necessities [...] like the famous Midas of the story, when owing to the covetousness of his prayer all the viands served to him turned to gold (P 1257b.10).

The myth of King Midas is presented in book XI of *Metamorphoses*, by Ovid (43 BC–17 AD). Midas, king of Pessinus, a city of Phrygia, when asked to choose a present from the god Dionysus, asked for a golden touch. The king then finds out in the worst possible manner the most basic factor in monetary theory: money holds no value. He was able to acquire a lot of gold, but drastically reduced his own welfare and even resulting in the murder of his own daughter, transformed into a gold statue.

This story furthermore symbolizes the dubious fascination with gold. Christopher Columbus, in a letter to Ferdinand and Isabella, rulers of Spain, on 7 July 1503, voiced this fascination by saying: "Gold is most excellent. Gold is treasure, and he who possesses it does all he wishes to in this world, and succeeds in helping souls into paradise." (Columbus, 1503) However, whilst this proves the psychological impact of money, the case of Midas is proof of the fragility and futility of that fascination. This leads us onto the most basic aspect of economic theory, the origin of value.

As is well known, economic value is based on utility, i.e. the importance we attribute to goods. This accounts for the psychological origin of all the value of goods and resources. Goods are useful for people and resources (e.g. labor, capital, energy, raw materials), which attain value by their ability to produce goods. Money represents the only factor, which, while neither a good nor a resource, also holds value. Indeed, there is only one thing with value but no utility: money. Money holds this value simply because we say it has value. This is the conventional aspect Aristotle also pointed out: "Demand has come to be conventionally represented by money [...] it does not exist by nature but by custom, and can be altered and rendered useless at will" (NE V, 5, 1133a.28 – 31).

Should the value of money be merely conventional, it is inherently, by its very own nature, very fragile. Proof of this volatility of money comes in financial crises, such as those experienced in 2008 and 2009, when a lot of financial wealth disappeared overnight. Physical capital and production remain the same, but the money evaporates.

This facet points to another crucial element to fiduciary money, which is patent in its own name. "Fiduciary" means trust-based and, in fact, trust forms the central base of all monetary and financial systems. Whenever there is any crisis of confidence in any financial system or in any currency in the world, such trust instantly disappears.

This also explains the role of the State, through the central bank, in managing the financial system. Central banks hold greater power over commercial banks than any other public office over private firms. The reason stems precisely from trust-building. In the financial collapse of 2008 and 2009, both aspects became very patent when the breakdown in public confidence brought the whole system to near collapse, which was only avoided through massive interventions by governments and central banks. Today, as in the time of Midas, money exerts a drastic fascination but its value always remains extremely fragile.

3 The rule of money

This takes us to a far deeper and highly influential aspect. In the treatment of economics in his treatise on *Politics*, Aristotle made a basic distinction, which, although absent in the more scientifically relevant analysis of *Nicomachean Ethics*, proved very influential historically. This is the separation between household management (οικονομικη, *oikonomikê*) and wealth-getting (χρηματιστιχη, *chrematistikê*).

We should start by the relationships existing between them: "whether wealth-getting is a part of the art of household management, or a different sort of science is open to debate" (P 1256a.13). However, they generally prove very different. *Oikonomikê*, the original word still used in our science, relates to the management of a family or a state: "One kind of acquisition, therefore, in the order of nature includes a part of the household art, in accordance with which either there must be forthcoming or else that art must procure a supply of those goods, capable of accumulation, which are necessary for life and of usefulness to the community of city or household." (P 1256b.26)

The other activity, *chrematistikê*, directly relates to the existence of money, and extends well beyond the needs of a household: "With currency now invented as an outcome of the necessary interchange of goods, there came into existence the other form of wealth-getting, trade. At first, this no doubt went on in simple forms but has latterly become more highly organised as experience discovered the sources and methods of exchange that would generate most profit." (P 1257b.1–5)

The definition of this second activity shows how intimately trade relates to money. There are indeed some important consequences. The main difference between "natural wealth-getting" (*oikonomikê*) and its unnatural peer (*chrematistikê*) is that the natural version contains limits whilst its peer does not (P 1256b.30, 1257b.30). "These riches, that are derived from this art of wealth-getting, are truly unlimited" (P 1257b.25). The lack of limits is connected to the desire for life: "as therefore the desire for life is unlimited, they also desire without limit the productive means of life" (P 1257b.40).

This idea, lost to later economic theory, proves very interesting. Its value, which is mostly ethical, results from Aristotle's basic intellectual attitude and allows us to relate this with other cultural approaches. For example, we may say that its meaning closely resembles the Gospel sentence: "No one can serve two masters. Either he will hate the one and love the other, or he will be devoted to the one and despise the other. You cannot serve both God and Money." (Mt 6, 24)

Furthermore, Adam Smith, another philosopher interested in economic issues and known as the founding father of economic science, makes some similar statements:

> Consumption is the sole end and purpose of all production; and the interest of the producer ought to be attended to only so far as it may be necessary for promoting that of the consumer. The maxim is so perfectly self-evident that it would be absurd to attempt to prove it. But in the mercantile system the interest of the consumer is almost constantly sacrificed to that of the producer; and it seems to consider production, and not consumption, as the ultimate end and object of all industry and commerce. (Smith 1776: IV, ch. 8)

Even John Maynard Keynes, the famous twentieth century economist, also reported on the dangers of *chrematistikê:* "Speculators may do no harm as bubbles on a steady stream of enterprise. But the position is serious when enterprise becomes the bubble on a whirlpool of speculation. When the capital development of a country becomes a by-product of the activity of a casino, the job is likely to be ill-done." (Keynes 1936: 159)

We may say that the extreme case of the *chrematistikê* attitude is found in pyramid schemes, where money is simply shuffled between uses, without any real use. This is a mechanism of pure distribution, where new deposits pay the interest on previous deposits. Operating according to the same system as chain-letters and similarly bound to fail, pyramid schemes inevitably encounter the inherent limits of physical growth. Sooner or later, the scheme will run out of new depositors to finance the interest on existing deposits.

These age-old schemes where made famous by Charles Ponzi (1882–1949), an Italian adventurer, who created a similar scheme in Boston in the 1920s. The debacle led to the naming of such scams as "a Ponzi-game." In Portugal, a similar case was run by Maria Branca dos Santos (1902–1992) in Lisbon in 1983–1984. However, history's biggest case was performed by Bernard Madoff (born 1938) in Palm Beach and New York over twenty years, from 1992 through to 2008. This scheme, involving 68 billion dollars, defrauded many banks and other sophisticated investors.

As stated, the most important aspect of pyramid schemes is that there is no economic application of the money, no investment, no insurance, not even any speculation. It is pure redistribution. This is pure *chrematistikê.*

4 The corruption of money

The Aristotelian distinction between *oikonomikê* and *chrematistikê* is a contribution, which as aforementioned, later scientific economic analysis did not greatly value and incorporate.[2] However, the differentiation simultaneously generated a terrible intellectual and political influence on practical economic considerations, mostly in the Classical Period and the Middle Ages, periods when Aristotle served as a particularly pre-eminent guide. In particular, the aspect under focus is ethical evaluation, which the moral condemnation of *chrematistikê* carried over to many money-related activities. This relationship is explicitly analyzed by Aristotle in the following sequence and explicitly stating that *chrematistikê* may lead to the corruption of the arts: "It not the function of courage to produce wealth, but to inspire daring; nor is it the function of military art nor of medical art, but it belongs to the former to bring victory and the latter to cause health. Yet, these people make all these faculties means for the business of providing wealth, in the belief that wealth is the end and that everything must conspire to the end." (P 1258a.13–14)

Much more relevant are the interconnected condemnations of trade and interest, which Aristotle identified and which had enormous consequences on at-

---

2 See, for example Gordon (1975), Lowry (1987), Lowry and Gordon (eds) (1998).

titudes towards economic activity until the industrial revolution. This simply bestowed intellectual dignity on some popular preconceptions.

The first, and probably the most relevant, is related to trade and merchants, attributed a negative moral repute by Aristotle: "The branch connected with exchange is justly discredited (for it is not in accordance with nature, but involves men taking things from one another)" (P 1258b.01). But the most famous of Aristotle's economic condemnations is of lending and interest, which were reprobated as usury:

> As this is so, usury is most reasonably hated, because its gain comes from money itself and not from that for the sake of which money was invented. For money was brought into existence for the purpose of exchange, but interest (tokos) increases the amount of the money itself (and this is the actual origin of the Greek word: offspring (tokos), resembles parent, and interest is money born of money) consequently this form of business of getting wealth is of all forms the most contrary to nature. (P 1258b.2–8)

The influence of these condemnations is long and wide. Many historical references confirm this and even opinions by such latter and eminent authors like Karl Marx are perhaps directly related to this aspect of the Aristotelian canon. Another similarity may be found in the religious condemnation of money even while important differences must be noted.

Islam takes a very extreme position on the subject. In particular, while there were no problems with trade, as the prophet Mohammed was a merchant for part of his career, lending and interest are explicitly condemned by the Holy Quran:

> Those who devour usury will not stand except as stand one whom the Evil one by his touch Hath driven to madness. That is because they say: "Trade is like usury," but Allah hath permitted trade and forbidden usury. Those who after receiving direction from their Lord, desist, shall be pardoned for the past; their case is for Allah (to judge); but those who repeat (The offence) are companions of the Fire: They will abide therein (for ever). (Holy Quran, Surah 2, The Cow, 275)

The Bible, although not sympathetic to the practice, has no similar drastic repudiation. For this reason, neither Judaism nor Christianity ever took up the doctrinal obstacle of Islam. Actually, we find in the Gospel some references that, although not economic in intent, mention the practice favorably: "You should have put my money on deposit with the bankers, so that when I returned I would have received it back with interest." (Mt 25, 27)

Among the Fathers of the Catholic Church there are some very interesting reflections on the ethical dignity of economic activities. We lack the scope here but would note that some authors, when able to step beyond Aristotle, revert these condemnations. Saint Augustine, for example, presents a very interesting analysis of the ethical question of trade and economic production in his comments on Psalm 71.

> A trader said to me: [...] If there is lying, of false swearing, this is the fault of me, not of trading: for I could, if I would, be able to do without this fault [...] I then, the merchant, do not shift my own fault to trading: if I lie, it is I that lie, not the trade [...] A trader might thus speak to me – Look then, O Bishop, how you understand the tradings which you have read about in the Psalms: lest perhaps you don't understand, and forbid me trading. Admonish me then how I should live; if well, it shall be well with me: one thing however I know, that if I shall have been evil, it is not trading that makes me so, but my iniquity. (Augustine LXXI: 15)

Even Saint Thomas Aquinas, generally considered to be the great medieval disciple of Aristotle, diverged from the philosopher on this point.[3]

The poisonous components to money were thus carried over into other social activities, thereby greatly enlarging the negative effects of the cultural life of money.

Conclusion: Money from Midas to Madoff

These very brief remarks serve to highlight how consideration of the monetary theory of Aristotle may guide us through the most important facets of the cultural life of money. In conclusion, we may quote one of the men who, in the late twentieth century, was most influential in the concrete life of one particular money, the American dollar. Alan Greenspan was chairman of the Federal Reserve Board, the American central bank, for almost twenty years (from 11 August 1987 until 31 January 2006). Summarizing his experience in his memoirs, he has some interesting things to say about the cultural life of money: "Human nature does not change. History is replete with waves of self-reinforcement enthusiasm and despair, innate human characteristics not subject to a learning curve." (Greenspan 2007: 490 – 491)

Works cited

Aristotle (1926) *Nicomachean Ethics*, trans. H. Rackham (Cambridge, Mass.: Harvard University Press). Title abridged NE.

---

3 See Neves (2000) for further discussion.

78 — João César das Neves

Aristotle (1932) *Politics*, trans. H. Rackham (Cambridge, Mass.: Harvard University Press). Title abridged P.

Augustine, Saint *Exposition on the Book of Psalms*. <http://www.newadvent.org/fathers/1801.htm> (accessed 9 January 2014).

Columbus, Christopher (1503) "Lettera Rarissima to the Sovereigns", 7 July 1503, in Julius E. Olson ed. (1906) *Original Narratives of Early American History*, http://www.gutenberg.org/files/18571/18571-h/18571-h.htm#Solomon (accessed 8 October 2014).

Gordon, Barry (1975) *Economic Analysis before Adam Smith* (London: MacMillan).

Greenspan, Alan (2007) *The Age of Turbulence, Adventures in a New World* (NY: The Penguin Press).

Keynes, John Maynard (1936) *The General Theory of Employment, Interest and Money* (London: Macmillan).

Lowry, S. Todd (1987) *The Archaeology of Economic Ideas. The Classical Greek Tradition* (Durham and London: Duke University Press).

Lowry, S. Todd and Barry Gordon (eds) (1998) *Ancient and Medieval Economic Ideas and Concepts of Social Justice* (Leiden: Brill).

Meikle, Scott (1995) *Aristotle's Economic Thought* (Oxford: Clarendon Press; NY: Oxford University Press).

Neves, J (Fall 2000) "Aquinas and Aristotle's Distinction on Wealth," *History of Political Economy* 32. 3, 649 – 657.

Schumpeter, Joseph A. (1954) *History of Economic Analysis* (Oxford, NY: Oxford University Press).

Smith, Adam (1776) *An Inquiry into the Nature and Causes of the Wealth of Nations*. <www.econlib.org/library/Smith/smWN.html> (accessed 9 January 2014).

Sutton, Willie (1976) *Where the Money Was: The Memoirs of a Bank Robber* (NY: Viking Press).

II The Arts and Finance

Joyce Goggin
Death and Diamonds: Finance and Art

Introduction

While contemplating the cultural life of money and the fraught relationship of art to capital, my mind has repeatedly been drawn back to one particular work of art that embodies many of the issues addressed in this volume. I am referring to an enormous canvas (5.4 m by 2.4 m) executed by Barnett Newman in 1976, hanging in the National Gallery in Ottawa, and composed simply of a shocking red band painted through the center of an ultramarine blue background. For visitors to the National Gallery, the work comes as something of a surprise – welcome or otherwise – as they follow the standard itinerary from one exhibition room to the next and where centuries of traditional Western art is on display. At the end of a path that leads from the early modern period, through hundreds of years of representational art and on to impressionism, one arrives quite suddenly in a remarkably cavernous room. In this echoing space, the visitor is confronted with only a few select pieces of high minimalism and abstract expressionism, including a typically manic Jackson Pollock and one of Mark Rothko's color fields. However, the entire central wall directly in front of the spectator is reserved for Newman's *Voice of Fire* which, for many, proves the highlight of their visit to the National Gallery.

For many others, however, this vibrant canvas serves as a reminder of the public debate surrounding its purchase, announced in 1990 by wary curators who had quietly acquired the piece from Newman's widow in 1989. The Gallery correctly anticipated the hostility that its acquisition would trigger, expressed most typically by Member of Parliament Felix Holtmann who complained that "[i]t looks like two cans of paint and two rollers and about 10 minutes would do the trick" (Barber et al. 1996: 29). In a similar spirit, the owner of a flower nursery painted his greenhouse in identical blue and red stripes on the same scale in an effort to voice his frustration that so much money had been spent on just one, very simple, painting. These derogatory comments and dramatic interventions were meant to criticize the purchase of *Voice of Fire* as a waste of taxpayer money on "useless art" that "anyone could have made" for a very small investment in time and materials. People bemoaned the $1.76 million that the federal government had "squandered" on this canvas and reeled off long lists of social ills that the same money could have put aright.

On the other hand, people who understand the art market argued that the curators had made the deal of the century knowing that, with time, this painting would become one of the museum's most valuable pieces. And indeed, prices for the work of American post-war abstract painters have sky-rocketed since 1989 and, in 2008, one small ink drawing by Newman sold at auction for over $5 million.[1] As Shirley Thomson, who was the Director of the National Gallery at the time of the controversy explained, "[w]e rarely have a chance in today's over-heated art market to purchase works of the scale and historical significance of *Voice of Fire*."[2] Put somewhat less delicately, Brydon Smith, who visited Newman's widow in 1987 to purchase the piece recalls a conversation in which she told him "you know about the market, you tell me what the value is," and Smith himself then made what he thought was a reasonable offer for this priceless work of art (*ibid.* 62). Thus, from the outrage over public spending on a painting that "anyone could do" to collectors who considered the painting's price tag a bargain, this anecdote illustrates the ambiguous relationship of art – which has no apparent use-value – to money, as well as to the principles of basic market practices, such as pricing.

1 Art and modern finance

The perceived antagonism between aesthetics, cultural production and the economy remains a topic of research with a growing number of studies by scholars such as Marc Shell, Mark C. Taylor and Peter De Bolla. Essential to the work of all of these scholars is the historic purview that takes into account the moment at which the relationship between art and money was called into question. Peter De Bolla, for example, locates the roots of the popular notion that art and money must necessarily occupy separate spheres in the movements and events to which we collectively refer as the beginnings of western modernity. Importantly, the seeds of this modernity were sown in the financial revolution that began in the seventeenth century and resulted in modern banking, along with the invention and development of various instruments of credit. These same instruments produced a surplus of wealth and fuelled the other revolutions that occurred in the eighteenth century, which, in turn, in one way or another, all contributed to class mobility. Thus, the increased wealth available to new segments of the population through the extension of credit and the availability of

---

1 See John Geddes, <http://www2.macleans.ca/2010/01/21/are-we-over-this-yet/>.
2 See John Geddes, <http://www2.macleans.ca/2010/01/21/are-we-over-this-yet/>.

various financial constructions such as mortgages, suddenly made it possible for members of the merchant classes to secure titles through means such as the marriage market, aided by their new-found ability to acquire wealth through various forms of credit and entrepreneurship. The result was the class of parvenus depicted in so very many eighteenth-century works of fiction such as *Tom Jones* (1749) or *Manon Lescaut* (1731), and works of art such as Hogarth's *Marriage à la Mode* (1743–1745).

Fig. 1: William Hogarth, *Marriage à la Mode*, Panel 1, "The Marriage Settlement," 1743.

While the financial revolution rendered the financial surplus facilitating social mobility, it equally gave rise to markets in goods through which the class-conscious bourgeoisie were able to demonstrate their superior tastes. The need to communicate the suitability of one's station in life through the acquisition of tasteful goods got satisfied in any number of ways, including the purchase of inexpensive "sketches" of valuable paintings, a practice and a word that would eventually morph into the contemporary expression, "kitsch."[3] Likewise, a booming market in cheap prints and copies of famous sculptures and paintings expanded alongside the financial revolution and was assisted by the new technologies of mass production. As De Bolla explains, by the mid-eighteenth century, Europe experienced a "growth in the audience for culture [that was] stimulated by greater capacities for reproducing and disseminating" aesthetic objects, and representing a powerful potential leveler of class distinction. The threat of the blurring of class distinctions was further exacerbated by the rise of museums and galleries in which "vulgar" people could rub shoulders with members of the upper classes, who "naturally" possessed more refined aesthetic judgment (De Bolla 2003: 6). Not surprisingly, the potential of such developments to erode class boundaries was the source of considerable paranoia and contributed to a hardening of a line that adherents were eager to define and maintain – a line ostensibly separating refined art from art for the masses.

In eighteenth-century Britain, authors such as Addison, Shaftsbury, and Richardson produced a surfeit of writings on aesthetics, the nature of beauty, and just who might be best positioned to appreciate it. Similarly concerned with the distinction between "high" and "low" or commercial art, Joshua Reynolds, himself a commercially successful painter, added his voice to Enlightenment discourses on taste but from the ambiguous position of owing his popularity and wealth at least partially to the classes he distained. Hence while Reynold's arguments about aesthetics contributed to the notion that high art enjoy popularity only among members of a restricted group of people who had genuine, aristocratic claims to refined tastes, he was nevertheless also obliged to appeal to a wider market through his art because a small audience also meant modest financial success. Reynolds, moreover, made his fortune from portrait painting, a genre that takes second last place on a scale of cultural value ranging from historical painting to still life and he addressed this consideration by arguing that his work portrayed persons of quality, on a noble scale and in noble settings, "raised into dignity...in the hands of a Painter of genius" (Reynolds 1997: 197). Throughout his *Discourses on Art* therefore, Reynolds's professional interests force him to draw such fine distinctions, as he meticulously parses the field in order to justify his own undeniable commercial success.

Reynolds contemporary, the popular artist and commercial sign painter William Hogarth, however, took the opposite approach in his contribution to eighteenth-century aesthetic debates. Having advertised for advance subscriptions to its publication, Hogarth collected his ideas on aesthetics in book form under the title *The Anal-*

---

3 On this point, see Giez 1994: 21.

ysis of Beauty, which also contained popular prints "suitable for framing."[4] For Hogarth, the aesthetic value of cultural objects resides neither in the nobility of the subjects depicted, nor in the artist's lack of commercial interest, but rather in the "Lines of Beauty" common to all aesthetic objects in varying degrees. Indeed, so confident was Hogarth of his thesis that in the first of the explanatory plates accompanying *The Analysis of Beauty* the artist illustrates his argument with a sketch of a yard filled with copies of classical statuary.

Fig. 2: William Hogarth, *The Analysis of Beauty*, Plate 1, 1753.

The statue yard depicted in this illustrative plate was owned by a friend of Hogarth, who specialized in cheap lead knock-offs of famous Classical statues, whose execution was "so monstrously wretched, that one [could] hardly guess at their Originals" (James Ralph, qtd in Paulson 1993: 101). Therefore, while

---

4 The book included what Hogarth advertised as "Two Explanatory Prints, serious and comical engraved on large Copper-Plates, fit to frame for Furniture" (See Paulson's introduction to *The Analysis of Beauty*, xvii). The prints out-sold the book and were often purchased without the accompanying text.

handily advertising his friend's shop, Hogarth argued that aesthetic value is grounded in the same Lines of Beauty that structure kitsch, commercial art and canonical art alike. Put differently, rather than calling for a culturally constructed, class-driven aesthetics that strives to separate art created for its sale value from art made for some higher purpose, Hogarth chose to resolve the aesthetic debate around Lines of Beauty found everywhere, regardless of the perceived status of the respective object.

2 Art and big money

As indicated, the relationship between art and money is, and has been, fraught with delicate hierarchies informed by what is often referred to as a "post-romantic" world view that carries on a tradition wherein art is tied to notions such as truth and originality rather than to reproducibility and marketability. As the public debate around Newman's *Voice of Fire* illustrates, eighteenth-century notions concerning aesthetics such as those to which Reynolds subscribed are still very much alive in the popular imagination. Typical of such post-romantic sentiment was a statement made by Canadian politician Jean Charest, who claimed that public spending on the arts is unnecessary because "any good artist would want to give his art to Canada". Thus, while images persist of the starving artist driven by his quest for beauty; the priceless masterpiece; and the notion that commercial art is not really art at all, there has, of course, been a postmodern move underway for many decades to deconstruct the high/low cultural divide. This has been accompanied by a concerted undoing of the notion that art should necessarily be divorced from money with many artists having taken to making both endlessly reproducible and highly lucrative works of art. Indeed, according to one critic who reported on the Art Basel fair in 2008, collectors, dealers and artists gathered at the event to "witness the endlessly renewable marriage of art and money" and "to be swept up in" compulsive cultural consumption.[5]

The enduring tension between money and art had already been around for centuries by the 1960s when Andy Warhol proclaimed that his goal was to be an "Art Businessman or a Business Artist," and claimed to look forward to a day when art museums and department stores would merge (qtd in Galenson 2007:14).[6] Like Hogarth, Warhol started out as a commercial artist who, rather than attempting to enter the elevated enclaves of high artistic endeavor, boldly

---

5 See Yablonsky, <themoment.blogs.nytimes.com/tag/barnett-newman/>.
6 On Warhol, art and the department store, see also Taylor 31–43.

proclaimed that, "[b]eing good in business is the most fascinating kind of art [...] making money is art and working is art and good business is the best art" (qtd. in Galenson 2007: 13). Fittingly then, in 1962 he responded to the question "what do you love most?" with drawings of paper money, which culminated in *Two Hundred One Dollar Bills*, one of his famous silkscreen prints.

Damien Hirst – a great admirer of Warhol – has, like his role-model, also enjoyed rock-star fame, and specifically for flaunting his relationship with money and the market. Hirst's highly performative career began by securing the services of advertising mogul Charles Saatchi, who launched the artist as a new product.[7] Indeed, rather than referring to a particular artist who produces original works, the "Hirst" name has virtually always designated a brand that represents a renaissance-style studio like Warhol's, where many assistants mass-produce works. For example, production of the trademark Hirst spot paintings has now been entrusted to an assistant whom Hirst refers to as, "the best person who ever painted spots for me," adding that "the only difference, between one painted by her and one of mine, is the money."[8] It is precisely Hirst's attitude along with a talent for business, that accounts for why he is best known as "the richest living artist to date."[9]

While the Hirst name refers to a mass-produced brand, the artist's name now equally refers to his corporate work and event-creation strategies as a particular sector within the art market. "The Hirst market" as it is called, boomed on 15 and 16 September 2008 as Lehman Brothers went bankrupt and markets everywhere collapsed. On those same two days, the Hirst auction, *Beautiful inside My Head Forever*, was organized to by-pass dealers and raised £111 million, along with "several questions about the relationship between the financial markets and the art market."[10] In particular, Hirst's business associates were rumored to have "propped up" the prices of his art and manipulated a massive profit in the face of a global financial catastrophe. In response, the Sotheby's *Art Market Review* explained that the success of

---

7 See <http://www.artchive.com/artchive/H/hirst.html>.
8 See <http://en.wikipedia.org/wiki/Damien_Hirst>.
9 See "For the Love of God" <http://en.wikipedia.org/wiki/For_the_love_of_god>.
10 Note that a similar sale of Picasso's work in 1988 raised only a fraction of this sum. See. <http://www.kennethafriedman.com/artist_bio.php?artist=Damien+Hirst&id=24&startLimit=0&limitPerPage=6>. The £111 million that the sale raised was "ten times higher than the existing Sotheby's record for a single artist sale" and it frequently noted that it occurred "as the financial markets plunged", in September 2008. See also "Hirst dealers bolster prices at record sale" (<http://www.timesonline.co.uk/tol/news/uk/article4795010.ece>), where one collector, convinced that Hirst manipulated the market, is quoted as saying, "[n]othing can convince me that on the very day banks were collapsing around us, collectors were buying these works at Sotheby's. I don't care how rich you are or where you're from. When it looks like the world is going under, nobody buys."

the Hirst auction represented the combined result of "world-wide marketing efforts and a frenzy of publicity [that] made the auction more than a sale of artwork. It became an international cultural event."[11]

In his work on banking and art, Michael Bzdak remarks that, "in many ways, art is like money" (Bzdak 2008: 320). According to Marc Shell, part of the reason for the rapprochement of art and money stems from "the trend toward dematerialization [which] has been a telling hallmark of twentieth-century economics as well as visual aesthetics" (Shell 107). Simply put, this is what infuriated the nursery owner who painted his greenhouse with Barnett Newman stripes even if he most certainly would not have expressed his frustration in these terms. The source of amazement or frustration with art and its ability to command outrageously high prices, is mostly connected with art's lack of intrinsic value or usefulness, which compellingly aligns it with money itself. Likewise – and this is very much the case with Newman's *Voice of Fire* – the high prices for art are most often not based on either the labor or the cost of materials, but rather on whatever inflated price people will pay for it. This represents the very source of Warhol's intended irony in naming a silkscreen print *Two Hundred One Dollar Bills* – a work that would quite obviously sell for much more than that two hundred dollars. Indeed, one of the prints sold in 2009 for $43 million, far exceeding its estimated price of $8 million.[12]

3 What does it all mean?

As Andy Warhol once famously remarked, "art is what you can get away with," and Damien Hirst's *For the Love of God* might be the perfect outing of Warhol's wit. As one art blogger complained, this "diamond encrusted head [...] speaks to little more than the amount of money it will sell for," which distinguishes it at a time when "every male artist in the Western world seems to be fascinated by" skull art.[13] The platinum based, diamond-encrusted skull cast from a real eighteenth-century skull with only the teeth eerily remaining, went on display in London with an asking price of £50 million in 2007. This made the Hirst skull the highest priced work of art by a living artist in history, a fact which the artist enthusiastically publicized. Moreover, as with the Hirst auction, the artist and his associates unabashedly manipulated the market in making *For the Love of God*

---

11 See <http://avvakoum.livejournal.com/9136.html>.

12 See Panero, <http://www.newcriterion.com/articleprint.cfm/The-art-market-explained-4337>.

13 On: <http://www.artfagcity.com/2007/10/25/1309/>, see "Joining the Style Revolution; Skull Art is Hot.",

market, and watched carefully "as the price of international diamonds rose while Bond Street gem dealer Bentley & Skinner tried to corner the market for the artist's benefit" (Pescovitz 2007).[14] In an equally savvy move, Hirst publicized how he personally financed *For the Love of God* and then sold it to an unnamed investment group while retaining partial ownership.[15] The artist's conditions of sale included the stipulation that the piece tour museums around the world for two years, before coming to rest in "some corporate death lounge."[16] These also ensured that the Hirst skull would not be retired to a safe to be traded on in absentia but would go on tour with "security more synonymous with an international airport than an art gallery".[17] Thus, *For the Love of God* was able to generate considerable profits as an attraction while heightening Hirst's "global name-recognition" and his status as an icon, as well as significantly contributing to the United Kingdom's "Cool Britannia" image.

However, just what, with *For the Love of God*, is the Hirst machine communicating about money and art by purchasing an eighteenth-century skull and encrusting its platinum cast with thousands of diamonds? This question has been answered by Hirst himself in various ways. For example, when the piece was exhibited in the Rijksmuseum in Amsterdam, Hirst chose sixteen seventeenth-century "masterpieces" containing memento mori such as skulls to be displayed with it and to communicate, in the words of the curators, "how the fear of death has been expressed aesthetically through the centuries."[18] The Dutch art works selected by the artist to surround *For the Love of God* obviously constituted a significant gesture, and communicated a great deal about the cultural politics of aesthetics. Moreover, as Hirst was surely aware, his choices would generate conscious as well as potential, unintentional meanings depending on the spectator. Politically, for example, this gesture might well be read as linking

---

14 See Thorpe, 2008, passim. For a detailed discussion of both Warhol and Hirst's relationship with the market, and the historical development of that relationship, see Galenson, passim. See also Mark C. Taylor's 2004: 15–43, and on the broader topic of art and the market, see, Shell 1995: 56–207.

15 I am grateful to Simon Lilly for directing my attention to many of the points on which my argument in this section is based.

16 *Art News Blog*, <http://www.artnewsblog.com/2007/08/damien-hirst-diamond-skull-sells. htm>. On how banks purchase, store and trade contemporary art, see Bzdak, passim.

17 See O'Hagan, <http://www.guardian.co.uk/uk/2006/may/21/arts.artsnews>.

18 See Schoonus, "*For the Love of God* en de keuze van Hirst uit de collectie van het Rijksmuseum, laten zien hoe de angst voor de dood door de eeuwen heen in schoonhied wordt gevat" (my translation) <http://www.8weekly.nl/artikel/6804/damien-hirst-for-the-love-of-god-mod erne-visie-op-de-dood.html>. See also <http://www.rijksmuseum.nl/pers/tentoonstellingen/for-the-love-of-god?lang=en>.

Hirst's skull to Europe's colonial past and to the phenomenal wealth of the Dutch Republic in the seventeenth century. Seen in this light, the diamonds that cover the platinum skull could be understood as a politically conscious commentary on contemporary colonialism along the lines of the popular Hollywood film, *Blood Diamonds*.[19]

However, while *For the Love of God* quite consciously engages with canonical seventeenth-century art, Hirst's work is also said to "democratize its meaning," and the piece may therefore equally suggest heavy metal and bling culture while referencing the contemporary fascination with Mexican and Aztec art.[20] Moreover, by specifically selecting an eighteenth-century skull from which to work, and later creating a cupboard full of skulls and calling it *Cornucopia: Enlightenment*, Hirst is aligning his pimped-up crania with the financial revolution that also occurred in the eighteenth century and the nature of the market to which it gave rise. In this case, Hirst's conscious choice of a skull from the eighteenth century on which to model his work self-consciously positions it as a statement on art's relationship to the market, just as manipulating both the diamond and art markets to create the piece draws attention to the relationship between art and money. One might, therefore, also read *For the Love of God* as a direct and intentional link to the discourses on aesthetics to which I referred earlier that mark the juncture at which the relationship of art to money becomes a matter of heated debate.

When asked why he called the diamond skull *For the Love of God*, Hirst explains that the name was his mother's expression of amazement at yet another outrageous project from a son famous for preserving animals in formaldehyde and calling them art. On a more sentimental note, the artist also stated in an interview that the piece conveys the difficulty in having to come to terms with death, claiming perhaps factitiously that his artful skull is about "how people throw money at death," so that it constitutes a sort of bittersweet, "money-can't-buy-happiness" statement. [21] When asked in the same interview whether he is an artist or a businessman, Hirst quickly replies, "what do you think? A businessman of course," and then explains that "since Andy Warhol, it's okay for artists to have money". Better still, when his interviewer suggests that suffering and poverty are an artist's inspiration, Hirst replies quite simply, "well, maybe for you."

---

19 See <http://www.avaaz.org/en/diamonds_for_love_not_hate/?cl=360086929&v=4404>.
20 See *The Artchive*, <http://www.artchive.com/artchive/H/hirst.html>.
21 See <http://www.youtube.com/watch?v=EbhH_Mjywmo>.

4 Diamonds are forever

Perhaps still more startling and significant is Hirst's choice of materials and his decision to work in diamonds, the quintessence of priceless-ness and rarity. Suggesting a parallel between art and diamonds is not, of course, simply become gratuitous because like art, diamonds have no intrinsic value and instead are rendered valuable by their aura, which has been carefully constructed over time. As Freud speculated, precious jewels are valueless by definition and money spent on them is therefore a form of economic waste associated with decay, dissipation and excrement. Picking up on Freud and Bataille on the relationship between precious stones and the subconscious, Paul Crosthwaite argues that the "constitutive invitation to dissipation [extended by *For the Love of God*] is inextricable from its status as a universal symbol of death" but instead of signifying "'wealth against death,' as Hirst himself claims, the skull's glittering covering reinforces the affinity between the one and the other" (Crosthwaite 2011: 87). Crosthwaite likewise advances the notion that the contemporary art market provides "an arena in which reserves of capital may be wantonly expended" and that the wastefulness expressed in Hirst's auction as well as in the skull "literally embod[y] waste – hence the prominence today of artworks that entail death, decay, mortification and abjection" (Crosthwaite 2011: 80).

However, more concretely, the scarcity-based value of diamonds in particular is the result of a concerted campaign undertaken by the industry and centered on an image constructed by marketing agents late in the nineteenth century. The purpose of the campaign was to impart the notion of rarity as a means of preventing the complete devaluation of diamonds when South-African gems began flooding the European and North-American markets. At the same time "the first chairman of De Beers [...] amalgamated the Kimberley Diamond Mines around 1890" with the object of regulating "diamond deposits and set[ting] up a common marketing scheme so that the mines wouldn't undercut each other" (Fleming 2006: 24). De Beers then set about establishing a "world price for diamonds – a monopoly price" through the Diamond Syndicate. When the artificial monopoly price of diamonds was again threatened between 1902 and 1940, when a number of vast diamond fields were discovered throughout Africa, De Beer's responded by hiring an agency to create magazine advertisements featuring recognizable paintings by Picasso and Dali; to metonymically propose value and rarity by interlinking one supposedly priceless commodity with another.[22]

---

22 See Epstein, <http://www.theatlantic.com/magazine/archive/1982/02/have-you-ever-tried-to-sell-a-diamond/4575>.

In later years, De Beers' efforts to monopolize the market and maintain the artificially inflated price of diamonds later took the form of a marketing campaign that ironically if unconsciously highlights diamonds' valuelessness. In this campaign, men were targeted by encouraging them to give diamond engagement rings with De Beers putting forward guidelines as to just how much disposable income should be spent on one's intended. The stones were advertised as an "integral part of any romantic courtship," with the tag-line notion that diamonds are forever, which association with eternity prevents people from flooding the market with second-hand stones.

Ian Fleming, who published a book on diamond smuggling, in 1957 further capitalized on this glamour by writing *Diamonds are Forever* featuring Bond getting a lesson in "Gem Quality" as he comes to understand "the myth of diamonds" (Fleming 2006: 13). Seemingly complicit in the process of constructing the value of diamonds, Fleming insists that the struggle in which 007 is enlisted is "not just [about] the millions of money involved, or the value of diamonds as a hedge against inflation, or the sentimental fashions in diamonds for engagement rings" (Fleming 2006: 14). Rather, the influx of diamonds smuggled into London, which would threaten their aura of rarity and value, is construed as a threat to British national security and to a business that "the British got hold of at the beginning of the century [...] and managed to hold [onto]" (Fleming 2006: 18).

And later, in the 1970s, when diamond prices were again threatened by an influx of stones from the Soviet Union, "DeBeers devised the 'eternity ring', made up of as many as twenty-five tiny Soviet diamonds, which could be sold to an entirely new market of older married women."[23] When the overwhelming success of this campaign began threatening the price of large stones, the solitaire diamond was promoted as the 1980s way of saying "I love you". Therefore, like the price of art, the price of the diamonds adorning Hirst's skull has been artificially established by the trade, and by Hirst himself, so that the meaning of *For the Love of God* was "in a sense, its price, the pure sublime display of exorbitant expenditure it elicited" (Crosthwaite 2011: 86).

Conclusion

In Oliver Stone's 1987 film *Wall Street*, entrepreneur and art collector Gordon Gekko (Michael Douglas) explains why art is such a fantastic commodity:

---

23 See Epstein, <http://www.theatlantic.com/magazine/archive/1982/02/have-you-ever-tried-to-sell-a-diamond/4575/>.

"Money itself isn't lost or made it's simply transferred from one perception to another like magic. This painting here, I bought it ten years ago for $60,000 dollars. I could sell it today for $600. The illusion has become real... capitalism at its finest. I create nothing – it's the free market and you're part of it." In essence, what Damien Hirst has done is perhaps not as innovative as often claimed, but rather more in keeping with a genealogy of painters who perceived themselves as part of the free market and the magical processes of art valuation so famously expressed by Gekko. This tradition reaches back to Rembrandt, who used to corner the market on his own prints to drive prices up – later Picasso would do the same and, of course, artists since Warhol have been very aware of the market. This could also be said of J.S. Boggs whose art is essentially money, or at least produced as facsimiles of such and that have been seized by the U.S. treasury due to accusations of counterfeiting.

However, having said that, Warhol does seem to have understood that a work of art called *Two Hundred One Dollar Bills* would ultimately draw attention to the artificiality of its own price, and J.S. Boggs openly produces his art with the goal of disrupting the market and drawing attention to how money circulates. Hirst, however, in "his capacity as a twenty-first-century hybrid of artist, collector and dealer," who established a consortium to purchase his own work in order to protect "the marketability of his works," seems to celebrate the market and its means of manipulating and inflating prices to almost religious heights (Crostwaite 2011: 86). Moreover, although his predecessors also intervened directly in the market, Hirst has raised the stakes by introducing a structural change in how art is brought to the market (i.e. by passing dealers and raising unprecedented sums) with his auction, *Beautiful inside My Head Forever*. Hence, as Hal Foster notes, while Hirst's record-breaking auction makes plain how the art and financial markets are connected where not synchronized, it certainly did nothing to subvert the mechanisms underpinning the art market.[24] Similarly, Irene Finel-Honigman asks whether "Damien Hirst's transformational objects sold at exorbitant prices in an art market rather than an art world [are somehow indicative of] a new symbiosis [that] exalt[s] and validate[s] economic progress, or has economic progress inspired [Hirst] to translate industry, money and commerce into art" (Foster 2008: 3).

Through the example of Hirst's diamond encrusted skull, I have shown how the market works together with culture and particularly in concert with contemporary artists of whom Hirst is the acting dean. Hirst is significant in this regard because he is so very openly complicit in processes whereby various aspects of

---

24 See Foster, <http://www.lrb.co.uk/v30/n19/hal-foster/the-medium-is-the-market>.

our lives, such as our notions of what constitutes art, are increasingly financial-ized.[25] Hirst's work, moreover, plays on standard issues that congregate around "postmodernism," such as commerciality and authenticity, while performatively interacting with the market, which itself is constitutive of his art. I would also suggest that Hirst's interventions in the processes of financialization, currently shaping both private and cultural life, become somewhat different to the ges-tures of previous artists involved in the market around their work in various ca-pacities. In so doing, I have shed light on some of the ways in which financial-ization has increasingly worked together with culture since their relationship was first contested in the eighteenth century. Currently, artists seem invariably obliged either to be openly complicit in finance or seeking to disrupt it, or both.

Works cited

Art Fag City (2007) "Joining the Style Revolution; Skull Art is Hot," 25 October 2007. http://www.artfagcity.com/2007/10/25/1309/ (accessed 10 October 2013).

Art News Blog (2007) "Damien Hirst Diamond Skull Sells". 30 August 2007. <http://www.artnewsblog.com/2007/08/damien-hirst-diamond-skull-sells.htm> (accessed 10 October 2013). "Diamonds for Love not Hate." <http://www.avaaz.org/en/diamonds_for_love_not_hate/?cl=360086929&v=4404> (accessed 10 October 2013).

Barber, Bruce, Serge Guilbaut and John O'Brian (1996) Voices of Fire: Art, Rage, Power and the State (Toronto: University of Toronto Press.)

Bzdak, Michael (2008) "Money in the Bank? Corporate Support of the Arts in Twentieth-Century American Art," in Money and Culture, ed. Fiona Cox and Hans-Walter Schmidt-Hannisa (Frankfurt: Peter Lang), 319–333.

Crosthwaite, Paul (2011) "What a Waste of Money: Expenditure, the Death Drive and the Contemporary Art Market," New Formations 72.6, 80–93. "Damien Hirst (1965–)." The Artchive. <http://www.artchive.com/artchive/H/hirst.html> (accessed 10 October 2012). "Damien Hirst – Beautiful Inside My Head Forever, London September 15 and 16, 2008" <http://avvakoum.livejournal.com/9136.html> (accessed 10 October 2012).

De Bolla, Peter (2003) The Education of the Eye: Painting, Landscape, and Architecture in Eighteenth-Century Britain (Stanford: Stanford University Press).

Epstein, Edward J. (1982) "Have You Ever Tried to Sell a Diamond?" The Atlantic Magazine. February 1982. <http://www.theatlantic.com/magazine/archive/1982/02/have-you-ever-tried-to-sell-a-diamond/4575/> (accessed 10 October 2013).

Finel-Honigman, Irene (2010) A Cultural History of Finance (London and New York: Routledge).

Fleming, Ian (1963) The Diamond Smugglers (New York: Dell).

Fleming, Ian (2006 [1956]) Diamonds are Forever (London: Penguin). "For the Love of God". <http://en.wikipedia.org/wiki/For_the_love_of_god> (accessed 10 October 2013).

---

25 On the financialization of daily life, see Martin 55–101 and Langely 20–43.

Foster, Hal (2008) "The Medium is the Market," *London Review of Books*, 9 October 2008. <http://www.lrb.co.uk/v30/n19/hal-foster/the-medium-is-the-market> (accessed 10 October 2013).

Friedman, Kenneth. <http://www.kennethafriedman.com/artist_bio.php?artist=Damien+Hirst&id=24&starLimit=0&limitPerPage=6> (accessed 10 October 2011).

Galenson, David (2007) "Artists and the Market: From Leonardo and Titian to Andy Warhol and Damien Hirst," *NBER Working Paper Series*. <http://www.nber.org/papers/w13377> (accessed 10 October 2011).

Geddes, John (2010) "Voice of Fire: Are we over this yet?" MacLean's.ca. Thursday, 21 January 2010. <http://www2.macleans.ca/2010/01/21/are-we-over-this-yet/> (accessed 10 October 2011).

Giez, Ludwig (1994) *Phänomenologie des Kitsches* (Frankfurt a. M.: S. Fischer Verlag). "Hirst dealers bolster prices at record sale," *The Sunday Times*, 21 September 2008. <http://www.timesonline.co.uk/tol/news/uk/article4795010.ece> (accessed 10 October 2011).

Hogarth, William (1997) *The Analysis of Beauty*, ed. Ronald Paulson) (New Haven and London: Yale University Press).

Langley, Paul (2008) *The Everyday Life of Global Finance: Saving and Borrowing in Anglo-America.* (Oxford: Oxford University Press).

Martin, Randy (2002) *Financialization of Daily Life* (Philadelphia: Temple University Press).

Mastrigt, Marja van "Art in Network over Damien Hirst". <http://www.youtube.com/watch?v=EbhH_Mjywmo> (accessed 10 October 2011).

O'Hagan, Sean (2006) "Hirst's diamond creation is art's costliest work ever," *The Observer*, Sunday 21 May 2006. <http://www.guardian.co.uk/uk/2006/may/21/arts.artsnews (accessed 10 October 2011.

Panero, James (2009) "The Art Market Explained". *The New Criterion.* <http://www.new criterion.com/articleprint.cfm/The-art-market-explained-4337> (accessed 10 October 2011).

Paulson, Ronald (1993) *Hogarth: Art and Politics, 1750–1764.* Vol. III (New Jersey: Rutgers University Press).

Pescovitz, David (2007) "Damien Hirst's diamond skull," *BoingBoing: A Directory of Wonderful Things.* 2 June 2007. <http://boingboing.net/2007/06/02/damien-hirsts-diamon.html> (accessed 10 October 2011).

Reynolds, Sir Joshua (1997) *Discourses on Art* (New Haven and London: Yale University Press).

Rijksmuseum. "Diamanten mensenschedel," Holland: ArtCities 2009–2010. <http://www.rijks museum.nl/tentoonstellingen/hirst?lang=nl> (accessed 10 October 2011).

Schoonus, Maykel (2008) "Damien Hirst – For the Love of God: Moderne visie op de dood," 10 November 2008. <http://www.8weekly.nl/artikel/6804/damien- hirst-for-the-love-of-god-moderne-visie-op-de-dood.html> (accessed 10 October 2011).

Shell, Marc (1995) *Art and Money* (Chicago: University of Chicago Press).

Taylor, Mark C. (2004) *Confidence Games: Money and Markets in a World without Redemption* (Chicago and London: University of Chicago Press)

Thorpe, Vanessa (2008) "Top critic lashes out at Hirst's 'tacky' art *The Guardian*, 7 September 2008. <http://www.guardian.co.uk/artanddesign/2008/sep/07/damienhirst.art> (accessed 10 October 2011).

Yablonsky, Linda "The Night Before the Day Before Art Basel 30" <themoment.blogs.nytimes.com/tag/barnett-newman/> (accessed 10 October 2011).

Films

Blood Diamond. Dir. Edward Zwick. Warner Bros. 2006.
Wall Street. Dir. Oliver Stone. Twentieth Century Fox. 1987.

Márcio Seligmann-Silva

Art and its Potentialities:
From the Virtual to Speculation

Counterfeit money

As we were walking away from a tobacconist's, my friend carefully sorted out his change: into his left vest pocket he slipped the small gold coins, into his right vest pocket the small silver coins; [...]

We encountered a poor man who tremblingly held out his hat to us. – I know nothing more disquieting than the mute eloquence of those supplicating eyes, which contain at one and the same time so much humility and so many reproaches, at least for the sensitive man who knows how to read them. He finds something approaching these depths of complicated emotion in the tearful eyes of dogs being beaten.

My friend's offering was much larger than my own, and I said to him: "You are right: next to the pleasure of being astonished, there is none greater than causing surprise." "It was the counterfeit coin," he replied tranquilly, as if to justify his prodigality. [...]

A publican or a baker might, for example, have him arrested as a counterfeiter or as a passer of counterfeit coins. But the counterfeit coin might also just as well serve as the seed for several days of wealth, in the hands of a poor, small-scale speculator. [...]. "Yes, you are right: there is no pleasure sweeter than surprising a man by giving him more than he had hoped for."[...]

I then saw clearly that he had wanted to both perform a charitable act and make a good deal at the same time – to gain forty sous and the heart of God; to get into paradise economically; finally, to earn for free the badge of a charitable man. I might almost have pardoned him for the desire for criminal enjoyment of which I had just recently supposed him capable. I would have found it curious and singular that he amused himself by compromising the poor, but I could never pardon him for the ineptness of this calculation. One is never excused for being evil, but there is some merit in knowing that one is – and the most irreparable of vices is to do evil through stupidity. (Baudelaire 1999)

I start this essay with this well-known and particularly witty prose poem by Baudelaire, "La fausse monnaie," first published in 1864 in the periodical *L'Artiste*,[1] because it carries important themes that deal with the relationship be-

---

1 *Le Spleen de Paris (Petits Poèmes en prose)*, in Baudelaire 1975: 273–274.

tween the aesthetic and the financial spheres, the subject chosen for this occasion. This short passage provides an account of a meeting between two bourgeois men with a beggar who asks for money. Furthermore, this text offers a sophisticated mise en scène of fundamental aspects of capitalism, exposed just where it meets with religion and setting a new mandate for the aesthetic field. The narrator of the anecdote could be understood as a kind of double of both the author and the reader himself: he acts as an observer who describes the facts and judges them from the point of view of a certain Judeo-Christian ethics. The scene described is of an individual who gives a beggar a counterfeit coin. The narrator reflects on the possible consequences of this act. That fake coin could "se multiplier en pièces vraies" ("be converted into real coins"), or in the hands of "un pauvre petit spéculateur" ("a poor, small-scale speculator") become "le germe d'une richesse de quelques jours" ("the seed for several days of wealth"), or it could even put the beggar in prison. The action is condemned as an attempt "de faire à la fois la charité et une bonne affaire" ("to both perform a charitable act and make a good deal at the same time"), or even as a way to "emporter le paradis économiquement" ("to get into paradise economically"). The man performing this act justifies himself in some way by saying that there is nothing more pleasurable than "surprendre un homme en lui donnant plus qu'il n'espère" ("surprising a man by giving him more than he had hoped for"). In this theatrical scene, Baudelaire not only dramatizes language itself with his hierarchy of "poor" and "rich" words (we recall that the bourgeois man, before handing the fake coin to the beggar, performs a careful triage of his coins distributing them between different pockets), but we can also see in this poem a presentation of the poet's activity in that a mere coin can become the beginning of poetic Fortune. The whole scene is a poem. In a way, when reading good literature, the reader is always surprised by the poetic offering which goes beyond what is expected. Rather than being a double of reality, the poem creates a reality, that is, a scene in which two "sophisticated" bourgeois men differentiate themselves from a beggar. The "sophistication" of the bourgeois men gets established as much by their ability to detach themselves from the moral rules as by a certain air of superiority which both men display in their total indifference to the beggar (who does not have a voice and is only described as someone who trembles and has "yeux suppliants" ["supplicating eyes"]), as well as by the moral discourse constructed by the narrator. It is as if a division of modular tasks is taking place here: a bourgeois individual, who positions himself as a "homme sensible" ("sensitive man") embodying the institutions of order such as religion, the state and its legal arm, and another who becomes the image of the bourgeois able to place himself above the laws that he himself establishes. In this character, we encounter the sovereign structure of power, which places those who create the laws beyond and above them. This figure is complemented by the image of the beggar as someone who inhabits a haunted frontier, where he can be both victim of the force of the law (he is at risk of going to prison), as well as being almost animal, more specifically a dog that has been beaten. This beggar-animal may today be read as a representation of what Agamben labeled *homo sacer*, or even, following Walter Benjamin's lead, the "bare life" – a being excluded from the circle of citizenship and politics, thus ensuring a frontier, a margin which shelters and dialectically determines both bourgeois men in our story.

The final paragraph of the poem is about the condemnation of the act of giving a fake coin (as charity). The so called "good bourgeois" claims he could almost forgive what he calls "criminelle jouissance" ("criminal enjoyment"), but could not forgive the "ineptie de son calcul" ("the ineptness of this calculation"). For him, the more unforgiveable vice is "to do evil through stupidity." However, for the reader nothing is certain: was the "bad bourgeois" really so ignorant and innocent of the consequences of his act? His words indicate that he simply thought he was making the beggar happy by surprising him "en lui donnant plus qu'il n'espère" ("giving him more than he had hoped for"). The beggar who saw himself as the lowest level of humanity, could not hope to be so much "valued" by a distinguished man – though in fact he was being made fun of. However, what if the words of this bourgeois person were only half-truths? What if he was capable of "fausse paroles" ("fake words") as well as being able to give "fausses monnaies" ("fake coins")? From the point of view of the "good bourgeois," this man who is seen as "méchant" ("evil") is also in debt as he cannot be forgiven. His situation is characterized both by his infinite capacity to pass on fake coins and by the fact that he can never be forgiven. In fact, we see in this poem one of the many examples of the vicious circle structure characteristic of this volume of Baudelaire's prose poems. It seems as though poetry gets presented as an enclosed autopoetic system, which is simultaneously perceived as a microcosm of the world around it. Thus, the aesthetic field endows new meaning to the "real" world both by describing it differently and by displacing it.

In Baudelaire's *Spleen de Paris*, we encounter the characteristics of this new capitalist society which later, in 1921, Walter Benjamin would scrutinize in his fragment "Kapitalismus als Religion." Here, Benjamin describes the four main characteristics of capitalism as a religion: first, it is a religion merely perceived as a cult (which does not have any dogma or theology); second, this cult has no end and no limit; third, one of the characteristics of this cult is that it draws us into debt. Everything revolves around *Schuld*, a term whose ambiguity has been widely explored by Nietzsche both in its sense of guilt and in its sense of debt. In fact, the subject is always in a state of irreparable guilt/debt. Finally, for Benjamin, capitalism as religion is marked by the occultation or concealment of God (GS VI, 100 – 101). In this passage, Benjamin also speculates about the similarities between bank notes and the images of saints (a subject he also addresses in his *Einbahnstrasse*) and notes how capitalism emerged in the West as a parasite on Christianity by appropriating its mythic elements (GS VI, 102). "La fausse monnaie" can be read as an allegory of this mythical force of capitalism while simultaneously revealing its Christian roots.

In this prose poem, we observe the paradigmatic intersection of the prosaic world of economic life with the aesthetic sphere. In his dedication of *Le Spleen de Paris* to Arsène Houssaye (originally published in the daily *La Presse* in 1862), Baudelaire wrote that "This obsessive idea owes its birth above all else to the frequenting of enormous cities, to the criss-crossing of their innumerable relations," Baudelaire 1999.[2] The prose poem genre, which is the subject of the introduction and of many of the poems included in the book, is presented as the offspring of modernity and big cities. Baudelaire states that in this new kind of poems he is searching for "the description of modern life, or rather of a modern and more abstract life" Baudelaire 1999.[3]

The prose of modernity proves simultaneously to be both the source and the subject of his poems. In "La fausse monnaie," we observe a sort of premonition of the disappearance of the *homo laborans* and the birth of two new species that later became touchstones in our world: the *homo aestheticus* and the *homo sacer*. The former incorporates many aspects of the new man envisaged since the end of the eighteenth century by thinkers such as the German romantics Friedrich Schlegel and Novalis. For them, the artist would represent the pinnacle of humankind and art would cure the wounds opened up by progress and alienation. The latter, the *homo sacer* is considered by Agamben to be scrap, a kind of waste in human form, rejected by society as a means of maintaining its sovereign power structure. This biopolitical landscape is not static and runs its own dynamics. We may say that one side of the coin sustains the other. The spectacle of violence, poverty and misery is part of our aestheticized world and not its opposite. In this way, the poem becomes a sort of microcosm of our world and of its new moneyscape.

Indeed, the idea of a "fake coin," which might provide the start of ephemeral or endless wealth, reminds us of a potential – which tends to be infinite – of the growth of wealth, as much in the capitalist society as in the "poetic fortune,"

---

2 "C'est surtout de la fréquentation des villes énormes, c'est du croisement de leurs innombrables rapports que naît cet idéal obsédant." (Baudelaire 1975: 276).
3 "[...]"la description de la vie moderne, ou plutôt d'une vie moderne et plus abstraite." (Baudelaire 1975: 275)

that is, within the aesthetic field and in the values attributed to works of art. Capitalism is founded on a monetary and value-creating system that clearly lacks a solid foundation, as the global crisis has more than demonstrated since September 2008. Despite its dubious foundations, its logic of exponential growth has yet to be abandoned even after these great financial crises. The artist occupies an ambiguous place within this capitalist system, grounded in utilitarianism and commodity fetishism. On the one hand, as he does not produce anything useful, the artist has been on the margins of society since the time of romanticism. In a way, the *Bildungsroman* shows him going through a metamorphosis, which culminates in acceptance into bourgeois society – or, sometimes, when failing acceptance, in exile or death. On the other hand, artists often continue to occupy a place of distinction in the symbolic economy of modern societies and, in fact, their symbolic capital has ever more increased. Their works of art may reach astronomical values of tens of millions of dollars. Recently, Damien Hirst's work, paradigmatically called *For the Love of God* – pure capitalism as religion and aesthetic performance – was put on sale for $100 million. Andy Warhol's *192 One-Dollar Bills*,[4] from 1962, was the first in a series of works which took as its theme the relationship between art, financial speculation, the cult of celebrities and also violence and death.

Thus, it should be considered that while Benjamin established a parallel between capitalism and religion, the same holds true of the relationship of this system with the aesthetic field. We are faced with the resounding permeability between capitalism, religion and the arts. The latter two serve as a place for reflection and a testing ground for the riskier adventures of capitalists. The Midas-capitalist sees in the Midas-artist a sort of more daring and rebellious brother who has managed to take the Midas gift to its ultimate consequences. On the one hand, Benjamin noted that the exhibition and the cult values in works of art relate to one another as inverted powers – the stronger the exhibition value, the weaker the cult value – ; on the other hand, he did not take into account the increase in monetary value resulting from exhibiting works of art. The fact that nowadays some works of art do sell for astronomical prices only emphasizes the ambiguous place that art occupies in our culture: works of art have literally no value, which means that anything can be projected onto them. The art system has served not only as a model for the self-reflection of modern, post-romantic man, but also as the self-reflection of the very capitalist

---

4 I recall one of Warhol's witty remarks on his affair with money: "I like money on the wall. Say you were going to buy a $200,000 painting. I think you should take that money, tie it up and hang it on the wall. Then when someone visited you, the first thing they would see is the money on the wall." (Warhol 1975: 133–134).

system that has increasingly become some huge speculative game without any solid foundations. While in the economy, there is a constant anxiety concerning the future and this same future is constantly being deployed as the screen on which the grounds of future speculation are projected, in the universe of the arts, we have instead built a place from which we would like to observe our future. Artists and their works are now conceived as windows through which we observe the future of humankind.

In the field of the arts, we can no longer separate the role of large exhibitions such as the Documenta and the Biennials from the big Art Fairs, the work of the powerful auction houses such as Sotheby's and Christie's, and also the actions of art critics and theorists. Today, art exists within this system and to deny this is simply to deny reality. Andy Warhol knew how to capitalize on this reality – again, literally – bringing to his works of art and artistic performances an awareness of this belonging both to the market and the religious fields, within this new religion that is pure cult, charged with what Benjamin, in his notes to the Arcades Project, called the "sex appeal of the inorganic." Benjamin's words in relation to fashion are enlightening in this context:

> Fashion reveals the dialectical point of transfer between woman and commodity – between pleasure and the corpse [...] fashion has never been anything but the parody of the colourful corpse, the provocation of death through a woman and, amidst memorable shrill laughter, a bitter murmured conversation with decomposition. This is fashion. For this reason it changes so quickly. (GS V, 111).

Also drawn from the same notes: fashion "connects the living body [*Leib*] to the inorganic world. Fashion sees in the living the rights of the corpse. Fetishism, which succumbs to the sex appeal of the inorganic, is its vital nerve" (GS V, 130). Fashion brings together a dialectic that evokes the tensions between libido and the pull of death. Within it, sex and death meet each other as a kind of absolute. Warhol brought this force of fashion into his own works of art exposing the cult of money and the aesthetic as the fields of speculation par excellence. The artist, ironically, serves as a vanguard to the speculative capitalism so prevalent today.[5]

Artists and their works, serving as a means of catching a glimpse of the future, make us consider the artistic potential to anticipate what is to come, while recalling the neo-platonic tradition that projected onto artists the capacity of ris-

---

5 The Brazilian artist Cildo Meireles with his work *Coca-Cola Project* (1970) reflects, like Warhol, upon this connection between art and capitalism, but from a different point of view, namely as a critic of the capitalist credo.

ing to the world of ideas. If, on the one hand, artists are considered as those who are able to give palpable shape to archetypes, to ideas, or to the origin of those things existing in derivative form on earth, on the other hand, we tend to see the field of the arts as the ante-chamber of the future. Artist are seen as prophets. This is the case both because of their capacity to play and speculate with values (symbolic and monetary) and because of their capacity to understand technology as an extension of our body. Something of the demiurgic is projected onto the artist, as we have seen since Mary Shelley's *Frankenstein* and Goethe's *Faust*. The Faustian force of modern man simultaneously proves an aesthetic, a technical and a monetary drive. This triad constitutes the new trinity of capitalism as religion organized around the cult of commodity and money. This cult, as Benjamin shows, leaves us in debt and feeling guilty and leading only to more devotion.

Above all, artists are those who transgress. Therefore, it is important to once again note the ambiguity of "La fausse monnaie," its profound and blatant irony. Baudelaire had good reason for initially baptizing this poem in prose as "Le Paradoxe de l'aumône" (Baudelaire 1975: 1336). Everything in *Le Spleen de Paris* revolves around the paradox, the oxymoron. In fact, this same paradoxical structure comes in the passage of the text "L'école païenne" which gave vent to "La fausse monnaie." Here, Baudelaire tells us that he did in fact meet an artist who, on receiving a fake coin, said he would keep it for a pauper ("pour un pauvre"; Baudelaire 1976: 49). Baudelaire's commentary makes clear how he identified himself with the narrator of the prose poem and later wrote: "The wretched man took an infernal pleasure in stealing from the poor and at the same time enjoying the benefits of a reputation for charity."[6] Thus, artists are described as men without morals, who invest their reputation on appearances. By dislocating this scene to his book of prose poems, what at first seemed a banal dichotomy – that is, the opposition between a moral and an immoral attitude, the union between a moment of enjoyment and false appearances – somehow has its structure dissolve. As seen, the final condemnation of the man giving the fake coin is not related to the act itself, which the narrator is willing to forgive, but to the agent's ignorance of this act. This ignorance, however, could also be pure simulation. In this sense, we could also ask whether our own society simulates ignorance when the fake coin of charity is given to its poor, only reinforcing a system that perpetuates itself by increasing the difference between rich and poor. The window of the aesthetic enables Baudelaire to "simulate" the hypocrisy of our society – which is so dear to us. The "fake" character of the aesthetic

---

6 "Le misérable prenait un infernal plaisir à voler le pauvre et à jouir en même temps des bénéfices d'une réputation de charité." (Baudelaire 1976: 49)

field allows for the deconstruction of dichotomies and polarities, as Baudelaire brilliantly shows in *Le Spleen de Paris*.

To conclude this exploration of the potentialities of the arts today, I would like to reiterate the so-called "moral" question broached by Baudelaire's poem. The narrator seems to hold firm ideas regarding just how we should deal with money. Within Western cultural history, besides the representations of good fortune and the beautiful and gracious Abundance – with her cornucopia symbolizing wealth and happiness – we may trace a long tradition preaching discretion and morality in handling money. The previously mentioned myth of Midas in Ovid also portrays a greedy character depicted as a donkey (and even given ass ears by Apollo). Midas is characterized by Ovid as "rich and poor" and almost dies of hunger because of his peculiar wish, a "disastrous gift" writes Ovid in an oxymoron, just as Baudelaire would later characterize his protagonist in "La fausse monnaie." From Ancient Greece – and later adopted by Christianity – comes the tradition of presenting greed as one of the seven deadly sins, along with gluttony, sloth, envy, anger, lust and pride. Mammon in this sense proves a paradigmatic figure within Christianity, seen as the one who embodies the diabolic side of the attraction to money. It was no coincidence that he was also seen as a false god (another version of the biblical golden calf), or as a (dis)simulator. Just as often, in the Christian world artists were condemned as dissimulators – especially actors.[7] During the Renaissance, and inspired by the humanist spirit, many artists represented this association between greed and evil. In these cases, art functions as a mnemonic device of *paidéia* whose role was to recall the virtues and admonish vices. *Avaritia* often gets depicted as an ugly and melancholic old woman, accompanied by an emaciated wolf, a "greedy and voracious" animal, as we read about in *Iconologia* by Cesare Ripa, quoting Christofano Landino (Ripa 1625: 58).

This movement of the arts towards moralization which had been ongoing up to the Enlightenment collapsed with Romanticism. Increasingly the arts became a device to present what had been censured, repressed and prohibited, what Freud, inspired by Schelling, would later call *das Unheimliche*. As we have seen, the artist becomes someone who puts values in general on hold: both in monetary and moral terms. The economic potential of the arts has never been as great as it is today. It has never been so close to the sciences and politics.

---

7 I leave aside the long anti-Semitic tradition, which has always tried to attribute the cult of the false god Mammon to Jews, from the Middle Ages to *The Protocols of the Elders of Zion*, through to our times (see Attali 2002, 2010). It would be interesting to look at the issue of the profound relationship between Judaism, not with Mammon, but with the arts in the twentieth century and with the aesthetic field in general. However I shall leave this theme for another occasion.

If it is true that Benjamin saw in the aesthetization of politics a fascist streak, then today there is no guarantee that we are free from fascism. The artist-demi-urge is as much an instrument of new onto-typological programs – helping design a new man that would mean the death and/or the extermination of those falling short of this category – as s/he can also critically be of service to the *Gestaltung* of a plastic world, where individuals are free to air their differences and contradictions. Just like Pascal, who in the seventeenth century advised us to back the existence of God by a wager, today we may feasibly back the possibility of a positive outcome for the creation of this *homo aestheticus*. Everything shall depend on our ability to also include the materiality of the *homo sacer* in our lives so as to integrate him, not as scrap, but as an equal.

Works cited

Attali, Jacques (2002) *Les Juifs, le monde et l'argent. Histoire économique du peuple juif* (Paris: Fayard). Trans. (2010) *The Economic History of the Jewish People* (Portland: Eska Publishing).

Baudelaire, Charles (1975) *Œuvres complètes*, vol. I (Paris: Gallimard-la Pléiade).

Baudelaire, Charles (1976) *Œuvres complètes*, vol. II (Paris: Gallimard-la Pléiade).

Baudelaire, Charles (1999) "Counterfeit Money," Trans. Cat Nilan. <http://www.piranesia.net/baudelaire/spleen/28monnaie.html> (accessed 10 October 2013). Benjamin, Walter (1972–1989) *Gesammelte Schriften*, ed. R. Tiedemann und H. Schweppenhäuser, 14 vols. (Frankfurt a.M.: Suhrkamp). Title abridged: GS.

Ripa, Cesare (1625) *Della novissima iconologia* (Padova: Pietro Paolo Tozzi). <https://archive.org/stream/dellanovissimaic00ripa#page/58/mode/2up> (accessed 9 January 2014).

Warhol, Andy (1975) *The Philosophy of Andy Warhol: from A to Z and Back Again* (New York: Harcourt, Brace, Jovanovich).

Alfred Opitz[†]

The Magic Triangle

Considerations on Money, Art and S***

In 1979, Joseph Beuys, the German artist then already on his way to the top of the worldwide art ranking,[1] signed banknotes of 10 and 100 marks with the statement "Kunst = Kapital" (Art = Capital), a visual abbreviation of his pictorial and social theory.[2] We may also discern in Beuys's statement a twinkling reference to Andy Warhol, who produced not only a sequence of multiplicated dollar notes but also a painting of a toilet and several piss paintings in the early 1960s. Warhol and Beuys met for the first time in 1979 in Düsseldorf. Whilst quite different in their understanding of art and society, they held one big common aspiration: to become a living myth in transforming their poor injured bodies into shining stars. Warhol dusted his silk screen portrait of Beuys (1980) with diamond powder, and Beuys replied with a multiple called "The Warhol-Beuys-Event."[3] At that time, they were not the only self-performers and prophets of their own overall mission on the art scene, but for some years, they were the greatest, the most famous and the most successful.

In the dirty context of this essay, I shall focus on the central element of the formula quoted (K = K), the equation mark which implies transformation or even, when considering the messianic and Christic features in Beuys's activities, transubstantiation; all this in the name of art and with the rather old-fashioned aim of redemption. In fact, Beuys became known as a charismatic master of transformation; he used dead and living animals, blood, honey, grease and felt, not to mention alchemic substances like copper and sulphur. For Beuys, the famous Feyerabend-slogan "anything goes" (Science in a free society 1978) represents an artistic project. In a 1973 interview, questioned on the limits of the aesthetic utilization of excrement, Beuys answers that everything human

---

1 In 1978, Beuys already occupied the second position in this ranking and in the following two years the first ("Kunstkompass," *Capital:* http://www.capital.de/guide/kunstkompass/100001645. html).

2 For Beuys's opinions on society and the economy, see Beuys, 1992 and his installation *Das Kapital Raum, 1970–1977,* documented by Versphol 1985. On social change by art, see also the megalomaniac *Aufruf zur Alternative*, published first in the *Frankfurter Rundschau* (23 December 1978) and reprinted at the first election for the European Parliament in June 1979 (available on http://www.impuls21.net/pdf/aufruf_zur_alternative.pdf, accessed June 2010).

3 The camouflage portrait was the only picture in Beuys's house in Düsseldorf. For more details on Warhol and Beuys see Billeter (1988) and Warhol (2009: 210–211).

can be – and must be – aestheticized and even proclaiming a polarity between cerebral and intestinal production (Murken 2006: 72–78).

Beuys's esthetic program, however, derives firstly from recycling alchemic and romantic ideas. With the staging of the artistic integration of common materials, Warhol and Beuys created an open artistic space liberated from the taboos of idealistic representation that still dominated a great extent of the nineteenth and twentieth centuries. At the center of this open space, these artists represent their public persona, in their performances and with their non-interchangeable outfits (the hat of Beuys, the silver white wig of Warhol). When Marshall McLuhan proclaimed in 1964: "the medium is the message," we may say in the case of Warhol and Beuys: "the artist is the medium," and the works are only material extensions of a mythified body.

In the specific case of artistic work about money, Beuys's signature imitates the gesture of the merchant or banker who signs a cheque or a bill of exchange, an act of magic that implies a moment that no longer requires the material presence of money. The signed paper is a transforming agent, a key to the world of commodities. However, Beuys's formula (Art = Capital) demands reflection, the seal of the signature and the new cultural and economic value of the bank note questions the economic system by means of art. This magic trick of transformation had already been executed by Marcel Duchamp when, in 1919, he signed a hundred-dollar cheque for his dentist (Schwarz 2000: 378). The piece of paper ended up in an art collection with the artist's signature more valuable than the amount of the cheque with many of the following conceptual artists replaying this productive shifting of systems to create new, traditional money. On his death, Andy Warhol left behind a $100 million fortune.

1 Blood, bodily discharges and exploding excrement: the sticky face of modern art

When, in 1973, Beuys insisted on the necessity of an esthetic use of excrement, those vulgar materials had already entered the domain of the artistic vanguard. In 1961, the Italian artist, Piero Manzoni produced 90 cans of *Merda d'artista*, 30 grammes each, numbered, signed and sold at the then current price of gold. Among other works, Manzoni had already produced *Fiati d'Aria* (*Breath of the Artist*), which reminded the viewer not only of the contingency of aesthetic values but also of very ancient metaphysical traditions. Some decades earlier, Dali and Duchamp had already thought about an art-edition of s*** and, in December 1919, Duchamp sent a glass recipient of Paris Air to the USA (Schwarz 2000: 379,

675). The lines of tradition are evident: they critique the Christian past worship of the bottled breath of Jesus and several saints. The modern artist, who assumes the role of a second creator and the *salvator mundi* mission, takes up these ritual objects. Manzoni's (unrealized) project to wrap dead bodies in transparent plastic for exhibition represents another response to relic rituals. Thirty years later, the German anatomist, Gunther von Hagens, launched an exhibition of plastinated corpses (see the catalogue *Körperwelten 2000 – Body Worlds*), which has hitherto been seen by 26 million visitors in Asia and several European countries.

Manzoni has now become part of the history of conceptual art. For Engler, one important aspect of Manzoni's work is the relationship "between an immaterial concept and the concrete materials of corporal remains" (Engler 2000:126) presented as an invisible idea that cannot be verified.[4] We must believe the content just like the pilgrim in front of the reliquary. Engler, by the way, does not believe the cans contain real waste, whereas Denis Dutton reports joyfully: "at least half of those [cans] bought by museums and collectors eventually exploded" (Dutton 2009: 202). Furthermore, where Engler sees a "creative revision of the concept of ready made" (Engler 2000: 129–131), Dutton welcomes its decline and fall (Dutton 2009: 202). Apparently, the mythical *Merda d'artista* remains good enough for art legends.

Manzoni died in 1963, at the age of 30, before he could realize his next project, *Sangue d'Artista*, containers with the artist's blood, which once more recalls the cult of relics and the floods of blood in traditional religious paintings.[5] Manzoni's idea was taken up in 1991 by the British artist Marc Quinn, who sculptured his self-portrait with five liters of his own frozen blood, a procedure repeated every five years with the last in 2009. The self-portrait of Quinn is a disturbing game with our concepts of identity and time. The vital relation between the portrait and the freezing container evokes the fragility of our mental and physical constructions; the impermanence of the body doubled up by our increasing dependence on machines and technical devices. This modern *memento mori* also recalls similar relic artifacts.

Considering the great importance of relic cults to modern conceptual art, we now take a closer look at the complex historical filiation of body and s***-art. When Manzoni transforms his breath, his blood and his excrement into artworks, as seen, he clearly refers to the relic cult, the history of which is full of dramatic events: robberies and rivalries, miracles and scandals. Relics were pro-

---

4 Engler's study situates Manzoni in the context of modern European concept art (Fontana, Yves Klein), but his history of the symbolic utilization of human excrement begins with Cézanne (127); the tradition of the (holy) body cult is not mentioned.

5 See, among other and former examples, the works referred to in Lang 2001.

duced (and falsified) in special factories and sold in markets (see also Geary 1996). We even find bottled Egyptian darkness and the body-fat of grilled saints. Clearly, the contemporary artist Teresa Margolles did not have to invent her disgusting procedures. The nineteen certified saints produced one hundred and twenty one heads and one hundred and thirty six bodies and other limbs. Believers apparently did not mind this multiplication. The breasts of Saint Agatha were worshipped in four different towns, and Saint John left behind sixty fingers. The relics were sacred and not at all the dead bodies of the saints. These would seem to have been immediately dismembered and transformed into relics, with the more pieces the better.

For hundreds of ages, millions of pilgrims circulated in Europe to see the famous relics, a permanent auto-hypnotic migration, which also brought about the mass production of religious souvenirs. Relics even served as collateral for bank loans, and the most famous collections accumulated phantastic amounts of redemption. The elector Frederick the Wise (1463–1525) applied his wisdom and his money to collecting in Wittenberg about 19,000 relics with an indulgence value of 1,902,202 years and 270 days. That nevertheless paled alongside the Halle collection with over 21,400 relics good for 39 million years of indulgence (Hermann 2003: 176).

The long history of the relic cult suggests that the European public was familiar with the ritual presence of dead bodies or body parts and with the pictorial representation of violence, blood, torture and extreme suffering. The atrocities displayed in Medieval and Renaissance paintings are not inferior to modern splatter movies or recent mainstream TV-series. There was technical progress, however; nowadays, the camera passes literally through the slaughtered, dismembered, triturated, decomposed and burned bodies, which Jerry Bruckheimer, amongst others, serves up in colourful close-ups every night at dinner.

On the other hand, body fluids and excrements have played an important role worldwide in popular medicine as well as in black and white magic. These prescriptions imply not only the external application of excrement but also its ingestion in various forms (Bächtold-Stäubli 1932–1933: V, 330–350).

The hunger for belief, the need for religious and profane relics is certainly present in the metonymic work on the body and on body components, which has dominated the art scene ever since the 1960s. Viennese Actionism (Nitsch, Brus, among others) is deeply impregnated with religious symbols and redemptive references; its violent art-practice proved highly scandalous before it became mainstream. In 1968, Brus got six months of jail time for a dirty performance at

Vienna University before he won the Grand Austrian State Prize for artistic life achievement in 1996.[6] This game of initial scandal and later fame repeats itself still today, with increasing acceleration.

The success of dirty metonymies of the body may be considered as a late counter-reaction to the restrictive idealistic art tradition, an attempt to reintegrate the real and to realize the fusion of truth and reality, the *vréel* beyond imaginary and symbolic codes. Once the conceptual constraints – imposed by decades of Puritanical esthetics – had been loosened, the imagination held no limits. The well-known turning point from pictorial representation to the material (and symbolic) presence of the object in its most abject forms is the Marcel Duchamp urinal, the famous *Fountain* of 1917. Even Dutton praises Duchamp's "ironic genius" (Dutton 2009: 242), and the American art philosopher Danto dedicates an entire book to *The Transfiguration of the Commonplace* (1981). Duchamp had experimented with all artistic trends in the waning century before going conceptual. In the light of cultural history, Duchamp's genial gesture seems far less original. Transcendental presence in vulgar objects is indeed a common-place in centuries of relic cult, and the remains of historical heroes (such as Frederick II of Prussia or Napoleon) were collected and exhibited long before Duchamp. He accomplished, with some delay, in the domain of art what was already current practice in other cultural fields. Nevertheless, his *Fountain*, exhibited in public for the first time in 1950, was imitated and subjected to variations, like other ready–mades he produced through to the end of the century. In 1986, Robert Gober (b. 1954) presented *Two Urinals* in a vertical position before Sherrie Levine (b. 1947) exhibited in New York six shining bronze urinals à la Duchamp in 1991. "The alchemist's interest in putrefaction is shared by contemporary artists, many of whom see something beautiful in natural decay," James Elkins writes. "There are hundreds of examples in fine art, each more nauseating and compelling than the last" (Elkins 2000: 70).

Here are just a few of the potential examples: Dieter Roth (1936 – 1998) was already working with rotting food (yoghurt, salami, chocolate) in the 1960s, he created *Literary Sausages* with shredded newspapers and the complete works of Hegel, his *Rabbit-Shit-Rabbit* is from 1972. Felix Droese (b. 1950), son of a former priest and Beuys's disciple, sold cow-dung as art and later made artistic objects of photos and newspaper pages stamped with the word *Geld* (money). In 1998, the Turner-Prize winner Chris Ofili (b. 1968) decorated some of his paintings as well as portraits of the Virgin Mary with elephant droppings. The blasphemous

---

6 For more details, see the commemorative exhibition of Viennese Actionism at the Staatsgalerie Stuttgart, 3 – 5 July 2009.

gesture has become a common place in contemporary art. Human waste was a frequent material for German artists Thomas Rentmeister and Anton Henning in their "bad paintings," as well as for the French outsider Gérard Gasiorowski (1930–1986), and the British art clowns Gilbert & George who created their very own *Dirty Worlds* (1977).[7]

The invasion of body fluids contaminated not only contemporary art but also theatre, cinema, TV, literature and photography. In 2009, German writer Charlotte Roche published a dirty bestseller entitled *Feuchtgebiete* (*Wetlands*), and a comedy by the Austrian Nobel Prize winner Elfriede Jelinek, *Die Kontrakte des Kaufmanns* 2009 – *The merchant's contracts*), stages the bloody face of almighty money.

While the first generation of conceptual s*** art is still deeply dominated by religious references, the second generation prefers more playful procedures. Thus, in 2000, the Belgian artist Wimm Delvoye created a monstrous machine, Cloaca, which imitates the process of digestion. And the American "Sprinkle Brigade" works on excrement found on the streets of New York (2007), creating, among others, the *Double Header* (Yankee Stadium 2006) and *The Last Supper* (West Village 2005), incidentally the subject of Warhol's last (rather conventional and self-referential) picture.

The two most radical followers of Manzoni are without doubt Andres Serrano (b. 1950) and Teresa Margolles (b. 1963). Serrano's photos involve blood, semen and human milk – his *Piss Christ* of 1987 travelled the world – , and his crude self-portrait as a pile of bodily discharge represents the human as crude matter. The Mexican artist Teresa Margolles, a student of the works of Viennese Actionism, frequently resorts to Christian traditions and local death cults. *Entierro/Burial* shows (or better: hides) a baby's corpse in a block of concrete. During her performance, *Ciudad en espera*, she painted public buildings in Cuba with the fat of corpses, *Vaporización* (Berlin 2002) is a room vaporized with the water used to wash dead bodies, this same water again used, in *En el aire* (2003) for beautiful soap bubbles. Other works directly apply the principle of contact relics, such as the famous shrouds of Christ in Turin and Trier. However, Margolles's shrouds display the fluid marks of homeless people's unidentified corpses (Vienna 2003).

The evolution of money in art represents a rather different story booming only in the 1990s following the global triumph of unrestrained capitalism. While many utopian projects with different trade practices and means of social exchange get discussed, money is denounced as a symbol of capitalism in order

---

7 Video-art too has not been spared. In 1998, Jennifer Nelson recorded *The 33rd Attempt at Symmetrical Shitting* for video.

to incite the public to consider its character and function. Artists print their own money or use it as aesthetic play material as do Victor Bonato (b. 1934) and Antonio Natale (b. 1965) in *L'artista delle banconote*. These tendencies were documented in an exhibition at the Kunsthalle Düsseldorf in 2000, with the title *The Fifth Element – Money or Art*, at the same time the review *Kunstforum International* published a special issue about money, titled *A Balance at the Turn of the Millennium*. Just like relics, money is – and always has been – a medium for hopes and desires; the German words for believer (*der Gläubige*) and creditor (*Gläubiger*) differ only in one tiny letter.

2 "Paint is s***" – the cultural history of colors

For the first cave and body paintings, nature provided the necessary colors: red and yellow ocherous earth, chalk, charcoal and soot, but no blue or green. The earliest artistic remains date from 350,000 BC, and, by 40,000 BC, prehistoric painters had already learned how to burn ochre to get redder pigments. The preparation of these early colors was simple but with the increasing need for different colors in the great urban cultures of the Middle East, from the Neolithic age onwards, new resources (animals, plants, metals, acids, etc.) were put into practice. The Egyptian empires applied colors on a large scale and they already knew how to produce synthetic pigments.[8] In ancient Egypt, the same artisans supplied pigments, medicines and face-paint with the medieval word "pigmentum" still combining these three meanings. Colors were integrated into well-defined symbolic and religious systems, and the rarest and most beautiful pigments sold at high prices, a situation continuing well into the Middle Ages and the Renaissance.[9]

The most precious pigment in history, purple, was used from 1600 BC onwards to dye fabrics for kings and emperors. The pigment was distilled from the glandular liquid of a sea mollusk, Murex, which lived along the Mediterranean coasts; for 1 gram of pigment 10,000 snails had to die. At today's prices, the market cost of this pigment would amount to €2,050 for a single gram. Emperors, kings and clerics not only enforced their exclusivity over usage of this color, they also claimed a substantial share of the economic profits from the trade in purple. Thus, millions and millions of snails had to die for their outfits

---

8 The recipe of the famous Egyptian blue remained a well-kept secret and only discovered by greedy and curious European scientists at the end of the nineteenth century.
9 For more details about the history of pigments, see Finlay 2008, and Delamare and Guineau 2009.

and benefit. We might recall here the inscription on the recent "Animals in War Memorial" in London: "They had no choice."

Another very expensive and highly praised pigment was made of blue rocks mined for over 6,000 years near the Chinese border with Afghanistan: lapis lazuli, the Fra Angelico blue, which still displays its transcendent beauty in medieval manuscripts and Renaissance paintings. The current price of the purest preparation: 15,594 euros/kilo.[10] A small gold-leaf coated book costs 23 euros. The preparation of these colors required not only knowledge and technological skills, but also raw materials in increasing quantities. The color red made of boiled insects, for example, turned into a major commodity. In 1560, Spanish ships imported not only gold and silver, but also about 115 tons of cochineal pigment from the American colonies (Delamare and Guineau 2009: 74). The eventful and violent evolution of the color trade is a history of fame and fortune, of the rise and downfall of monopolies and industrial empires, a sequence of commercial wars, espionage, exploitation and slave work in mines and factories.

In the complicated procedures of producing more and better pigments, alchemical techniques played a key role. Still in use today, Prussian blue was invented in around 1710 by two German alchemists, thus enabling Elkins to affirm: "Painting is alchemy" (Elkins 2000: 9). He bases the similarities on two levels: a number of identical ingredients such as realgar, oripigment, lapis lazuli, lead and gold, but also body liquids and discharges, like blood, urine and horse dung, part of the materia prima, called "carbon humanum" by Paracelsus (149).[11] Also identical are not only the many procedures and technical devices for distillation and purification but also the act of painting whose "means are liquid" and "whose ends are solid" (1–2). "In the studio it can feel as if paint is not just reminiscent of shit, but it is shit. The alchemists realized that excrement cannot be denied, that is has to be used" (136). Beuys, a dedicated follower of the esoteric tradition, could not agree more. On a different level, we also find a cognitive and performative similarity. The alchemist conceives of his person as a "surrogate of God," working on transformation, sublimation and resurrection (125). He aims to create other, better worlds "out of the morass" (72), "the labor is about redemption" (75). For Elkins, both in painting and alchemy, "the underlying act is spiritual," and this also proves valid for modern and post-modern art whose "buried spiritual content" may be, he says, "the great un-

---

10 According to Michael Baxandall, the quality and price of blue pigment were stipulated in many Renaissance contracts and thus customer controlled (1999: 19–21).
11 This polarity is furthermore reflected in the Dirt and Gold Paintings of Robert Rauschenberg (1953) (see Bois and Krauss 1997: 235–236, figures 6 and 7).

explored subject in contemporary art history" (75). This perspective, however, requires some further historical and anthropological considerations.

3 The magic triangle

The cultural history of money, art and s*** may be condensed in three versions of the same magic triangle. The most ancient version, from the Neolithic age through to the fourteenth century, sought to integrate the mortal body in ascendental programs within their respective typical death cult and semantic border-crossing systems. These programs have hitherto been characterized by the increasing commercialization and specialization of training devices. The basis of this triangulation is the material world (dirt, excrement), which must be purified and sublimated. The second version (from the fifteenth to the nineteenth century) places art (and, furthermore, redemption) at the top of the triangle. Romantic art idealizes the body, proclaims artistic autonomy and emphasizes the mythical persona of the artist, inhabiting the material (and dirty) matter of life. Even if contemporary art is dominated by money (the third version of the magic triangle), traditional forms of illusory schemes still prevail in the various forms of conceptual and body art; even the recent "abject art" is shaped by aesthetic sublimation and very ancient taboos. The "recent multiplication of 'shit' in actual art works," concludes Menninghaus in his extensive study on disgust, appears in the light of tradition "as perfectly harmless" (Menninghaus 1999: 566).

The first manifestations of art were certainly a reaction to a hostile and dangerous environment, an attempt to understand and dominate a chaotic and fascinating world. At the dawn of human history, the first aesthetic feelings were, according to Leroi-Gourhan (1980: 452), identical with pre-scientific behavior and implying the creation of a meaningful order. This objective still dominates Schiller's aesthetic theory. The imaginary worlds created by art throughout history were not only alternatives to a limited, painful and often boring reality, they were also attempts to deny or to veil the ultimate border, the point of no return. In this context, the god-like artists gained a new aura, their works and their presence provided hope and consolation in hopeless cases. Furthermore, and also for the same reason, transformation proves to be the basic concept of art and religion. Baudrillard may consider "l'alchimie transubstantiatrice" one of the most primitive and regressive myths of mankind (Baudrillard 2008: 53), but it nevertheless remains a basic driver of cultural evolution. The perception of death implies a dynamic and holistic vision of the body whose finality is daily experienced in bodily discharges. This evidence creates a double division of body and soul, of normal, mortal and eternal bodies such as saints, angels, gods and demons, which allows for all sorts of fantasies of eternal survival. The respective rituals of sublimation and, eventually, transition to a better world, promise the transformation of base materials, such as the fetid and mortal human body into eternal youth and pure essence. For sociology, the cultural invention of the "soul", for example, results from the liminal experience of the observed death of others, according to Luhmann, thereby leading to the highly plausible, efficient and therefore universal construction of a border-crossing concept enabling the proclamation of an identical substratum for life and eternity (Luhmann 2002: 267).

To sum up, when the human species became *sapiens*, it was confronted by two primary situations: permanent exposure to aggression and accidents, hunger, disease and all sorts of material needs and suffering, and the evidence of its own death. *Cogito ergo moriturus sum.* There must have been, some 150,000 years ago, a negative epiphany when the *homo sapiens* became aware of his mortality. Culture tries to overcome and compensate: 1) the need for material shelter and food and 2) the metaphysical hunger, the need for a meaningful world, a lasting structure for a limited life. All these challenges converge in the (vulnerable and mortal) human body, which is divided into dualistic entities, devalued in its material and spiritual impermanence (s***, sin and karma) and submitted to machines and mental programs of ascendance, as described by Peter Sloterdijk in his 2009 study: *Du mußt dein Leben ändern* – You must change your life.

We may now ask whether art is possible without this ascendant background. What is s*** without aura, art without technical skills and the transcendent beauty of artifacts? The production of alternative worlds will continue, as will the bio-medical attempts at genetic improvement and transformation in order to overcome the basic/elemental limitations of life, but so will the human instincts of destruction. Perhaps the practice of illusion and self-hypnotic insanity is not only, as Sloterdijk says (Sloterdjk, 2009: 166), an indispensable right of modern societies but also, and primarily, a basic need for dirty human animals who know what they are and that they must die.

Works cited

Appadurai, Arjun (1996) *The Social Life of Things. Commodities in Cultural* (Cambridge: Cambridge University Press).

Baudrillard, Jean (2008) [1968] *Le Système des objets* (Paris: Gallimard).

Bächtold-Stäubli, Hanns (1932/33) *Handwörterbuch des deutschen Aberglaubens,* vol. V. (Berlin und Leipzig: De Gruyter).

Baxandall, Michael (1999) *Die Wirklichkeit der Bilder. Malerei und Erfahrung im Italien der Renaissance*, trans.Hans Günter Holl (Darmstadt: Wissenschaftliche Buchgesellschaft).

Berns, Jörg Jochen (2007) *Himmelsmaschinen / Höllenmaschinen. Zur Technologie der Ewigkeit* (Berlin: Semele Verlag).

Beuys, Joseph (1992) *Kunst = Kapital. Achberger Vorträge* (Wangen: FIU-Verlag).

Billeter, Erika (1988) "Andy Warhol – Joseph Beuys," *Die Zeitschrift für Kunst und Kultur* 8, 44 – 45.

Bois, Yve-Alain and Rosalind E. Krauss (1997) *Formless. A User's Guide* (New York: Zone Books).

Celant, Germano (2007) *Anselm Kiefer* (Bilbao: Guggenheim).

Chirat, Nicol (ed.) (2009*) Warhol. Le grand monde d'Andy Warhol* (Paris: Éditions de la Réunion des Musées Nationaux).

Delamare, François and Bernard Guineau (2009) *Les Matériaux de la couleur* (Paris: Gallimard).

Danto, Arthur C. (1981) *The Transfiguration of the Commonplace: A Philosophy of Art* (Cambridge, Mass.: Harvard University Press).

Dutton, Denis (2009) *The Art Instinct. Beauty, Pleasure & Human Evolution* (Oxford, New York: Oxford University Press).

Elkins, James (1999) *Pictures of the Body. Pain and Metamorphosis* (Stanford: Stanford University Press).

Elkins, James (2000) *What Painting Is. How to Think about Oil Painting, Using the Language of Alchemy* (New York, London: Routledge).

Engler, Martin (2000) *Piero Manzoni – Metonymien des Körpers* (doct. Diss., U. Freiburg)

Finlay, Victoria (2008) *Das Geheimnis der Farben. Eine Kulturgeschichte*, trans. Charlotte Breuer und Norbert Möllemann (Berlin: List).

Geary, Patrick (1996) "Sacred commodities: the circulation of medieval relics," Appadurai 1996: 169 – 191.

von Hagens, Gunther (2000) *Körperwelten. Katalog der Ausstellung: Die Faszination des Echten* (Heidelberg: Institut für Plastination).

Hermann, Horst (2003) *Lexikon der kuriosesten Reliquien vom Atem Jesu bis zum Zahn Mohammeds* (Berlin: Rüttgen & Loening).

Kiefer, Anselm (2005) *Heaven and Earth*, ed. Michael Auping (Munich, London, New York: Prestel).

Kris, Ernst and Otto Kurz (1995) [1934] *Die Legende vom Künstler. Ein geschichtlicher Versuch*, preface Ernst H. Gombrich) (Frankfurt am Main: Suhrkamp). (2000) *Kunstforum international* 149 (Das Schicksal des Geldes. Kunst und Geld – Eine Bilanz zum Jahrtausendwechsel).

Lang, Walther K. (2001) *Grausame Bilder. Sadismus in der napolitanischen Malerei von Caravaggio bis Giordano* (Berlin: Reimer).

Leroi-Gourhan, André (1980) *Hand und Wort. Die Evolution von Technik, Sprache und Kunst*, trans. Michael Bischoff (Frankfurt am Main: Suhrkamp).

Luhmann, Niklas (2002) *Die Religion der Gesellschaft*, ed. André Kieserling (Frankfurt am Main: Suhrkamp).

Menninghaus, Winfried (1999) *EKEL. Theorie und Geschichte einer starken Empfindung* (Frankfurt am Main: Suhrkamp).

Moura, Leonel (2009) *30 gramas* (Lisboa: LXXL Edições).

Murken, Axel Hinrich, Volker Rattemeyer and Hans Peter Wipplinger (2006) *Joseph Beuys. Heilkräfte der Kunst. Werke aus der Sammlung Axel Hinrich Murke* (Altrogge: Verlag Murken).

Schwarz, Arturo (2000) *The Complete Works of Marcel Duchamp* (New York: Delano Greenidge Editions).

Sloterdijk, Peter (2009) *Du mußt dein Leben ändern. Über Anthropotechnik* (Frankfurt am Main: Suhrkamp).

Versphol, Franz-Joachim (1985) *Beuys, das Kapital Raum, 1970–1977: stratégie pour réactiver les sens*, trans. François Renault (Paris: Éditions Biro).

III Literature and Money Matters

Paulo de Medeiros

Phantom Counterfeits: Credit and Betrayal in a (Post)-Modern Polity

> "And the brothers, then really looking at
> the bills,
> saw that not even the blind
> would have accepted them".
>
> Fernando Pessoa, "A Great Portuguese"[1]
>
> "Fixing prices, setting values, working out
> equivalents, exchanging – this preoccupied
> man's first thoughts to such a degree that in a
> certain sense it *constitutes* thought"
>
> Friedrich Nietzsche. *On the Genealogy of
> Morality.* Transl. Carol Diethe, 1994, 45.

Taken thus, isolated and out of context, these two statements, one by Fernando Pessoa from a seemingly uncharacteristic short story (Pessoa 1986), the other by Friedrich Nietzsche, from his second essay on *The Genealogy of Morality* (Nietzsche 1999), at first seem unconnected both mutually and to my chosen topic. However, as I hope to make clear, they are crucial for reaching an understanding of the logic of counterfeiting or, better said, the logic of spectral counterfeiting, which I would argue our contemporary age both inscribes and subscribes to. In order to begin with, I will invoke another kind of text that, even while not as crucial as the two above, and even if circumstantial, might more readily make clear what I mean by phantom counterfeits and how they relate to our contemporary polity. On 16 July 2009, *The Guardian* published a cartoon by Steven Bell, depicting what looks like a five-euro bill with the effigy of former prime-minister Tony Blair behind the bars of the stylized monument that graces the bill, with the caption reading: "First President of Europe & War Criminal at Large." The cartoon is a response to the voicing of a wish for Tony Blair to become the first European Union President, which, given Britain's relationship with the rest of Europe, and its non-acceptance of the Euro as its national currency, is certainly ironic in itself. What caught my attention in this cartoon was the immediate link between money and politics – a certain kind of politics, and not just money, but counterfeit money – as well as between credit and be-

---

1 All the translations from the Portuguese unless otherwise indicated are my own.

trayal, credibility and criminality. Moreover no one would mistake the cartoon for a real five-euro bill. Hence, even though it pretends to be a (counterfeit) bill, in reality it proclaims loudly its quality as art, a certain kind of art. I classify this cartoon and its content as a phantom counterfeit, i.e. a counterfeit that rejects from the outset the main purpose of counterfeiting, which is to pass on false money or other goods as real.

The connection between Steven Bell's cartoon and other examples of phantom counterfeits with clear political messages becomes obvious when looking, for instance, at the example of the Bush zero-dollar bill, a bill that looks much more like a real one-dollar bill than the Steven Bell image looks like a real five-euro bill, but that, its realism notwithstanding, loudly proclaims itself as political commentary and not as legal currency, by explicitly stating that "This note is not legal tender, it is a joke just like George Bush" and by deploying a simulated serial number to raise political consciousness ("B4YOUVOTE-THINK") and by its denomination as "Zero" dollars with the additional comment: "just like Bush [it is] not worth a damn." Furthermore, whereas the question of "bad" faith or "lack of" credit was subtly implied by Steven Bell, with his mention of the role of Blair's government in the wars in Iraq and Afghanistan, the zero-dollar bill is overtly explicit, by replacing the motto printed on real dollar bills, "In God we trust" with "In George Bush we disgust," which makes a further link between faith, credit and betrayal on the one hand, and the questions of taste, aesthetic or moral judgment – or rather their absence –, on the other hand. A radical difference between the "Bush Dollar" and the "Blair Euro," however, is that whereas one proclaims itself as a joke, the other is deadly serious and that is the distance between claiming one politician to be worth not a damn and the other a war criminal, even while one could, of course, easily – some would say justly – invert those claims. What the fake euro note proclaims is the link between a certain form of current politics and cruelty, something the fake dollar manages to avoid all together. The zero-dollar bill is a call for voters to think, the Blair euro bill, astonishingly, recalls the blood attached to it.

All of these steps are already contained in the second essay on guilt and consciousness in *The Genealogy of Morality*, where, among many surprising and lucid pronouncements, Nietzsche claims that thinking not only derives from, but actually is, the process of setting prices and making traded exchanges. The whole second essay starts from the equally disconcerting proclamation that human beings are animals taught to forget and to promise, and that, as much a comment on ethics as it is a political statement, might indeed even seem to apply more directly to politics. In an essay on *The Merchant of Venice* that reads Shylock as Nietzsche and Nietzsche as Shylock, Simon Critchley and Tom McCarthy duly draw attention to the astonishing quality of many of

Nietzsche's pronouncements in that second essay and show how the text is replete not so much with economic metaphors as with statements directly linking economics to thought and morality, while also making clear how much of such moral trading is based on cruelty and bloodshed. They cite Nietzsche's famous passage on the second section of the essay: "Ah, reason, seriousness, mastery over emotions, the whole gloomy business called reflection, all these privileges and ceremonies of human beings – how expensive they were! How much blood and horror is at the bottom of all 'good things'." (Nietzsche ZGdM 2.3)

One of the most emblematic texts concerning not only the relationship between counterfeit money and culture but the very notion of modernity is Baudelaire's "La fausse monnaie" (Baudelaire 2006), an oft analyzed text and the subject of one of Derrida's most stimulating books. The main points are well known: upon leaving a tobacco shop, two friends meet a beggar; one of them gives the beggar a fake coin as a practical joke. One of Derrida's most extended arguments concerns the title, "Counterfeit Money," for, in its duality, it already encapsulates both the story and counterfeit money itself:

> Every thing that will be said in the story of counterfeit money (and in the story of counterfeit money) can be said of stories, of fictive texts bearing this title. This text is also the coin, the piece of counterfeit money provoking an event and lending itself to this whole scene of deception, gift, forgiveness, or non-forgiveness. It is as if the title were the very text whose narrative would finally be but the gloss or a long note on the counterfeit money of the title, at the bottom of the page. (Derrida 1992: 86)

The actual coin in Baudelaire's story is counterfeit, that is, a false coin passed on as if real money. That is the grounding upon which the narrator chastises his friend. But the reason for non-forgiveness, as is also well known, is not the crime or the evilness of passing on the false coin to the beggar, with all the potential consequences this might bring to the poor man, and not even how the friend was attempting to buy himself a reputation as generous without actually having to pay for it, but rather that the evil so committed would have been unconscious. Perhaps one can say that Baudelaire's modernity resides precisely in that act of judgment that targets not so much evil itself, but rather that lack of consciousness about it: "It is never excusable to be wicked, but there is some merit in knowing that one is; and the most unredeemable vice is to do evil through stupidity". Baudelaire, 2008: 59.[2]

---

2 "On n'est jamais excusable d'être méchant, mais il y a quelque mérite à savoir qu'on l'est; le plus irréparable des vices est de faire le mal par bêtise" (Baudelaire 2006: 173).

The counterfeit money in this text, however, remains just that and is not yet a phantom counterfeit as it never pretends to be anything else but real, just as the friend does not ever pretend to have passed it on to the beggar with being aware of the cruelty of his act. Derrida's interpretation of the title as already counterfeit money itself, at once the naming of the coin and the coin itself, "as if the title were the very text" would seem to point out the scope of also reading Baudelaire's text as a form of phantom counterfeit inasmuch as the title would possibly already present itself as counterfeit and as such deny any claims at passing for real. However suggestive that might be, I believe the opposite holds true. Precisely by hiding away in itself, or folding into itself, its very own nature as counterfeit, the title does not give this away. As such, what Baudelaire does, and Derrida lucidly explains, is to bring forth a direct equivalence between text and counterfeit money that one can assume as the hallmark of modernity.

This may be tested in that other exemplary text of modernity and counterfeit money – one is almost tempted to say of modernity as counterfeit money –, Gide's *Les Faux-Monnayeurs* [*The Counterfeiters*]. The often-cited passage details the conversation between two friends, Bernard and Éluard, in which the latter first asks the former to imagine a false ten franc piece and then proceeds to show it to him, asking the friend to admire how real it looks and sounds and emphasizing its interest as a curious object: "Just hear how true it rings. Almost the same sound as the real one. One would swear it was gold [...] but it's made of glass. It'll wear transparent". Gide, 1973: 192.[3]

The equation between text and coin was already transparent, as was the one between the fiction and the counterfeit money that many critics have also pointed out and that should not surprise us. However, perhaps even more explicitly than in Baudelaire's text, Gide emphasizes how good the counterfeit coin is – it even has a slight covering of gold, "so it's worth more than two sous," we are told. Éluard's interest in the coin might be as a curiosity, as an artefact, but that in the first instance stems from its mimetic properties, the effectiveness of its imitation of a real coin. Therefore Gide might thereby not only equate text and counterfeit, but also criticize notions of realistic representation, demonstrating them as counterfeit even while the emphasis is here again on how well the counterfeit simulates the real. Thus, there is still no question of a phantom counterfeit because neither the ten-franc piece nor its text proclaims itself a priori as a counterfeit. Even though one may read the text as a critique of the value of realistic representation, there is no fundamental critique of the process of equiva-

---

3 "Écoutez comme elle sonne bien. Presque le même son que les autres. On jurerait qu'elle est en or. [...] mais elle est en cristal. A l'usage, elle va devenir transparente" (Gide 2009: 189).

lency between reality and its representations. Modernity might no longer blindly accept the equivalency between value and object, but the fiction of the gold standard is not yet completely abandoned.

I now turn to yet another key modernist text – at least his author saw it as a key text in his own works and continuously included it in the incessant lists he made of future projects, some of which he never came to realize. I am referring to Pessoa's well-known novella, *The Anarchist Banker* (1922). It also involves a dialogue between two friends, this time after dinner, following a question by one of them designed to rekindle the conversation that had, in the meanwhile, died, and which gets punctuated by the renewed lighting of the banker's cigar. What the conversation entails is the detailed explanation by the banker of how he is an anarchist, how he sees no contradiction between being a banker and an anarchist, and how he even considers himself to be a truer anarchist than those others, trade-unionists and bombers, who claim to be anarchists but really are not. This too is a text that should be read alongside Baudelaire's and Gide's as an exemplary setting out of modernity's preoccupation with money and with its relationship to both thought and politics. There is no counterfeit money in this story; rather, what is at stake is the possibility of reconciling the activities of the banker and speculator with the ideals of justice and liberty that he claims to profess in the extreme. The title itself already announces what would seem paradoxical, almost aporetic, the nature of the text and of the relationship between capital and social justice, but this does not serve the double duty of Baudelaire's title. Fascinating as the logic of that story is, we may perceive it as a reiteration precisely of modernity's emphasis on the individual: while it seems to put forward a critique of capitalism, it ends up by folding in the realization that given the human condition in which men always naturally attempt to dominate others and limit their liberty, the only possible means of achieving liberty is by foregoing solidarity. Read this way, the text proves not so very modern even while seeming to spell out the conditions of extreme greed we have now come to see exposed but only when beginning to threaten the whole system of credit and speculation on which they were themselves based. Important as *The Anarchist Banker* might be to the context of modernism, and the canonical status it has come to embody, it is not the most interesting of Pessoa's writings on money. Its inclusion here stems from its representation of a stage of thinking about the relationship between money and culture, a stage totally aligned with modernity in its critique of capital that stops short of questioning money's essence.

Another more interesting text by Pessoa, that I see as a sort of intermediary stage between a modernist approach to money and one that might be considered more post-modern, in which that relationship is characterized by the figure of the phantom counterfeit, is the short poem "Ai, Margarida," curiously attributed to his heteronym Álvaro de Campos, who would have been "communicated" with while in a state of alcoholic inebriation (Pessoa 2002). In many ways a simple poem, the poet addresses a woman and asks her what she would do if he would give her his life and then proceeds to detail the possible meanings of such a gift, ranging from the metaphorical to the very real one of dying, and coming to a sense of it as poetry. It is precisely this last aspect I find significant because when the poet asks Margarida what she would do if the giving of his life to her were poetry, she answers that then she does not want to have anything to do with it because "nesta casa não se fia" [This house makes no loans] (Pessoa 2002: 317). The conjoined meaning of extending credit and having faith are inseparable in such a statement that actualizes what Nietzsche pointed out when remarking that the moral concepts of guilt and belief are inseparable from their material origins: guilt (*Schuld*) is also a debtor and a creditor (*Gläubiger*) is also a believer. When Margarida refuses the poet's gift of his life as poetry she in a sense, both says that she – or rather her house, which reflects a commercial establishment dimension – will not extend credit and that she neither believes in poetry nor in life as poetry. I mention this small, witty poem because it already makes more explicit that the relationship in question is not only one of reality but primarily one of art than the more acclaimed story. Hence, it is neither life nor even death that Margarida refuses to accept as a gift, but rather, poetry.

The Pessoa text of most interest here is yet another short story, closer to Baudelaire's notion of a *petit poème en prose*, that is or was far more obscure, at least until the lapsing of copyright inspired myriad cheap reproductions of all kinds of his smaller texts. First published in 1926 entitled "Um grande Português" (A great Portuguese man) and then reprinted in 1929 under another title, "A Origem do Conto do Vigário" (Pessoa 1986), the plot is rather simple: a farmer, named Vigário, buys a bunch of counterfeit "cem mil réis" notes and later, while under the pretense of being drunk, uses them to settle a debt owed to two brothers. The brothers think they are taking advantage of the inebriated Vigário in actually receiving double that owed as Vigário refers to the notes as being of fifty thousand réis even as they glimpse the hundred thousand réis note denomination. Thus, they gladly sign a receipt for the transaction. When the next day they realize the bills are forgeries, they confront Vigário with the police and he then produces the receipt as proof of his innocence. In many ways, one could say this is but a simple variation on the supposed cunning of country folk, or even a moralistic tale on human greed. However, there is far more within. To begin with, the title doubles itself and not in the way that Derrida unfolds Baudelaire's title, but rather in the opposite direction as the same text is published twice but under different titles. What was "A great Portuguese man" then becomes, "The origins of the tale of Vigário." The second title itself is also a double title in a Baudelairian sense: it could be said to be like a counterfeit since the text that then serves as a gloss is already false in relation to the previous title as well as to its own claim of presenting the "origins" of the text itself. The two titles also operate an interesting exchange in which being a great Portuguese man is equivalent to presenting the origins of the narrative and to swindling. The name of the protagonist of course also partakes precisely of such a doubling and at the same time plays on the notion of belief and credit. The term "Vigário," applied here as a surname, is firstly the person who stands in for another, or more specifically the official who stands in for Christ and, as such, a guarantor of true belief. However, it has also come to signify its opposite, as "vigarista" refers precisely to the Portuguese for a swindler. Whereas Baudelaire's title insists on hiding its function as counterfeit money – even as it is precisely that – the titles of Pessoa's story draw attention to their exchangeability and their shifting value. Furthermore, just as with Baudelaire's text, the title, or titles, also already function as stand-ins for the entire text that depends for its effect not only on the successful swindle but also on the counterfeit notes, their object being visibly counterfeit. As Vigário initially said to the counterfeiter when first refusing the transaction, the forged notes were of such poor quality, "imperfeitíssimas," that they could not even be passed to the blind, something the two brothers also express on realizing their mistake: "And the brothers, effectively looking at the bank notes, saw that not even the blind would take them" (Pessoa 1986: 96)[4].

In effect, what Pessoa does in such a text involves not only raising doubts about mimetic representation and the possibility of equating justice with liberty – in the end, to all intents, Vigário not only gets away with it but also takes the moral high-road: showing the brother's signature on the receipt, mentioning the non-existing fifty thousand notes before adding that, had it happened as the brothers claim, neither would he have been so drunk as to pay double nor would the brothers have been so dishonest as to take it. Far more than that, Pessoa questions the whole process by which the legality of money gets established. As Marc Shell notes, the determination of the legality of money is not necessarily dependent on its material properties: "What does matter in considering whether a coin is genuine or counterfeit is the issuing authority. A coin as money is counterfeit when the stated place of origin does not correspond to the actual place of origin [...] It is treason for a private citizen to mint coins." (Shell 1982:160)

---

4 "E os irmãos, olhando então verdadeiramente para as notas, viram que nem a cegos se poderiam passar"

Obviously, the notes passed on by Vigário are counterfeit but that becomes precisely the point as they are so visibly false they do not even pretend to be real and, as such, are phantom counterfeits questioning the entire process by which the legality of money is established. When Vigário buys the counterfeit notes from the forger, he does so willingly and in full knowledge that they are counterfeit. Had he simply done that out of curiosity, as Éluard does in Gide's novel with the ten-franc coin, he would be purchasing – even if illegally – a curious object, an artifact. However, when Vigário in turn passes them on to the brothers, he is not strictly using them as counterfeit money because he does not claim their stated value. What he does in turn is again assign a fictitious value to the artifacts, by stating they are bills of fifty thousand. The brothers are done in, because of their greed, of course, but also, and crucially, because of their belief in the stated value of the notes. That is, in the course of this series of transactions the text presents, only the brothers actually believe in the system and that becomes their undoing. The initial transaction between the forger and Vigário is illegal, treasonous even, but neither man is deceived, there is no faith in either the monetary system or the state authority behind it; there is simply an extension of credit by one man to the other, redeemed by the object acquired. The second transaction, however, depends on the asymmetrical nature of exchange as Vigário knows the bills are not what they pretend to be but also does not claim them to be either. Yet the brothers believe in what they see – or think they see – rather than in what Vigário tells them, and as such they are in fact betrayed by themselves. Good money is used to buy bad money and then bad money in turn is bought as if good money. Had the notes been excellent forgeries, this would be yet another text in line with the others, making an equivalency between art, and specifically literature, and money. However, since the forgeries are so bad that even "a blind person would notice," they cannot be claimed as art, nor are they effective as counterfeits. This should be seen in line with a long-standing concern about the relationship between literature and money: Marc Shell mentions Melville as one of several key examples as well as a concern over "ghost" money when legal tender was first issued by a large variety of banks and commercial institutions in the United States. This text by Pessoa goes further as it proclaims the discrediting of state authority – and in that it proves more anarchistic than *The Anarchist Banker*, given the troubling relationship between belief and betrayal and the spectral condition of commodities, be they money or writing.

In conclusion, I would mention one further case, that of *Thirty Pieces of Silver*, an exhibit by Cornelia Parker from 1988–1989 and that was purchased in 1998 by Tate Modern where it can now be seen. It is also an example of a phantom counterfeit as the objects contained are clearly painted in silver color and not of silver; and of course are not the thirty coins of the title. Parker assembled a large number of discarded household objects, including what were at one time and still are nowadays referred to as "silvers," forks, knives, spoons, and after spray-painting them silver, they were then flattened with a steam roller. These objects were subsequently mounted in groups of thirty circular structures that hang in suspension from the ceiling. It is thus only explicitly figuratively that these objects can be said to pretend to be thirty coins since they so obviously are not. It is also equally clear that they are not silver either. The title is crucial because, in a sense, only the title allows us to even begin "recognizing" the objects as representing coins, so that one could again speak of a Baudelairian "counterfeit money" effect to the title. However, the title of course also carries yet another meaning in the allusion to Judas' thirty pieces of silver and the narrative of the betrayal of Christ so the title itself forces the viewer to also consider the aspect of faith and betrayal behind the realization of art objects. That the objects in question themselves were not only simple and discarded household implements, trash, in other words, is also significant inasmuch as the way Parker could be said to both recuperate those discarded objects and highlight the arbitrariness of the system of values inherent both to western tradition as well to our consumerist society. It is certainly ironic that the note accompanying Parker's exhibition must spell out the title's connotations, but it is even more ironic that Pessoa, whose life was marked by a lack of money, and who so wittingly criticized it, would end up as the effigy on the Portuguese 100 escudo note that preceded the adoption of the Euro. Perhaps it represents too much of a step to claim that objects like the Blair five-euro note, or Pessoa's "Vigário" and Parker's thirty pieces of silver as more representative of a postmodern polity in which capital itself has become commodified to such an extent that it only survives as speculation for the future, while repeatedly forgetting how all "good things," to refer to Nietzsche's biting irony, are the result of immense cruelty and caked in blood. However, that is a wager I am willing to take.

Works cited

[Anonymous] "Bush Inspires Zero Dollar Bill." <http://bitsandpieces1.blogspot.com/2007/12/bush-inspires-zero-dollar-bill.html> (accessed 17 March 2013).

Baudelaire, Charles (2006) [1869] *Le Spleen de Paris: Petits poèmes en prose* (Paris: Gallimard).

Baudelaire, Charles (2008) "Counterfeit Money" In *Paris Spleen and La Fanfarlo*. Transl. Raymond N. MacKenzie (Cambridge, MA: Hackett Publishing).

Bell, Stephen (2009) "Tony Blair is our man for EU president, says minister." Cartoon. *The Guardian* 16 July 2009. <http://www.guardian.co.uk/theguardian/cartoon/2009/jul/16/steve-bell-tony-blair-cartoon> (accessed 17 March 2013).

Critchley, Simon and Tom McCarthy (2004) "Universal Shylockery: Money and Morality in *The Merchant of Venice*," *Diacritics* 34.1, 3–17.

Derrida, Jacques (1992) [1991] *Given Time I: Counterfeit Money*, trans. Peggy Kamuf (Chicago and London: The University of Chicago Press).

Gide, André (2009) [1925] *Les Faux-monnayeurs* (Paris: Gallimard).

Gide, André (1973) *The Counterfeiters* (New York: Vintage).

Nietzsche, Friedrich (1999) [1887] *Zur Genealogie der Moral*, in *Kritische Studienausgabe* 5, ed. Giorgio Colli and Mazzino Montinari (Munich and Berlin: De Gruyter).

Parker, Cornelia (1988–1989) *Thirty Pieces of Silver*, Silver and Metal Sculpture, London, Tate Modern. <http://www.tate.org.uk/servlet/ViewWork?workid=26446> (accessed 17 March 2013).

Pessoa, Fernando (1986) [1926] "Um grande português ou A Origem do Conto do Vigário," in *Obra em Prosa de Fernando Pessoa: Ficção e Teatro*, ed. António Quadros (Lisboa: Europa-América), 95–96.

Pessoa, Fernando (2001) [1922] *The Anarchist Banker*, in *The Selected Prose of Fernando Pessoa*, ed. and trans. Richard Zenith (New York: Grove Press), 167–196.

Pessoa, Fernando (2002) [1927] "Ai, Margarida," in *Obras de Fernando Pessoa 16, Álvaro de Campos: Poesia*, ed. Teresa Rita Lopes (Lisboa: Assírio & Alvim), 316–317.

Pessoa, Fernando (2007) [1922] *O Banqueiro Anarquista*, Obras de Fernando Pessoa 9, ed. Manuela Parreira da Silva (Lisboa: Assírio & Alvim).

Shell, Marc (1982) *Money, Language and Thought: Literary and Philosophical Economies from the Medieval to the Modern Era* (Berkeley and London: University of California Press).

Vivaldo Andrade dos Santos
From Miser to Capitalist: An Economic Reading of Aluísio Azevedo's *O Cortiço*

> Money is the estranged essence of man's
> work and man's existence, and this alien
> essence dominates him, and he worships it.
>
> Karl Marx, *The Economic and Philosophical*
> *Manuscripts of 1844*

The first major global economic crisis of the twenty-first century, in 2008, brought economics back onto the scene of our daily lives. The crisis has certainly proven extraordinary both given its historical timing and the sheer scope of its effects in post-industrial societies and the globalized contemporary world. Within the dynamics of capitalism, the extraordinariness of crisis is natural. The history of capitalism has shown us how economic crises force a shift and readjustment in financial practices involving capital.[1] By the same token, the relationship between literature and economics is also no novelty, as an interdisciplinary conference organized around the theme of money for which this article was written suggests.

Just over fifteen years ago Mark Osteen and Martha Woodmansee edited a collection of essays entitled *The New Economic Criticism: Studies at the Intersection of Literature and Economics* (1999), in which they point out that the emergence of "economic criticism" in the intellectual field in the 1990s continued a trend that had begun in the 1970s. This new research area was connected to a scholarly field focused on the relationship between literature, culture and economics (Osteen and Woodmansee 1999: 3). According to them, such emergence within literary studies stems from several reasons, in particular the return to historicist approaches, distant from deconstruction, semiotics, and the traditional formalist tendencies that reigned in the 1970s and early 1980s. Other factors include the crisis in the academic publishing industry and its corresponding search for new critical approaches; the influx of cultural studies, and their emphasis on interdisciplinary methodologies, in this case the work of economists; the role of economics in society, starting in the 1980s, along with discussions around stock markets, interest rates, bonds, speculation, and so forth – otherwise not seen in our society since the 1930s (3–4). This article proposes to exam-

---

1 See Kindleberger's discussion in *Manias, Panics, and Crashes* (2005).

ine the naturalist novel *O Cortiço* [*The Slum*, 1890] by Aluísio Azevedo (1857–1913) in light of economics, with the aim of identifying the dynamics of capitalism in modern Brazil. I argue that the main character's motivation (João Romão) reveal the development from a primitive to a modern form of capitalism, especially from avarice to speculation, from a miser to a rentier.

1 The dynamics of capital

O Cortiço[2] by Aluísio Azevedo describes the story of João Romão, a greedy Portuguese immigrant, who inherits a small tavern, buys a small piece of land and establishes a tenement that starts growing day by day in a suburban neighborhood in Rio de Janeiro. The story of João Romão is linked to the story of the tenement itself and the lives of all his property's inhabitants. Azevedo's novel is indebted to nineteenth-century naturalism, an aesthetics that attempted to apply scientific principles to literature. *O Cortiço*, highly influenced by Émile Zola's works, seeks to prove that human beings are governed by their instincts and passions as hereditary instincts and the environment in which they live define their character and morality.[3]

O Cortiço tells the story of João Romão and his ambition to be rich. In the novel, João Romão is a character for whom no social or ethical conception impedes the desire for financial accumulation. After working from the age of thirteen to twenty-five for a vendor in the Botafogo neighborhood in Rio de Janeiro who then left him fifteen hundred milréis in cash on retiring, João Romão is described thus:

> An established owner in his own right, João toiled even more feverishly, possessed by such a thirst for riches that he patiently endured the cruelest hardships. He would sleep on a

---

2 Most of the studies about *O Cortiço* have examined the novel in the context of the naturalist period. Antonio Cândido's brilliant article, "De cortiço a cortiço," in which he reads the novel as an allegory of nineteenth century Brazilian society, is the first to address the question of economics in Azevedo's novel. In his essay, Cândido examines the relationship between Aluísio Azevedo's *O Cortiço* and Émile Zola's *LAssommoir*, pointing out that, despite the borrowing of the form (the naturalist novel) from a peripheral or colonized country, Azevedo's novel content (the place of the poor Portuguese immigrant in Rio de Janeiro in the 1880s, the race relations, and the economic dynamics, for example) are Brazilian, par excellence. For Cândido, an art work is a product of the environment where it is created, and in this way, *O Cortiço* can be read as an allegory of Brazil. A second article addressing the novel's theme of capital is "Zola in Rio de Janeiro: The Production of Space in Aluísio Azevedo's *O Cortiço*," by Lúcia Sá (Sá 2010).
3 See Cândido 1991 and Sá 2010.

straw mat laid out over his own sales counter, using a burlap sack stuffed with straw for his pillow. His meals were prepared for 400 réis a day by Bertoleza, a black slave some thirty years old. (Azevedo 2000: 1)[4]

The opening scene of Azevedo's novel warns the reader of what João Romão's motivation in life will be. More than any physical description, the first account of the novel's main character portrays his mental drive: his mania to be rich, his "delírio de enriquecer" (delirium to become rich[5]). In João Romão's universe, every action leads to economic growth, in which money is the only object of desire. In this way, accumulation equates to deprivation: "apertando cada vez mais as próprias despesas, empilhando privações sobre privacies" [paring his own expenses down to the bone, heaping privation upon privation]. Such deprivation translates into asceticism, as Marx notes in the *Grundrisse:* "The cult of money has its asceticism, its self-denial, its self-sacrifice – economy and frugality, contempt for mundane, temporal and fleeting pleasures; the chase after the eternal treasure" (Marx 1973: 232). The pursuing of the "eternal treasure" that money represents translates in the novel not only into the self-deprivation of material goods or working seven days a week ("como uma junta de bois" [like a yoke of oxen (4)]) with his black partner-wife-former slave, Bertoleza, but also in stealing:

Always carelessly dressed, unaware of Sundays and holidays, never missing a chance to get his hands on another's money, leaving his debts unpaid whenever he could but always collecting whatever he was owed, cheating his customers with short weights and scant measures, and buying for a song whatever slaves could steal from their masters' houses.(4)[6]

Money as the object of greed differs according to Marx from the desire for "clothes, weapons, jewels, women, wine, etc.," as individualized forms of craving. Like greed,

---

4 I will quote the 2000 English edition throughout, and will refer to the original text in note. "Proprietário e estabelecido por sua conta, o rapaz atirou-se à labutação ainda com mais ardor, possuindo-se de tal delírio de enriquecer, que afrontava resignado as mais duras privações. Dormia sobre o balcão da própria venda, em cima de uma esteira, fazendo travesseiro de um saco de estopa cheio de palha. A comida arranjava-lha, mediante quatrocentos réis por dia, uma quitandeira sua vizinha, a Bertoleza, crioula trintona, escrava de um velho cego..." (Azevedo 1967:19)
5 In the English translation, this reads "possessed by such a thirst for riches." I decided to translate this phrase literally in keeping with the medical reference of the original, which is typical of the naturalism of the time.
6 "Sempre em mangas de camisa, sem domingo nem dia santo, não perdendo nunca a ocasião de assenhorear-se do alheio, deixando de pagar todas as vezes que podia e nunca deixando de receber, enganando os fregueses, roubando nos pesos e nas medidas, comprando por dez réis de mel coado o que os escravos furtavam da casa dos seus senhores..." (Azevedo 1967: 25)

"money is there as not only the object but also the fountainhead of greed" (Marx 1973: 222). From the standpoint of money as greed, João Romão's desire for these individualized forms of desire is, in essence, motivated by money as a transcendent form of the immediate craving. In this sense, João Romão distances himself from that which represents immediate bodily satisfaction. Comfort as in a bed or a pillow or food are refused on the grounds of wealth accumulation:

> Ever since this fever to possess land had taken hold of him, all his actions, however simple, had pecuniary ends. He had one purpose only: to increase his wealth. He kept the worst vegetables from his garden for himself and Bertoleza: the ones that were so bad that no one would buy them. His hens were good layers but he himself never ate eggs, though he loved them. He sold every single one and contented himself with whatever food his customers left on their plates. It had gone beyond ambition and become a nervous disorder, a form of lunacy, an obsessive need to turn everything into cash. (8)[7]

The novel dramatizes the process of pecuniary accumulation tied not only to moral or ethical value, but also to deception and forgery:

> After a while, he began to buy less from wholesalers and ordered some products directly from Europe – wine, for example. Before he had purchased it in demijohns, but now he bought barrels straight from Portugal. He turned each barrel into three by adding water and rum. Likewise, he ordered kegs of butter, crates of canned goods, big boxes of matches, oil, cheese, crockery, and much else besides.(10) [8]

João Romão imagines an economy in which he would have full control of the economic machine. Despite being against middlemen, João Romão has no interest whatsoever in echoing what might be producer concerns about the capitalist system. On the contrary, he sees himself as the only bridge between producers and the market. As a financial master, João Romão is nothing other than the one "[...] who has produced nothing, over production and over the product.

---

7 "Desde que a febre de possuir se apoderou dele totalmente, todos os seus atos, todos, fosse o mais simples, visavam um interesse pecuniário. Só tinha uma preocupação: aumentar os bens. Das suas hortas recolhia para si e para a companheira os piores legumes, aqueles que, por maus, ninguém compraria; as suas galinhas produziam muito e ele não comia um ovo, do que no entanto gostava imenso; vendia-os todos e contentava-se com os restos da comida dos trabalhadores. Aquilo já não era ambição, era uma moléstia nervosa, uma loucura, um desespero de acumular; de reduzir tudo a moeda." (Azevedo 1967: 31)

8 "Afinal, já lhe não bastava sortir o seu estabelecimento nos armazéns fornecedores; começou a receber alguns gêneros diretamente da Europa: o vinho, por exemplo, que ele dantes comprava aos quintos nas casas de atacado, vinha-lhe agora de Portugal às pipas, e de cada uma fazia três com água e cachaça; e despachava faturas de barris de manteiga, de caixas de conserva, caixões de fósforos, azeite, queijos, louça e muitas outras mercadorias." (Azevedo 1967:32)

Just as he estranges himself from his own activity, so he confers ownership over this activity to a stranger, which does not really belong to him," as Marx suggests in his *Economic and Philosophic Manuscripts* of 1844. According to the narrator, João Romão's action held no relationship whatsoever to economics but was, indeed, "a nervous disorder, a form of lunacy, an obsessive need to turn everything into cash" (8). Marx maintains that greed is neither a disease nor a natural behavior, but is instead an historical process: "The mania for possessions is possible without money; but greed itself is the product of a definite social development, not natural, as opposed to historical" (Marx 1973: 222). Marx discusses how this conception of greed interlinks with the end of tradition and the "fall of ancient communities." He argues that whenever money develops beyond its function of measuring trade and circulation, the owner of money, the individual, loses his individuality for the sake of enhancing the forces of production, better known as the industrial process. According to him, money is thus tied to a developed moment of production only where and when wage labor exists. Paradoxically, should money be seen as destructive of the old communities, it is simultaneously transformative of the social formation, becoming "a condition for its development and a driving-wheel for the development of all forces of production, material and mental" (Marx 1973: 223). Following the dissolution of the individual within this new economic process, greed as an individual drive gets replaced by general greed, "the urge of all" to make money under wage labor conditions and thereby becoming a kind of "self-reproducing wealth" (Marx 1973: 224).

Critics have very often missed this point by focusing only on João Romão's character, overlooking his actions within the framework of capitalism's development as shown in his arrangement, to live as a couple with Bertoleza, a black slave and his neighbor, whom he pretended to have freed from slavery. From Bertoleza's perspective, João Romão represents the promise of salvation, love and freedom; however, the relationship proves nothing more than a form of pecuniary priority.[9] Should João Romão free Bertoleza, by marrying her, he is able to turn her into his free employer within the logic of capitalism. The end of slavery opens the space for the free subject within the production process that João Romão represents:

---

9 Georg Simmel, in *The Philosophy of Money* (1900), states that marriages for money "are particularly common among primitive groups and conditions where they do not cause any offence at all." For Simmel, in contemporary times, there is a sense of dignity that "arises to every marriage that is not based on personal affection – so that a sense of decency requires the concealment of economic motives" (Simmel 1990: 80).

> Henceforth, João Romão became Bertoleza's banker, lawyer, and advisor. Before long, he controlled all her earnings, paying and collecting her debts and sending her master twenty milréis a month. He opened an account for her; and whenever she needed money, she hastened to his tavern and received it from his hands – from "Seu João," as she called him. Seu João noted these small transactions in a little book on whose brown cover one read, half in clumsy handwriting, half in letters clipped from newspapers: "Bertoleza: Deposits and Withdrawals." (2)[10]

The pragmatic tone of this passage suggests a tripartite relationship through economics, law and friendship, represented by financial advice. At the core of this equation is the logic of trust, established between João Romão and Bertoleza: "João won the woman's trust so completely that after a while she made no decision without him and accepted all his advice. Later on, anyone wanting to discuss business with her would not bother to seek her out but rather went straight to João Romão." (2) [11]

Why does she trust him? Love might be the answer. However, would love be the only answer to explaining her blind trust in him? In the naturalist logic, this could get explained by her desire for a superior race, as the narrator says: "Bertoleza wanted to keep away from blacks and instinctively sought a mate from the superior race." (2) This question, one might add, proves crucial to the logic of economics, in which faith, confidence, reliance and dependence are fundamental to economic growth, as suggested by Paul J. Zak and Stephen Knack in their studies on the role of trust in economics and social interactions (Zak and Knack 2001: 295–321). From the reader's standpoint, understanding João Romão's motivation based only on financial gain, for whom she represents just another currency of exchange while Bertoleza becomes trapped in her condition as slave: from her former master to her new husband-lawyer-entrepreneur. Thus, her new owner has access to her physical body as her "husband/lover," to her social body as a slave made employer, and her economic body, regulated through her

---

10 "Daí em diante, João Romão tornou-se o caixa, o procurador e o conselheiro da crioula. No fim de pouco tempo era ele quem tomava conta de tudo que ela produzia e era também quem punha e dispunha dos seus pecúlios, e quem se encarregava de remeter ao senhor os vinte milréis mensais. Abriu-lhe logo uma conta corrente, e a quitandeira, quando precisava de dinheiro para qualquer coisa, dava um pulo até à venda e recebia-o das mãos do vendeiro, de 'Seu João,' como ela dizia. Seu João debitava metodicamente essas pequenas quantias num caderninho, em cuja capa de papel pardo lia-se, mal escrito e em letras cortadas de jornal: 'Ativo e passivo de Bertoleza'." (Azevedo 1967: 20)

11 "E por tal forma foi o taverneiro ganhando confiança no espírito da mulher, que esta afinal nada mais resolvia só por si, e aceitava dele, cegamente, todo e qualquer arbítrio. Por último, se alguém precisava tratar com ela qualquer negócio, nem mais se dava ao trabalho de procurá-la, ia logo direito a João Romão." (Azevedo 1967: 20)

money loans. However, João Romão's trust is broken at the end of the novel when forced by law to return Bertoleza to her former master's heirs. Facing these options, Bertoleza chooses death:

> She recognized her former master's eldest son, and a shudder ran through her. In one horrible flash, she grasped the entire situation: She understood, with the lucidity granted the condemned, that she had been fooled [...]
> Bertoleza leapt back as swiftly as a startled tapir and before anyone could do anything to stop her, ripped open her belly with one swift slash. (207–208) [12]

Bertoleza's universe is reduced to two choices: to become a freed slave and be part of the new economic system, in which capitalism is just emerging or is manifested in its more primitive form of accumulation, represented by João Romão, or return to the old order of slavery, represented by the claim to own her by her master's heir.[13]

In her excellent article, Sá has studied the production of space in *O Cortiço* and has pointed out how in the novel the population of the tenement shows "a new, free working force that had slowly been replacing slave labor in the few years that preceded abolition" (Sá 2010). The critic points out that "The novel gives a clear view of the relationship between the tenement and the new economic conditions that are producing urban sprawl." In consonance with Cândido's historical and materialist analysis of *O Cortiço*, Sá's astute article draws attention to the social transformations taking place in the city of Rio de Janeiro in the last quarter of the nineteenth century. In this sense, capital is the force behind the creation of space and the social dynamics emanating from it.

As Marx points out, "Circulation is an inescapable condition for capital, a condition posited by its own nature, since circulation is the passing of capital through the various conceptually determined moments of its necessary metamorphosis – its life process" (Marx 1973: 658). [14] Thus, once in circulation, capital is

---

12 "Reconheceu logo o filho mais velho do seu primitivo senhor, e um calafrio percorreu-lhe o corpo. Num relance de grande perigo compreendeu a situação; adivinhou tudo com a lucidez de quem se vê perdido para sempre: adivinhou que tinha sido enganada; [...]
Bertoleza então, erguendo-se com ímpeto de anta bravia, recuou de um salto e, antes que alguém conseguisse alcançá-la, já de um só golpe certeiro e fundo rasgara o ventre de lado a lado." (Azevedo 1967: 266)
13 Cândido states that "A originalidade do romance de Aluísio está nessa coexistência íntima do explorado e do explorador, tornada logicamente possível pela própria natureza elementar da acumulação num país que economicamente ainda era semicolonial." (Cândido 1991: 113)
14 Marx also asserts that "The circulation of money, regarded for itself, necessarily becomes extinguished in money as a static thing. The circulation of capital constantly ignites itself anew, divides into its different moments, and is a *perpetuum mobile*" (Marx 1973: 516).

constantly transforming, metamorphosing. This is a view that Fernand Braudel somehow shares when he states that money is the agent for the market economy as it hastens exchange and creates a network of trade among the inhabitants of a city. Braudel argues that cities only exist because of money, and both are responsible for the fabrication of modernity which he defined as "the changing mass of men's lives, promoted the expansion of money and led to the growing tyranny of the cities."[15] The expansion of money in *O Cortiço* expands the initial small tavern to a large bazaar, the few small housing complexes to larger tenements, the small streets into an avenue, and last but not least, the incorporation of the Botafogo neighborhood into the city of Rio de Janeiro, as Sá suggests:

> There were many new tenants like him, wearing neckties, shoes, and socks. The ferocious, tireless cogwheel had sunk its teeth into a new social stratum, which it dragged into São Romão. Poor students began to appear... government workers, bartenders, singers and actors... Italians [...] João Romão had surpassed his neighbor [...]The big old front wall, with its broad gate that wagons could pass through, was replaced...There was a new sign, much larger than the old one, and instead of "Hostal São Romão," its fancy letters read: "SÃO ROMÃO AVENUE". (Azevedo, 2000: 182–183). [16]

---

15 According to Braudel, "The truth is that money and cities have always been a part of daily routine, yet they are present in the modern world as well. Money is a very old invention, if one subsumes under that name every means by which exchange is accelerated. And without exchange, there is no society. Cities, too, have existed since prehistoric times. They are multicenturied structures of the most ordinary way of life. But they are also multipliers, capable of adapting to change and helping to bring it about. One might say that cities and money created modernity; but conversely, according to George Gurvitch's law of reciprocity, modernity – the changing mass of men's lives – promoted the expansion of money and led to the growing tyranny of the cities. Cities and money are at one and the same time motors and indicators; they provoke and indicate change." (Braudel 1977:15)

16 "E, assim como este, notavam-se por último na estalagem muitos inquilinos novos, que já não eram gente sem gravata e sem meias. A feroz engrenagem daquela máquina terrível, que nunca parava, ia já lançando os dentes a uma nova camada social que, pouco a pouco, se deixaria arrastar inteira lá para dentro. Começavam a vir estudantes ... surgiram contínuos de repartições públicas, caixeiros de botequim, artistas de teatro, condutores de bondes, e vendedores de bilhetes de loteria... italianos [...] João Romão conseguira meter o sobrado do vizinho no chinelo... Foi abaixo aquele grosso e velho muro da frente com o seu largo portão de cocheira, e a entrada da estalagem era agora dez braças mais para dentro,[...]. e na tabuleta nova, muito maior que a primeira, em vez de "Estalagem de São Romão" lia-se em letras caprichosas: "AVENIDA SÃO ROMÃO". (Azevedo 1967: 238–239)

2 Money and distinction

At the end of the novel, the sudden and tragic death of Bertoleza shocks João Romão for a short time. Nevertheless, his moment of sadness is washed away by the title given to him by the authorities and with which Azevedo, in a sarcastic tone, ends his novel: "At that same moment, a carriage pulled up outside. It was a committee of abolitionists in dress suits, who had come to respectfully deliver a certificate declaring him an honored member and patron." (Azevedo 2000: 208)

The end of the novel illustrates what Marx wrote about the power of money in his *Economic Manuscripts:* "I am bad, dishonest, unscrupulous, stupid; but money is honoured, and hence its possessor. Money is the supreme good, therefore its possessor is good." (Marx 1973: 324) The title of distinction given to João Romão takes us into another dimension in the dynamics of capitalism. As the narrator puts it, the excitement of the miser is lost when accumulation of money becomes an end in itself: "In the end, his lack of self-confidence and his conviction that he was incapable of aspiring to anything except money and more money poisoned his thoughts, turning his ambitions to ashes and dulling the luster of his gold." (96). João Romão's ambition for distinction emerges at the moment his rich neighbor, Miranda, receives the title of baron. The desire to possess material things is now replaced by the symbolic, that which things represent, translated here as envy:

> But such was the case! That tavern-keeper, apparently so wretched and humble, that skinflint who dressed as poorly as a slave in a cheap shirt and wooden clogs; that animal who ate worse than a dog so he could set aside everything he earned or extorted; that miser devoured by greed who seemed to have renounced all his privileges and sentiments as a human being; that poor devil who had never loved anything but money now envied Miranda...(93)[17]

The steady transformation of João Romão from miser, from small vendor to rentier proves insufficient. For the "future viscount" or baron, money was not everything. In addition, he dreamed of " [...] a noble life, luxurious and sumptuous, a life lived in palaces amid costly furnishings and splendid objects...There he was not and never had been the owner of a slum who went about in clogs and a cheap shirt,

---

[17] "Sim, senhor! aquele taverneiro, na aparência tão humilde e tão miserável; aquele sovina que nunca saíra dos seus tamancos e da sua camisa de riscadinho de Angola; aquele animal que se alimentava pior que os cães, para pôr de parte tudo, tudo, que ganhava ou extorquia; aquele ente atrofiado pela cobiça e que parecia ter abdicado dos seus privilégios e sentimentos de homem; aquele desgraçado, que nunca jamais amara senão o dinheiro, invejava agora o Miranda..."(Azevedo 1967: 136)

he was a baron! A baron of gold!..." (95). No longer was he the small vendor, but the "famous and wealthy businessman! A mighty landowner! A banker..." (95). However, distinction has a price, and João Romão is very aware of this as it would require him to put money back into circulation: "I would have spent more, it's true! I wouldn't be so rich! But hell, now I could do what I liked with my money! I'd be a gentleman!" (97) Social distinction is equated here with civilization. And this indeed means a change in João Romão's view of existence and of his way of managing money. Once a miser, João Romão now becomes a spender in order to obtain distinction: "He ordered fine clothes, and on Sunday donned a white jacket and proper shoes and socks. Thus attired, he sat in front of his store reading newspapers." (127) Thus, from João Romão's perspective spending money is also a form of gaining, through the symbolic capital that distinction represents. João Romão's actions have been transferred from the material goods to, as Pierre Bourdieu suggests, the "economy of cultural goods." (Bourdieu 1984).

Interestingly, João Romão's concept of time also changes. While time for him, at the beginning of the novel, was defined only by labor, production and the accumulation of capital, now it is dedicated to a non-productive concept of time, e.g. leisure. His transformation is also a makeover: "He would then go out for a walk wearing his jacket, fancy boots, and a cravat. He gave up his crew-cut and clipped his beard, almost eliminating his moustache" (127). This is a complete change of life style that involves taking dance lessons, decorating his house, drinking good wine, learning table manners to eat, going to the theater, and reading French literature in translation!

In his study of the relationship between money, social distinction, and individuality in *Philosophy of Money*, Georg Simmel states: "we value the distinct formation of individuality, the mere fact that a personality possesses a specific and concise form and power" (Simmel 1990: 390). Because possessions carry a great deal of influence and distinction, they somehow shape individuality. Owning (or having) "a power of disposal over objects enters into the circle of our Ego. The Ego, our desires and feelings, continues to live in the objects we own" (389). Through the lens of psychology individuality is linked to money. Distinction displays the resistance "of being interchangeable, of the reduction to a common denominator and of 'common activity'" (389). Simmel also ties the definition of social distinction to a mathematical and economic discourse. From this perspective, distinction resists that which characterizes a commodity.[18] Hence "distinction should not be so conspicuous as to entice what is distinguished

---

18 Marx defines a commodity as "an object outside us, a thing that by its properties satisfies human wants of some sort or another" (Marx 1967: 215).

away from its independence, its reserve and its inner self-containment and to transpose its essence into a relationship to others, be it only a relationship of difference." From this perspective, distinction stands out due to its characteristics of exclusiveness, and of differentiation, since "[the] distinguished person is the very person who completely reserves his personality. Distinction represents a quite unique combination of senses of differences that are based upon and yet reject any comparison at all"[19] (390).

Let us conclude by stating that for João Romão, in the end, distinction does not necessarily imply renouncing money. Before changing his life style, João Romão dreamt about himself being recognized as "the famous, the grand capitalist! the mighty proprietor! the incomparable financier" (Azevedo 2000: 95).[20] His ideal for distinction also changes the dynamics of capital: "He hired three more clerks. He rarely waited upon the blacks who came to shop, and indeed was hardly seen behind the counter of his store." (127) In this way, money takes on a different logic and establishes a new dynamic in the tenement:

> He did, however, soon become a frequent presence on Rua Direita, at the stock exchange and in banks, his top hat pushed back and an umbrella tucked under his arm. He began to get involved in bigger deals: He purchased bonds offered by British companies and only loaned money for well financed mortgages. (127)[21]

O Cortiço indeed pays its dues to naturalism. Azevedo, influenced by Zola, attempts to make a coherent, oriented, and scientific critique of a corrupt reality. As a result, the novel demonstrates that João Romão becomes a villain, interested only in exploiting the weak in order to succeed, validating the maxim of the survival of the fittest in terms of the logic of economics. Therefore it is not by chance that the author-narrator denounces the protagonist and his behavior as "a disease, a mania to possess." The miser and seminal businessman turned

---

19 However, Simmel points out that the tendency of distinction is to disappear in the dynamics and development of capitalism, once objects are produced based on their monetary value: "Yet the more money dominates interests and sets people and things into motion, the more objects are produced for the sake of money and are valuated in terms of money, the less can the value of distinction be realized in men and in objects." (Simmel 1990: 390–391)
20 I have substituted the indefinite article "a" with "the," from the English translation to emphasize the sense of distinction that features in the Portuguese original.
21 "E em breve o seu tipo começou a ser visto com freqüência na Rua Direita, na praça do comércio e nos bancos, o chapéu alto derreado para a nuca e o guarda-chuva debaixo do braço. Principiava a meter-se em altas especulações, aceitava ações de companhias de títulos ingleses e só emprestava dinheiro com garantias de boas hipotecas." (Azevedo 1967: 178)

into a rentier finally ends up as a lender and speculator. In short, *O Cortiço* is the *Bildungsroman* of an emerging capitalist.

Works cited

Azevedo, Aluísio (2000) *The Slum*, trans. David H. Rosenthal (NY: Oxford University Press).

Azevedo, Aluísio (1967) *O Cortiço*. (São Paulo: Martins).

Bourdieu, Pierre (1984) *Distinction: A Social Critique of the Judgment of Taste*, trans. By Richard Nice (Cambridge, Massachusetts: Harvard University Press)

Braudel, Fernand (1977) *Afterthoughts on Material Civilization and Capitalism* trans. Patricia M. Ranum (Baltimore: The Johns Hopkins University Press).

Cândido, Antonio (1991) "De cortiço a cortiço." *Novos Estudos CEBRAP* 30: 111–129.

Kindleberger, Charles Poor (2005) *Manias, Panics, and Crashes: A History of Financial Crises* (Hoboken, N.J.: John Wiley & Sons).

Marx, Karl (1973) *Grundrisse: Foundations of the Critique of Political Economy*, trans. Martin Nicolaus (NY: Penguin Books).

Marx, Karl (1867) *Capital* Volume One, "Part I: Commodities and Money." <http://www.marx ists.org/archive/marx/works/1867-c1/ch01.htm#S1> (accessed 5 July 2013).

Marx, Karl (1844) *Economic and Philosophic Manuscripts of 1844*. <http://www.wsu. edu:8080/~dee/MODERN/ALIEN.HTM> (accessed 5 July 2013). Sá, Lúcia (2010) "Zola in Rio de Janeiro: The production of space in Aluísio Azevedo's *O Cortiço*," *Portuguese Studies* 26:2, 183–204.

Osteen, Mark and Martha Woodmansee (1999) *The New Economic Criticism: Studies at the Intersection of Literature and Economics* (London: Routledge).

Simmel, Georg (1990 [1900]) *The Philosophy of Money*, trans. Tom Bottomore and David Frisby (London: Routledge).

Zak, Paul J. and Stephen Knack (2001) "Trust and Growth," *Royal Economic Society Economic Journal* 111.470: 295–321.

Helena Gonçalves da Silva and Teresa Seruya
Not So Far Apart: Thomas Mann's
Buddenbrooks and Martin Amis's *Money*

According to Max Weber, "unlimited greed for gain is not in the least identical with capitalism, and is still less its spirit. Capitalism may even be identical with the restraint or at least a rational tempering of this irrational impulse" (Weber 2001: 160). Although this affirmation may still be valid in many ways, striving for "profit, and forever renewed profit" (Weber 2001: 160) has been the predominant endeavor of a culture of money that emerged alongside modern capitalism.[1] With the "globalist turn," liberalism arose as the last victorious ideology.[2] Henceforth, money has rivaled, or even exceeded political power as the preeminent goal of social activity.

The fact that money is capable of evoking a whole range of emotions, as a measure of identity and self-worth, as fetish and as a religious icon, explains why sociology, psychology, economics as well as the arts, including literature, and philosophy from classical times have undertaken to deal with its power. Although separated by eight decades, Thomas Mann's novel, *Buddenbrooks* (1901), and Martin Amis's novel, *Money: A Suicide Note* (1984), share a sharp focus on money. The former, which was instrumental in the award of the Nobel Prize for Literature to its author in 1929, belongs to the German literary canon and exemplifies European realist and naturalist aesthetics. The latter has been acknowledged as a major achievement of postmodern literary production. Whether they are associated with the commercialization of goods, as is the case for Mann's novel, or involving a more abstract mechanism, with money standing in for a "pure form of exchangeability" (Frisby 2004: xxvii), in the case of Amis's fiction, both texts endow visibility on the interrelatedness of economics, social and cultural values. In addition, they display the subtle (and not so subtle) ways in which the value of money interferes with one's freedom and consciousness.

---

1 Along with industrialism, coordinated administrative power and military power, capitalism is, in Anthony Giddens's view, one of the four institutional dimensions central to modernity (Giddens 1990).

2 In Francis Fukuyama's words, for example, "[...] a remarkable consensus has enveloped the world concerning the legitimacy and viability of liberal democracy" (Fukuyama 1989–1990: 22).

1

At the onset of Mann's novel, the eponymous Buddenbrooks enjoy an elevated social status and a high standard of living, thanks to the large amount of money the family has accumulated through inheritance, successive dowries and, above all, the specialization, diversification, and expansion of the family firm over three generations. The novelist engaged in painstaking research on commercial accounting and financial trading in order to ensure a high level of accuracy and sophistication regarding the business and financial facets that are depicted in the novel (Ridley 1987: 22).[3] He also conveys moments of strenuous difficulties, for example, during the Austrian-Prussian war of 1866, when the Buddenbrooks have to cope with the bankruptcy of a company with which they had a major partnership. Consequently, the novel follows the evolution of the Buddenbrooks's own firm, throughout its respective different phases, which include risky measures as well as decisions on lending and raising capital, ending with its liquidation in the face of fierce competition from a new form of capitalism (Ludwig 1979: 9).

The family story of the Lübeck Buddenbrooks covers the period from 1835 to the mid-1870s. Their business extends its commercial reach basically from Lübeck to Russia, Sweden, Britain and Holland. The family fortune, however, also stems from the prudent administration of its assets, which are always controlled by social and family values as well as beliefs involving the firm. These values configure a set of codes and rituals, "enduring dispositions" or habitus, that are passed on down through generations.[4] They prove vital insofar as they avoid the fragmentation of the family firm over a century.

Amongst other characteristics, these values disclose a growing and not always pacific separation between the inner and outer world – and a far greater one than between the private and public spheres. They include a pleasure in high-value acquisitions, which is exhibited on special occasions, particularly at the dinner table, an accumulation of capital, and a clear allocation of gender roles (Müller-Funk 2000: 59). Simultaneously, these values are imbued with a business ethics inherent in the notion of a rationally-structured society with social class confines that are well established and rooted in an individually-inbuilt

---

3 Mann even provided insight into the relationship between public finances, public enterprises and the stock market.

4 According to Pierre Bourdieu, the concept of "habitus" permits an understanding of beliefs and opinions – referred to as *doxa* – that shape people's views of the world precisely on the basis of "that system of enduring dispositions which I call *habitus*" (Bourdieu 1990: 190).

sense of duty and dignity. The best example is Johann Buddenbrook's advice to his son that business zeal must never prevent one from peaceful sleep (Mann 1982: 46). Other samples include Tony's subordination of her personal inclinations regarding love and marriage[5] to the business and family interests, and Thomas's dismissal of Anna, the flower girl, just before his decision to get engaged to Gerda Arnoldsen (Mann 1982: 147). Tony, in particular, is the best illustration of values inculcated from an early age, including the idea that renunciation is a duty owed to one's family. Mann's bourgeois novel anticipated, even if only by four years, Max Weber's connection between the spirit of modern economic life and the rational ethics of Protestantism. Mann himself acknowledged the affinities between *The Protestant Ethic and the Spirit of Capitalism* (1904–1905) and his own novel (Ridley 1987: 27).

The decline of the Buddenbrooks's firm and family comes about with their economic and social displacement by a class of dynamic business entrepreneurs, who uphold a more hard-line form of capitalism, represented in the novel by the nouveau riche, the Hagenströms. When they buy the Buddenbrooks's business and family mansion, they signal the emergence of monopoly capitalism and the end of an era characterized by the growth of industrial capital in largely national markets.[6] In this sense, the Buddenbrooks story is embedded not only in the German, but also in the broader context of European economic history. Yet the signs of this decline are manifest inside the Buddenbrooks's household right from the outset of the novel, as, for instance, in the pervasiveness of the symbolism of the grey color, which is "[...] intimately linked with a process of inner collapse" (Sheppard 1994: 920). [7] Christian's dissident lifestyle and nervous

---

5 When Tony falls in love with the leftist Morten, someone who does not belong in her social class, she is struck by the ingrained notion of the importance of family duty. A letter from her father has a similar effect on her: "We, my darling daughter, were not born for what we consider, in our short-sightedness, to be our small personal happiness, since we are not unbounded, independent and self-sufficient individuals, but members of a chain [...] inconceivable without those who came before us and showed us the ways while also following with firmness, without looking right or left, an experienced and dignified tradition" (Mann 1982: 123; see also chapters 13 and 14 of the third part of the novel).

6 Jameson distinguishes three periods in the development of capitalism: market capitalism, characterized by the growth of industrial capital in largely national markets (from the 1700s to the 1850s); monopoly capitalism in the age of imperialism, when European nation-states developed international markets, exploiting the raw materials and cheap labor of their colonial territories; and most recently (as from the 1960s), the phase of late capitalism, the multinational corporations with global markets and mass consumption (Jameson 1991: xviii).

7 In German, the noun "das Grau" means not only the color grey but also a feeling of emptiness and lack of hope. On the other hand, "das Grauen" means the fear or terror when faced with something disturbing or threatening.

sensibility also foreshadow the decline of the family business and ethics. Later on, these signs become clear symptoms of an inescapable aversion to all matters connected with business, such as Thomas's pervasive stress, melancholy and escapism – by his reading of Schopenhauer –, and Hanno's musical talent, physical frailty, and premature death.

All these signs and symptoms contrast with the confidence and energy of the elder Johann Buddenbrook for whom running the family business came naturally. Instead, for Thomas, the responsibility and the tough competition with the Hagenströms becomes unbearable (Mann 1982: 98), even though, at an earlier stage, he had managed to expand the firm and gain substantial profits. From the building of the new family house – which marks both the culmination of the family's success and the turning point in the Buddenbrooks's fortune – to his death, Thomas faces setbacks that reveal his inability and lack of will to run the firm. This is also the period when he grows particularly aware of the break-up of those ideals that guided the family over several generations. Moreover, the loss of traditional values and the vulgarization of taste that come along an emergent commodity culture defy Thomas's sense of decorum, as he admits, when referring to institutional politics: "[...] Standards are being lowered – yes, the general social niveau of the Senate is on its way down [...]. It offends something in me. It's a matter of decorum, it's simply bad taste" (Mann 1982: 100).

In line with Mann's symbolism that pervades most of his literary works, vital decay and a stressed or failing will to carry on with the family business become the symptoms of the inevitable agony of the bourgeois era, which characters both embody and precipitate through their search for self-expression via philosophical reflection and psychological and aesthetic refinement. In spite of the fact that the Buddenbrooks are not fully representative of *Bildungsbürgertum*, such symptoms symbolize the moment when the contradictions between the civic program of the *Bildung* ideal and the demands of capitalism reach a critical point. In other words, they reveal the decline of the bourgeoisie as a way of life at the point in time when the "affirmative culture" of the secularized German-Jewish *Bildungsbürgertum* makes way for the advent of mass society, metropolitan life and cultural industry, examined among others by Georg Simmel, György Lukács, Ernst Bloch, Siegfried Kracauer and Walter Benjamin. In one of their essays from *The Dialectics of Enlightenment*, a book in which they also react to the impact of Nazism, Theodor W. Adorno and Max Horkheimer discuss the political implications of this decline in "high art," whose essence was its potential for "aesthetic sublimation," the "[...] representation of fulfillment as a broken promise" (Adorno and Horkheimer 1999: 38). Abandoning the ideal of spiritual advancement, which the aesthetics of Kant and Hegel fostered, or any other form of liberating social aesthetics, the new culture industry was "repressive," "pornographic and prudish" (38) because it was at the service of organized capital. Alternatively, as Müller-Funk puts it, the end of the bourgeoisie brought about the end of modern art as the latter lost the object of its combat, the bourgeoisie itself (Müller-Funk 2000: 60).

Seen from Müller-Funk's perspective, the symptoms of the bourgeois decline comprise in *Buddenbrooks* – the most autobiographical of Mann's work – a repertoire of leitmotifs, which he builds, with incisive irony, into a cultural critique of this historical transition and evolution of capitalism. Although permeated by nostalgia for the patrician bourgeoisie of Mann's own origins, these motifs integrate into the critical process inherent to modernity. In addition, they carry Mann's writing well beyond nineteenth-century realism and onto the threshold of the self-reflexive modernisms of the twentieth century.

What this novel manifests is the unsustainable tension between the apparently stable values of a German Bildungsbürgertum (including Mann and the world from which he came), and an environment of mounting volatility and contingency resulting from the dynamics of capitalism. This tension also testifies to the presence of a distinctively German dichotomy between culture and civilization, which stretched back to the eighteenth century, as Norbert Elias explained in *The Civilizing Process* (1939). The last part of Mann's novel clearly symbolizes the split between culture and civilization in the falling apart of the inner and outer worlds. Such dichotomy became unmistakably manifest some years later, particularly in his conflict with his brother Heinrich, in Mann's public defense of the "*machtgeschützte Innerlichkeit*," or the inner world protected from politics.[8] Although specifically German, the valorization of culture over politics and economy, in *Buddenbrooks*, renders more intelligible and tangible the difficulties of coping with the various changes taking place between the late nineteenth century and the early years of the twentieth century.

These economic, social and cultural changes continued and picked up pace in the wake of the Second World War. They left behind the "solidity" of Mann's (or Stefan Zweig's) bourgeois world in favor of a post-industrial modernity with a "liquid" (Bauman 2000) and "disjunctive" quality as a "complex transnational construction of imaginary landscapes" (Appadurai 1996: 31), a world of signs wholly unmoored from their social meaning visualised by Jean-François Lyotard and Jean Baudrillard. Such is the world depicted in Amis's novel.

---

8 See the chapter entitled "Bürgerlichkeit" in Mann's *Betrachtungen eines Unpolitischen* (1918). Later on, already in exile in America, Mann reexamined this subject with a critical eye in some of his political essays such as *Schicksal und Aufgabe* (1944) and *Deutschland und die Deutschen* (1945).

2

Martin Amis's *Money: A Suicide Note* is a refined literary artefact that combines a profusion of postmodern artifices and narrative devices with a depiction of the 1980s and beyond. The image of a new form of modernity, which is at the core of the novel, indirectly echoes the effects of the 1980s reform processes that took place in Central and Eastern Europe in the context of the rapid move towards political and economic liberalism and globalization. As a result, the extension of the Western liberal-democratic model as the final form of government, which Fukuyama announced in his polemic essay "The end of history" (Fukuyama 1989), is inscribed in the globalized commodity culture of the novel, along with the rapidly changing order that undermines all bourgeois notions of permanence and progress as an evolutionary, unilinear process. Accordingly, what emerges in Amis's novel is a sense of rootlessness in all forms of social construction, of the disembedding of foundational structures that reduce the social realm to a mere diversity of scenarios, defusing the old system of social classes and the very meaning of social change while creating still more instability of collective and personal identity as well as new forms of alienation.

The spatial conception of Amis's fiction thus grows out of the landscape of London and New York, codified as the space of our world urban culture. Belonging to the "literature of the metropolis" genre, the novel discloses a stock of typical characters moving mostly in the contemporary traveler's and homogenized "non-places." As the antithesis of the anthropological locus, the "non-place" (Augé 1995: 86) is only suitable for contingent and transitory experiences and anonymous solitude. In its assertion of the impossibility of dwelling, in sharp contrast with the importance of the family house in *Buddenbrooks*, Amis's literary conception can only tolerate occasional locationary action and still less family life. Hence, the main character, John Self has neither family nor friends, travels incessantly between two of the largest Western capitals, interlinking the old continent with the new world, moving between airports and motorways, living mostly out of hotels, eating junk-food and drinking without restraint. His portable behavior projects an image of abstract, blind, senseless mobility, on the whole associated with sensations of dislocation, haziness, anxiety and fear of self-dissolution. In this respect, he stands at the opposite pole of the Buddenbrooks' restraint and decorum. Nor is Self a sample of the classic flâneur. Although an urban being accustomed to the streets of the megalopolis and the "infinite fluidity," which Simmel saw as a characteristic of modern life in his Viennese lecture on Rodin (1911), Self's hunt for money and sex cancels out any prospect of flânerie.

The interpretation, that views Self as "a representative child of the eighties, for whom money has to compensate for a total absence of culture" (Finney 1995: 4), conflicts with the fact that he is the narrator of his own story, which he also comments upon. His own words do seem to back such a view, for example when he states: "I chose not reading. Not reading – that's where I put my money" (Amis 1986: 42), or when he declares his hatred for "the beneficiaries of a university education [...] people with degrees, O-levels, eleven pluses [...]" (58). Should we consider that reading was for centuries – and still remains – the initiating ritual in the process of the individual's formation (or *Bildung*), which entailed a self-referential dimension and stimulated a critical perception of society, Self's attitude is, on the whole, a denial of any desire for a consistent culture. John Self, however, is not devoid of critical consciousness and would like to be admitted into the sphere of what he sees as "high culture" (326), which those like his "intellectual" friend and lover, Martina Twain, can access. In fact, he cannot rid himself of the cultural notion that reading or going to the opera are actually relevant matters. Therefore, he is both aware of his difficulties with books and intrigued by them, insisting, over and over again, on reading George Orwell's *Animal Farm* – a present from Martina. He also tries hard to improve his film script, and there are occasions when he displays a capacity for critical self-analysis, evident in the perception of himself as "addicted to the twentieth century" (91). Hence, he may want to fool himself and others with constant justifications for not reading, as when he claims that he cannot wear contacts because it "hurts his nerves" (42), or advances the excuse that he has no time, but in reality Self is frustrated, resentful and, sporadically, even humiliated for not being culturally more refined. Aware as he is of his shortcomings, he appears as the malformed product of a combination of lower middle-class origins and post-bourgeois culture. In addition to adopting a portable behavior suited to the new times, Self falls prey to the trappings of the same industrial cultures Adorno and Horkheimer criticized in their *Dialectics of Enlightenment*. In his addiction to television, publicity and all sorts of cheap magazines, particularly pornographic, he is the embodiment of experience as it is mediated by the mass media and images that amount to a series of unrelated presences in time. Such images explain the loss of depth and the surface appearances of contemporary culture (Jameson 1991: 9).

The utopia of an art, which would be aesthetic and morally superior, rather than subordinate to the ordinary world of the market and the dematerializing effects of the media, no longer seems possible. Ironically, Amis, who also appears in the novel as a writer paid by Self to revise the autobiographical film script he is supposedly directing, is unable to endow the script with quality. Averse to consumerism, the writer cannot prevent the script from becoming a pornographic project that operates along gendered categories and stereotyped images of the body, mostly dictated by the actors' fantasies and ambitions. The reference to an ideologically-framed book such as Orwell's *Animal Farm* is particularly relevant in as much as it reveals Self's incapacity to switch from the publicity code to an aesthetic level of representation, a logic Adorno and Horkheimer also analyzed in their essay on the culture industry and the mystification of the masses. Self is a successful producer of commercials and as such belongs, in Raymond Williams's words, "perhaps [to] the largest organized body of writers and artists, with their attendant managers and advisers, in the whole society" (Williams 1999: 421). The expertise in advertising that, according to Williams is "the official art of modern capitalist society" (421), stands for social alienation and lack of historical memory in Amis's fiction. As such, *Money*'s protagonist and narrator is both a victim and an agent of the dynamic global forces of production and consumption, the general system of signs and codes embedded in the cultural industries. Consequently, Self falls easy prey to rapacious swindlers like Fielding Goodney, a specialist in the tricks of virtual finance, who uses Self's film for accommodating financiers and assembling money. With sophisticated methods of exhibiting prêt-à-porter signs of wealth (chauffeured limousine, first-class travel, servants, expensive clothes, sophisticated meals and above all credit cards), he represents a case of hyper-inflated individualism and ephemeral success in the magic world of finance and film industry.

Living in a fantasy space of commodity-induced daydreams, Self indulges in multiple addictions to publicity, television, pornography and prostitutes, thus becoming the outcome of a system whose principle is that "the material object being sold is never enough" (Williams 1999: 422). However, by exhibiting the object of one's desire as being something always "new," the media only stimulate the preliminary desire, which is converted into masochistic behavior insofar as the desire is continuously denied and never sublimated. As we know from Michel Foucault's *History of Sexuality* (1976–1984), sexually explicit media is never subversive and its contents should not be mistaken for political liberation. In fact, Self "is consistently helped to believe that he [...] is an actor where in fact he [...] is at best a chooser," as Appadurai puts it in his study of globalized financial systems (1996: 42).

Self is well aware of the repulsiveness of his body, recalling images of Francis Bacon's paintings. He also knows how the body mediates the relationship between people's self-identity and their social identity and wishes therefore to undergo radical plastic surgery in California just as soon as he gets rich. His enslavement by unfulfilled desire and consumerism as the source of his troubles is never seriously questioned in Self's narration. Self loves money, he is turned on by money and his behavior is mostly conditioned by the desire to possess it.

For him, as for most of the characters in the novel, money generates the utmost value granting them a sense of freedom, no matter how illusionary this might be. Additionally, he wants to believe money is democratic because it has no favorites: "I truly love money. Truly I do. Oh, money, I love you. You're so democratic: you've got no favourites" (Amis 1986: 238). With Selina, his promiscuous lover and fellow addict to money, he constantly experiences the excitement of living a joint-venture of money, sex and voyeurism, which feeds on the usual repertoire of porn images.

Obsessed with masturbation, pornography and its fetishes, addicted to booze and fast food, and soaked in hyper-reality, mainly television, film, and publicity, Self, who made a successful career in publicity, is an extreme case of social alienation, evident in his basic numbness to history and politics. The irony inscribed in the name "Self" also indicates that post-modern societies have no room for alienation in the classical Marxist sense, but only as "psychic fragmentation," to use Jameson's apt formulation (1991: 90).

The world view Amis constructs thus offers no sense of redemption for the individual. Perhaps for this very reason, in the role of a writer, Amis is totally devoid of any aura. As the characters base their lives mostly on fabricated standards, on signs with pre-established meanings according to systems of signification, there is hardly any space for authenticity and individual development. Even Self's biography, the object of his artistic ambition, proves in the end to be spurious and based on lies. The novel is thus anchored in the radical idea that the nature of identity is inevitably fictional. As the masks of social performance crumble one after the other, as Rilke had already envisaged in *The Notebooks of Malte Laurids Brigge* (1910), nothing remains intact. Self ends up losing all critical aptitude, becoming incapable of understanding the causes of his own doom. In this perspective, the narrative logic appears deprived of any sense of teleology.

Nevertheless, ethics remain intrinsic to Amis's fiction precisely because it displays, with a penetrating eye and shocking language, the phenomenon of money as fulfilling the universally supreme value that, in a vicious fashion and ever more than before, drives the world round and round, dematerializing everything that was once solid. Viewed from this perspective, John Self becomes our post-modern Everyman about town.

Conclusion

In Mann's and Amis's novels, the main characters strive to relate successfully to the world through the symbolic power invested in them by money. The possibility of either losing it or simply not having it explains their anxiety and fear. Whilst through different devices and narrative strategies, both novels may be read as configurations of their historical time and cultural critique on the modern and post-modern conditions. Together, they allow for a clear insight into different moments in the development of cultural and economic change in the twentieth century. *Buddenbrooks* is associated with bourgeois modernity and its suggestive resilience in terms of social structures, practices and standards, whereas *Money* already belongs to a post-industrial and an informational future, to a rapidly changing order that undermines all notions of durability, rootedness and identity.

Are we then before two worlds apart? The answer is no. In both novels, we recognize signs of continuity rather than rupture, and such continuities could be compared with those David Harvey revealed between the Fordist-Keynesian era and the globalist expansion of financial systems (Harvey 1989: 170). Mann's novel is linked to a particular form of industrialism that developed in the late eighteenth century and reached its most dynamic expression in the post-war boom, leading to the success of liberalism on a universal scale. This occurred in spite of paradigm shifts within this process, each characterized by distinct social and political scenarios as well as cultural and economic patterns. What we find in Amis's novel is the portrait of a late form of capitalism in which culture has already been "commodified" or integrated into commodity production (Jameson 1991: 4). While post-modern culture corresponds to a stage in the development of capitalism, the ideological seeds coming to fruition in Amis's world were sown in the world of Mann's *Buddenbrooks*.

Works cited

Adorno, Theodor W. and Max Horkheimer (1999) "The Cultural Industry. Enlightenment as Mass Deception" [1947], in *The Cultural Studies Reader*, ed. by Simon During (London and NY: Routledge), 31–45.

Amis, Martin (1986), *Money. A Suicide Note* (Hardmondsworth: Penguin).

Appadurai, Arjun (1996) "Disjuncture and Difference in the Global Cultural Economy," in *Modernity at Large. Cultural Dimensions of Globalization* (Minneapolis, London: University of Minnesota Press), 27–47.

Augé, Marc (1995) *Non-Places: Introduction to an Anthropology of Supermodernity*, trans. John Howe (London & NY: Verso).

Bauman, Zygmunt (2000) *Liquid Modernity* (Cambridge: Polity).

Bourdieu, Pierre (1990) *In Other Words: Essays Towards a Reflexive Sociology*, trans. Matthew Adamson (Cambridge: Polity).

Finney, Brian (1995) "What's Amis in Contemporary British Fiction? Martin Amis' *Money* and Time's Arrow." http://www.csulb.edu/~bhfinney/Amis1.html, 1–9 (accessed 9 June 2011).

Frisby (2004) "Introduction," in Georg Simmel, *The Philosophy of Money*, the third enlarged edition, ed. David Frisby, trans. Tom Bottomore and D. Frisby (London: Routledge).

Fukuyama, Francis (1989–1990) "A Reply to my Critics," *The National Interest* 16, 21–28.

Fukuyama, Francis (1989) "The End of History," *The National Interest* 16, 3–18.

Giddens, Anthony (1990) *The Consequences of Modernity* (Cambridge: Polity Press).

Harvey, David (1990) *The Condition of Postmodernity: an Enquiry into the Origins of Cultural Change* (Cambridge, Mass: Blackwell).

Jameson, Fredric (1991) *Postmodernism, or, the Cultural Logic of Late Capitalism* (London & NY: Verso).

Mann, Thomas (1982) [1901] *Buddenbrooks. Verfall einer Familie* (Frankfurt am Main: Fischer Taschenbuch Verlag).

Müller-Funk, Wolfgang (2000) "Paternaler Hausvater und hässlicher Kapitalist," *Wespennest. Zeitschrift für brauchbare Texte* 31, 58–62.

Ridley, Hugh (1987) *Thomas Mann. Buddenbrooks.* (Cambridge: Cambridge University Press).

Sheppard, Richard (1994) "Realism plus Mythology: a Reconsideration of the Problem of 'Verfall' in Thomas Mann's *Buddenbrooks*," *The Modern Language Review* 89, 916–941.

Simmel, Georg (2004) *The Philosophy of Money*, ed. David Frisby, trans. Tom Bottomore and D. Frisby (London: Routledge).

Weber, Max (2001) *The Protestant Ethic and the Spirit of Capitalism* (London: Routledge).

Williams, Raymond (1999) "Advertising: the magic system" [1961], in *The Cultural Studies Reader*, ed. by Simon During (London and New York: Routledge), 411–423.

Filomena Viana Guarda
"Outside, the yellow lions are grinning"

Drugs, Crime and Ethnic Cleansing in Juli Zeh's
Eagles and Angels

> I make use of my right to explain the world
> to myself.
> Juli Zeh, 2002.

The global and flexible form of capitalism stamped on contemporary society at
the turn of this millennium has substantially changed man's relationship with
the world. The concepts of "neoliberalism" and "globalization," which have res-
onated in the discourses of the economic gurus over the past few years, characterize a new form of capitalism causing very different outcomes and effects from
those evident in its earlier versions. Nowadays, it is no longer tenable to speak
about man's enslavement to the machine or about the labor force composing the
exchange value in manufacturing or even about the depersonalization of human
life as a result of the growing dependence on money. These were circumstances
inherent in the industrialized society Georg Simmel so eloquently described in
The Philosophy of Money (1900). Often resorting to arguments of a moral nature,
Simmel describes the relationship between people and money, which he considers as having usurped God's place. In his examination of the situation, he interpreted money's central role in developed societies as a "tragedy of [modern] culture." Nevertheless, in the one hundred plus years that have since elapsed,
Simmel's study of modern civilization lost some of its relevance for an era of flex-
ibility such as ours. In fact, the capitalist society that developed and consolidat-
ed in the thirty years following the Second World War took shape as a new kind
of economy altogether at the end of the twentieth century, and one that is being
geared to short-term rather than long-term results and to very immediate pros-
pects. In its new embodiment, globalized capitalism has given rise to societies
typified by migration whose motto is moving on rather than settling in, as Richard Sennett argues.[1] In *The Culture of the New Capitalism* (2006), Sennett focuses on the research he has undertaken over thirty years regarding man's relationship with labor in the contemporary capitalist world, taking note of changes
in social capitalism over the first half of the twentieth century.

---

[1] Throughout this essay, when referring to Sennett's *The Culture of the New Capitalism*, I will use
the letter S followed by the page number.

At this time, the businesses and institutions of civil society were organized according to rank and the marked division of labor ensured each person occupied a set position and each place meant a well-defined function. The pyramidal organization gave people a sense of stability and the feeling that they were socially integrated despite the fact that their personal freedom was conditioned. This is why Max Weber deployed the expression "iron cage" in his well-known book *The Protestant Ethic*, an expression that Sennett recalls here. However, we should note that this "iron cage," which not only meant prison but also home, had long since been destroyed (Sennett 2006: 31–32). The new capitalism, arising mainly from "the shift from managerial to shareholder power" in many companies (Sennett 2006: 37), led to "the separation of ownership from control"[2] and to a growing interest in fast, short-term success that received solid backing in the information revolution. Hence, the former pyramid structure gave way to flexible organizations and certain qualities such as loyalty, informal trust and adaptive experience ceased to receive support (Sennett 2006: 63–71). As a result, Sennett insists, "the social has been diminished" even while "capitalism remains" (Sennett 2006: 82). The new work culture, characterized by change and speed, has robbed life of its stability and led to superficial human relationships and above all, to people feeling disoriented as a result of displaced inherited family values, now given over to values cultivated by the new world of labor. In other words, how are the enduring moral values cultivated by the family, and thus long-term values, supposed to harmonize with a short-term society that demands only a token link between things and people? How does one manage to develop a strong sense of identity and a coherent life story in a society that fails to esteem the experience accumulated throughout one's life? In looking at the current situation, Richard Sennett concludes: "The people I've interviewed [...] are too worried and disquieted, too little resigned to their own uncertain fate under the aegis of change. What they need most is a mental and emotional anchor; they need values which assess whether changes in work, privilege, and power are worthwhile. They need, in short, a culture" (Sennett 2006: 183). In fact, in his complex study of the effects brought about by today's new kind of world capitalism, Sennett does not rule out the way the individual's scope for maneuver has grown alongside the new kind of organization put forward by businesses and institutions, and he suggests that establishing a "cultural anchor" may well rely upon the rapid enhancement of three essential values which he calls narrative, usefulness and craftsmanship (Sennett 2006: 183).

---

2 Mark Roe, "The Inevitable Instability of American Corporate Governance," working paper, Harvard Law School, 2004 (qtd. Sennett 2006: 71).

The social and human outcomes of this lack of culture, which, as Sennett explains, should be understood in the anthropological sense here and not solely in the artistic sense, are made even clearer every time we read books written by contemporary writers who attempt to describe our society and its disturbing elements. In *Eagles and Angels* (*Adler und Engel*, 2001), the first novel by German writer Juli Zeh (born 1974), we come face to face with the "psychogram" of a mentally disturbed young man and his generation living in a capitalist, post-industrial society where material interests command and corrupt not only the people themselves, but also the most unsuspecting of institutions.[3] In the world Zeh introduces us to, there are neither consistent values nor absolute truths; the law is corrupt and morality absent. A lawyer, with a Master's degree in European and International Law,[4] who is also well informed about the political situation in the Balkans, about which she had published a travelogue following a journey through Bosnia in August 2001,[5] Juli Zeh has been an attentive observer of her society and is in constant demand by the German mass media.

In her debut novel,[6] the reader is introduced to four young characters aged between 23 and 33: three of them – Max, Jessie and Shershah – have been friends since their boarding school days; the fourth person, Clara, is a radio announcer interested in dissecting the life of Max, who is the only survivor of the trio of former schoolmates. The narrative plot starts unwinding eight weeks after Jessie's suicide, the love of the narrator's life. Shershah too, Jessie's great love, had already died by this point. The narrator is Max, a brilliant 33 year-old lawyer who is a specialist in international law and an expert on Balkan affairs. After completing a degree in law, he was immediately offered a well-paid job in the prestigious Vienna offices of Rufus, located in the heart of the UN building area of the Austrian capital. After Jessie's suicide at the age of 28, Max quits his job and loses himself in the grief of his loss, spending his days snorting coke and longing for his own death while simultaneously trying to understand just why Jessie took her life. Needless to say, the novel is shot through with both physical and mental pain as well as with the violence and

---

3 The term "psychogram" was used by Gudrun Boch in her speech praising Juli Zeh when she was awarded the Bremer Literature Prize (Bremer Literaturpreis) in 2002.

4 In 2002, Zeh published a book on the widening European Union membership into Central and Eastern Europe: *"Recht auf Beitritt?" Ansprüche von Kandidatenstaaten gegen die Europäische Union*, Schriften des Europa-Instituts der Universität des Saarlandes, Rechtswissenschaft, Bd. 41 (Baden-Baden: Nomos Verlagsgesellschaft, 2002).

5 *Die Stille ist ein Geräusch. Eine Fahrt durch Bosnien* (2002).

6 Juli Zeh received the prize for the best debut novel and the *Bremer Literaturpreis* for this novel. Translation rights were sold to 28 countries, including Portugal. Rights were also sold to a German film company in 2003.

corruption that seem to have contaminated all the characters and institutions mentioned in it.

Jessie was a strange, problem-ridden young woman, who blew her brains out while speaking to Max on the telephone and after she had uttered an enigmatic phrase in terror: "Cooper, I think the tigers are there again" (EA 10). The novel therefore starts with an inexplicable death, which the protagonist Max seeks to untangle step by step, revealing how his own private tragedy is involved in something much deeper that touches upon international political corruption and ill-gotten wealth. The narrative structure is also complicated and intermeshes not only recollections of past experiences with present-day occurrences, but also the private lives of characters with international political events.

We should stress that all of the novel's main characters enjoy a very high standard of living and do not have any financial concerns: either because they hold extremely well-paid jobs or because they belong to the world of highly profitable wheeler-dealing. Nevertheless, their privileged economic status fails to prevent them from feeling unhappy and hemmed in. Indeed, throughout the discourse of this lengthy novel, evil seems to know no end: characters are killed and/or beaten up while man-handled, family relationships are always problematic and behaviors are selfish. Examples abound. Herbert, Jessie's father, uses his two children as drug runners, refusing to let them off even when he sees how desperate his daughter has become. Rufus, Max's boss, uses his prestigious law firm and co-workers to bring off lucrative deals, all in the name of successful political business. Shershah, the handsome, charming, yet neglected son of an Iranian diplomat, lives by exploiting Jessie's enormous attraction to him. Clara, the radio announcer, mercilessly delves into Max's pain in order to get enough material on which to base her academic work. Max, who uses Jessie to fill the void in his emotional life, dedicates and protects the young woman, thus making up for his own loneliness and the trauma of a loveless childhood punctuated by severe eating disorders and various kinds of complexes. Even Jessie, a delicate small-boned girl whose hair is "short and blonde, sticking out in all directions," thus giving her an angelic appearance despite her hard gaze (EA 39), only becomes friendly with Max because she feels lost and frightened and does not know who to turn to. There is also the enigmatic Professor Schnitzler, Clara's PhD supervisor who seems to hide dubious interests. In short, readers fail to meet any balanced character who would display the strong and enduring values that might can guide them through life.

Cocooned in his personal drama of loss, which he fails to understand, Max needs to talk with someone and, as he has no friends, calls Clara's Bleak World, a radio program that goes on air every Wednesday and Sunday, aimed at "the desperate, the nihilistic, the ones left behind and the lonely, for atomic scientists, dictators and any jerk off the street" (EA 49). In immediately grasping the fact that Max and Jessie's story would be useful for her academic study on the pathology of organized crime, and never, it should be stressed, with the purpose of helping him, Clara visits Max so that he can tell his story into her tape-record-er (Leis 2001: 7). The relationship between Max and Clara (whose real name is Lisa Müller) composes the outer narrative, a sort of framework in which to explain Jessie's suicide through building up the story of the three school friends used as drug runners by the girl's father who, from a distance, seems always to have controlled the choices they made about life (Rüb 2001: 21).

During her visit to Max, Clara finds "three hundred thousand deutsch-marks," money unbeknownst to Max, resulting from drug dealing and hidden under the floorboards in the corridor by Jessie. Faced with so many situations that need explaining, Max decides to travel with Clara to Vienna, a pivotal city in the narrator's relationship with Jessie. While there, he attempts to unveil all the secrets that are wrapped around the young woman's life.

Indeed, in the world described here, where easy money does the rounds without difficulty and where human values and feelings are absent, it is not only the lives of the characters that are horrible, but also the environment in which they move that is drab: the houses are described as half-empty and over-look poorly-lit inner courtyards both in Leipzig as well as in Vienna, the plot's two urban settings. In the latter city, despite Max's and Clara's bag full of bank-notes in their car, the pair hole up for three weeks in a dark shack offering no kind of comfort or hygiene whatsoever and in use by Mafia gangs for storing drugs. Max shows no kind of interest in life and Clara is open to anything includ-ing being beaten up, taking drugs and being humiliated just so she can acquire the material necessary for her work, all the more so because she believes that "you can research someone's inner life by taking on their outward appearance" (EA 239). The characters Zeh introduces us to in her novel illustrate the loss of values of a still-young generation which, because it believes in nothing, is dis-posed to doing everything.

Max, the main character and narrator, has indeed overcome the traumas of his adolescence by concentrating first on his studies and later on his job and blossoming career, all of which become visible in his greatly improved physical appearance. However, when Jessie makes a second entrance into his life after a 12-year absence, the falseness of the yuppie life he has been leading dawns on Max: "Jessie was tiny in my arms; I hadn't held anyone so small in ages. I sud-denly realized that I'd missed her, that the life of titans at Rufus's side hadn't been perfect. Big things like Rufus or even whole nations could be marveled at, listened to or fought against, but they couldn't be loved" (EA 178). It should also be noted that for some time, Max had been pondering the moral principles of international law, which, based on the principle of safeguarding state sovereignty, had overlooked war crimes. However, Max continued working in this field and was well paid in the process.

In committing suicide without leaving any explanation, Jessie leaves Max bereft of feeling, which pushes him into heavy cocaine abuse when he concentrates on his physical senses as witnessed throughout the book: nausea, several kinds of aches and pain, dizziness, weariness and frequent bowel trouble (Falcke 2001: 22). When in Vienna, he discovers that some dirty business is being plotted by organized crime (weapons and drug trafficking) at the time of the Balkan wars and just at the time the European Union opens up to Eastern European countries. He finally becomes aware that he himself has helped this state of affairs by providing the legal coverage required for the business to advance. His boss, Rufus, belongs to a criminal network and is associated with Herbert, Jessie's father, and actually his long-time crony. It should be recalled that Rufus's law firm worked with the UN in drawing up peace agreements between parties at war in the Balkans whilst also helping set down the rules for opening up European Community membership to Eastern Europe (Neutwich 2001: 33). Arkan, another Rufus associate in these shady dealings, is involved in the "Gunsfor drug operation" (EA 227) making it possible for the Serbs to fund most of the Balkan wars. By taking advantage of the information network run by Rufus and Max's skilful legal wrangling egged on by his boss (EA 186–187), Arkan ends up obtaining international political protection. Nonetheless, when Max understands the intricate network of the relationships at work and is faced with the crude facts, the immense admiration he feels for his boss starts to wane: behind the façade to defend national sovereignty and human rights, Rufus has made a pact with organized crime.

Jessie, who has been trafficking in cocaine since a very young age, developed a fanciful imagination capable of protecting her from the harsh reality of a world dominated by economic interests in which "transactions" have replaced "relationships" (see S 25). But when she has to do business directly with the "Tigers," who are the paramilitary Serbian Volunteer Guard serving under Arkan, the Serbian criminal, also responsible for the spasm of ethnic cleansing, and when she personally witnesses the way in which a young Bosnian woman is slain for refusing to serve as a drug runner, her escape into fantasy is no longer effective. Jessie then starts experiencing severe panic attacks preventing her from leaving the house during daytime. The fact that Shershah, her lover, has disappeared with a large quantity of money also aggravates her mental balance and leaves her psychologically weakened. It should be pointed out, however, that it is not the lack of money that makes Jessie so vulnerable but rather, the inability to find one's way in the world, and as the narrator tells us: "I slowly began to understand that what Jessie was short of wasn't money itself but the ability to use money to get the necessary things in life" (EA 183).

As the novel progresses, the reader perceives that history and fiction become intertwined when the real-life panorama of the Bosnian wars intermeshes with the fictitious story of Max and Jessie. The character embodied by Jessie plays her role in a town called Sanski Most in 1995, which then housed an important "Tigers" general headquarters and only six months before the Dayton Agreement on Bosnia got signed, as the novel explicitly reminds us (EA 223). It is there that Jessie meets Franko Simatovic and Zeljko Raznatovic, better known as Arkan, who were two real-life men involved in the war in ex-Yugoslavia and later sought by The Hague International Court of Justice. After the unexpected death of Jessie, who was his only affective link with the world, Max becomes cynical about life and people and his routine is guided by "the coke and the hatred" as he himself confesses (EA 235), all the more so because behind his personal loss and his unfulfilled love story, there is also a political tragedy casting a shadow over the dubious world of EU case law, and above all shedding light on European disenchantment (Boch 2002: 22). As Peter Henning writes, we are faced with a society that has ceased having any kind of scruples (Henning 2001: 32).

As the novel ends, both the main character and the reader finally discover the reason Jessie committed suicide: she was panic-stricken over dealing with the drug mafia with whom she no longer wanted to do any business. In order to protect herself, she had secreted away a large amount of money and had coded the computerized access to a new plan for drug-trafficking to Poland and subsequently tattooed her password onto her dog's ear. After having cleared up the mystery, and in an altruistic act that proves so unusual in the world described here, Max takes upon himself to reveal the password in exchange for Clara's life. The final scene closing the book gives us the picture of the main character, stripped naked under heavy rainfall in the filthy Viennese courtyard where he has spent the previous few weeks, hoping the rain will wash his body and spirit clean. His last altruistic act after all reveals that he still has a shred of feeling even if the diagnosis is not comforting.

This fictional world shows us a solitary, misguided society lacking in either values or goals. Juli Zeh's second novel *Spieltrieb*, published in 2004, also shows a drifting younger generation: yet again, good and evil are hard to tell apart and the text's young characters are incapable of showing moral rectitude. Hence, young German literature does seem to carry with it a picture of present-day society that leads us back to the study by Richard Sennett. Although the American sociologist is not exactly optimistic in the conclusions he draws, he does leave us with a small ray of hope: "Since people can anchor themselves in life only by trying to do something well for its own sake, the triumph of superficiality at work, in schools, and in politics seems to me fragile. Perhaps, indeed, revolt against this enfeebled culture will constitute our next fresh page" (S 197).

Works cited

Auffermann, Verena (28 July 2001) "Und der Mond sank auf den Grund der Sahneschüssel". *Süddeutsche Zeitung* 172, IV.

Boch, Gudrun (2002) "Laudatio auf die Förderpreisträgerin Juli Zeh," in *Verleihung des Bremer Literaturpreises 2002* (Bremen: Geffken & Köllner), 21–24.

Falcke, Eberhard (4 October 2001) "Kinder des Kapitalismus," *Die Zeit* 41, 22–24.

Henning, Peter (23 August 2001) "Visionen vor dem Tode," *Die Weltwoche* 34, 31.

Köhnke, Klaus Christian (1990) "Die Verdrängung der Werte durchs Geld," *Universitas* 4: 328–333.

Kraft, Thomas (ed.) (2003) *Lexikon der deutschsprachigen Gegenwartsliteratur seit 1945*, vol 2: K-Z (Munich: Nymphenburger), 1365–1366.

Leis, Sandra (6 October 2001) "Hässliche Welt sprachlich schön verpackt," *Der Kleine Bund* 233, 7.

Neutwich, Andreas (6 September 2001) "Das grosse Achselzucken," *Neue Zürcher Zeitung* 206, 33.

Rüb, Mattias (9 October 2001) "Verkokste Roadshow," *Frankfurter Allgemeine Zeitung* 234, L21.

Sennett, Richard (1998) *The Corrosion of Character. The Personal Consequences of Work in the New Capitalism* (New York: Norton).

Sennett, Richard (2006) *The Culture of the New Capitalism* (New Haven & London: Yale University Press).

Simmel, Georg (1989 [1900]) *Philosophie des Geldes*, in *Gesamtausgabe*, vol. 6 (Frankfurt am Main: Suhrkamp).

Wehdeking, Volker (2007) *Generationenwechsel: Intermedialität in der deutschen Gegenwartsliteratur* (Berlin: Erich Schmidt Verlag).

Zeh, Juli (2003) *Adler und Engel. Roman* [2001] (Munich: btb Verlag).

Zeh, Juli (2002) *Die Stille ist ein Geräusch. Eine Fahrt durch Bosnien.* (Frankfurt am Main: Verlag Schöffling & Co.).

Zeh, Juli. (2003) *Eagles and Angels*, trans. Christine Slenczka (London: Granta Books). Abridged EA.

IV Cognitive Moneyscapes

Vera Nünning

Meanings of Money in Literature: D. J. Taylor's Novel *Kept* (2006) as a Test Case for Exploring Cognitive Functions of Literature

Why novels are able to present us with valuable information about 'the cultural quality of money' is anything but self-explanatory. After all, fictionality is one of the defining features of literature, and we might do well not to believe that there was a village in Latin America in which it rained continuously for a hundred years, or that a man called Don Quijote enjoyed fighting windmills, for instance. When one acknowledges that the references to reality even in 'realistic' novels are not necessarily correct and that the aesthetic quality and poetic function of literature does not relate to the real world, then it seems highly improbable that any contemporary novel may provide us with meaningful information about our culture.

Nonetheless, a quite heated discussion about the knowledge of (or in) literature[1] has been ongoing for some time now. Literary critics assert – and dispute – that literature 'contains' knowledge about life; that the data we find in literature also tells us something worth knowing about 'real life.' Although scholars seem to agree that one can determine what kind of knowledge has been introduced into a literary work by the author (that is concentrating on the process of production) or what kind of knowledge readers have to be in command of in order to understand a text (Jannidis 2008: 376), it seems doubtful whether a work of art like a novel presents us with knowledge about anything beyond the realm of art.

In this essay, I want to pursue another route and start from the premise that literature is, as Catherine Elgin puts it, a "thought experiment." In a very thoughtful essay, Elgin begins by disputing that cognition equals knowledge. Instead, she emphasizes that we need to "organise, synthesize, properly orient ourselves toward, and judiciously ignore known facts" (Elgin 2007: 44) in order to understand a person or an event. One may be in possession of various data

---

1 See, for instance, the discussion in and contributions to *Zeitschrift für Germanistik* XVII (2007, 2008), which was triggered by Tilmann Köppe's article "Vom Wissen *in* Literatur." (Köppe, 2007: 398–410), the seven volumes of studies concerned with *La conoscenza della letteratura/The Knowledge of Literature*, ed. by Angela Locatelli, 2005; Claus-Michael Ort 1992: 409–441; and Ottmar Ette 2007: 7–32.

on photosynthesis, for instance, but still not make sense of the actual process; in order to achieve an understanding we have to ignore many facts, and "duly accommodate p's salient properties and relations" (44). The fact that literature neither sports any direct references to the real world nor provides us with data about a phenomenon like money thus does not detract from the value of literature as a means of cognition. Rather, we can conceptualize literature as a kind of 'thought experiment', which is as divorced from reality as the setup of a laboratory is from conditions in the real world. The facts which literature represents at the level of the story or through the narrator's comments cannot be directly related to any situation in real life; however, in their mutual relations, these facts exemplify selected events, agents and circumstances in the real world and provide us with a dense description of them. This again enables readers to identify the salient properties more easily than when faced with a mass of data surrounding them in the real world – and it may make it easier for them to identify salient data and concentrate on the important factors in similar situations in real life.

Should this suggestion provide an adequate understanding of the function of literature, then it should be possible to gain insight into the qualities of money by looking at literary texts. This should not be confused with one-to-one references to the real world, with isolated facts about the gold-standard or the economic value of different currencies. We do not get any reliable pieces of information, any additional data that we usually define as 'knowledge' about a phenomenon. What we might expect, instead, are representations of some salient properties of money and how they relate to each other, as far as their meanings and functions in human life are concerned. Moreover, these representations always imply particular views on, particular perspectives of money. Literature does not provide us with 'objective' knowledge, untainted by subjectivity. This is a characteristic of literary texts; one of the main differences between a thought experiment in the natural sciences and philosophy on the one hand and a literary text on the other is that the latter is not concerned with an "objective stance" or "a view from nowhere" (Elgin 2007: 51). On the contrary, novels deal with characters; they represent events and circumstances in so far as they impinge upon these characters' lives and shape their perceptions and feelings. What we might gain from concentrating on literature are therefore not facts concerning the 'objective' properties of money, but various perspectives on money, perspectives that are different from our own – and probably also different from those of experts on business and economics. It may turn out that with regard to money, the "item's important properties are [...] the ones the view from some other perspective encloses" (51) and not the 'objective' knowledge provided by financial experts. To become aware of the various meanings money may hold for people may be just as important as knowledge of certain 'objective' facts about currencies.

With a conceptual framework in mind, I now turn to contemporary literature in order to gain some insight into the cultural qualities of money. Faced with the problem of selecting from among a host of books in which money plays an important role, two quite famous works – which focus on money to such an extent that the word even makes it into their titles – are obvious candidates for in-depth analysis: Martin Amis's novel *Money: A Suicide Note* (1984)[2] and Carol Churchill's play *Serious Money* (1987). Both works have the advantage of featuring protagonists obsessed with money and focusing on a representation of the cultural consequences of late capitalism in contemporary Britain. To concern oneself with such texts is certainly rewarding and it is therefore pertinent that at least one of the articles in this volume deals with Amis's *Money*. From the point of view of literary studies, however, it may be just as interesting to focus on a less famous contemporary work that does not put money in the foreground. D. J. Taylor's *Kept. A Victorian Mystery* (2006), a historical novel set in the 1860s, might seem an unlikely choice as the financial conditions at that time are certainly far removed from those we face today. Judging from the point of view of verisimilitude, for instance, it would be difficult to say to what extent the depiction of the condition of a character such as a servant girl living on the estate for which she works contributes anything about the cultural quality of money in present-day Britain. Nevertheless, should we take the idea of literature as a thought experiment seriously, it does not actually matter whether there is a wealth of fictional facts which directly relate to 'real life.' When faced with a significant description of salient properties and relations exemplified and placed in specific circumstances, we should be able to enlarge our horizon about the meaning and workings of money even while there are few gains in terms of verisimilitude. I therefore turn to Taylor's novel in order to find out to what extent the fictive literary world, the ordering of events, the constellation of characters, their perspectives on money and narrative techniques enhance our understanding of money.

In Taylor's novel, money is present in tangible as well as intangible ways. The material aspect is highlighted by several means, ranging from the spectacular robbery carried out by the gentleman-like Mr. Pardew and his associates that brings them into the possession of a large amount of gold bars – which later have to be melted down in order to become exchangeable specie – as well as foreign coins from France, which they keep in a bank and which thus pro-

---

2 See the essay by Silva and Seruya in this volume.

vide the police with a valuable clue. Moreover, the possibility of deceit is related even to specie, as becomes clear when Mr. Pardew's "clerk" Grace tosses a faked florin to a beggar, whose future difficulties with this coin are only hinted at (Taylor 2006: 149). In these instances, the novel seems merely to repeat or exemplify common knowledge about money as a means of exchange, which levels the meanings of substances and makes them interchangeable. In order to turn money into such a means of exchange, which initiates an unbounded flow reducing the distance between people, the gold bars have to be melted down. In Marxist terms, this leads to a process of abstraction, which reduces the substance not only of the objects traded, but also of human beings. As Terry Eagleton puts it, money is "a realm of chimerical fantasy in which all identity is ephemeral" (Eagleton 1990: 201). Applying this premise in order to gain insight into, for instance, Amis's novel *Money*, one comes up with interesting results: the claim that postmodern identities are 'invaded' by money and that money becomes a kind of surrogate identity. This has been done by Stephan Laqué with regard to Amis's *Money*. Yet I would propose one can find out more about the qualities of money in contemporary fiction when one considers less specific examples and more characters than one idiosyncratic protagonist.

1 Salient facts: the attitudes to and functions of money within this novel

True to its Victorian forerunners, Taylor's novel *Kept* sets out a panoramic view of society, encompassing a host of different characters in quite heterogeneous situations. In contrast to Victorian novels, however, this also includes the perspective of a servant girl. Thus, it becomes possible to assess the way in which money impinges upon the lives and attitudes of different characters who appear in separate chapters and who, for the first hundred pages or so, do not seem related to each other. It turns out, however, that nearly all are somehow connected to the murder of the gentleman Henry Ireton, which took place shortly before, and the fate of his widow Isabel, who is diagnosed as mad and placed as a ward in the attic of the estate of Mr. Dixey – who, it turns out, has no other motive for this act other than getting his hands on her money. Connected to this crime are, among others, not only the main perpetrator Mr. Pardew and the rather mixed bag of people whom he deploys as his instruments, but also distant relations of Isabel, who want to help her, alongside the servants of Mr. Dixey's estate. These characters are linked not only by means of the plot, which slowly becomes discernible to the reader, but also by the main motive of the novel, which is highlighted in the title: *Kept*. Kept, under the power and thrall of others, are, for instance, Mr. Dewar, whose wife is so ill that he can be forced to do just about anything to get money for her; Jemima, Pardew's literally "kept" mistress; and Mrs. Ireton, who is confined to her attic.

What – apart from being a "means of exchange" – are the qualities of money in this set-up? First of all, the material aspects arising from the exchange of money are highlighted: even before the young servant girl Esther has reached her new place as a servant in Dixey's estate, she hears that this gentleman does not take proper care of his belongings, that the greenhouses and the estate are falling into decay. Money would be the means to set this right, but money is lacking. As the number of servants diminishes, Esther is required to add more and more to her already substantial number of chores and has to fear for her livelihood: "In which case [...] what will become of us all?" (259) However, it is made quite clear from the beginning that Dixey does have money – only that he spends it on other things, paying large sums to people who acquire 'natural specimens' for him, such as the eggs of rare birds or the corpses of nearly extinct species. Whereas Dixey does seem to have choices, though his decisions are questionable, these opportunities are non-existent in the case of Dewar, a former grocer, who cannot continue working because he wants to care for his mortally-ill wife and who is forced to take part in Pardew's criminal schemes.

There might seem a great gap between characters like Dewar and Dixey, for the former appears to have few choices regarding the acquisition and spending of money, whereas the latter freely chooses his financial habits. However, the novel suggests that the facts of the matter are more complex as other factors need considering. For instance, knowledge about money and the world of finance becomes an important factor as we find that unawareness may lead one into otherwise avoidable situations if one had been able to foresee the consequences. Thus, Dewar, just like the servant girl Esther, becomes implicated in crimes because he does not understand them: the world of money (and deceit) remains inexplicable to this pair of characters. Yet both of them do sense that they are letting themselves into something illegal and wrong: "All this Dewar saw, or rather did not see, for his mind was lost in ceaseless calculation. He knew little of the money world, the world of Grace and his master, but he knew sufficient to be aware that the tasks he had been commissioned to perform could not, of their nature, be legitimate." (150) Even Esther, who tries hard to ignore how her lover William is doing something wrong, has to realize that he has been melting down gold in their house. Both Esther and Dewar risk facing imprisonment at the end; but although their actions do not quite fit prevalent moral standards, the narrative ordering of events makes it easy for readers to understand the characters' predicament because they find themselves in situations similar to those of these comparatively naïve figures, and have to wait rather a long time until they are in full possession of the facts enabling them to understand Pardew's criminal schemes. Money may be a neutral means of exchange but the novel makes quite clear how its different usages are charged with moral significance.

The difficulties of understanding (the loopholes in) the system of exchange are most obvious with regards to the "bills" and "cheques," which abound in the novel partly because Pardew is a "bill broker." What this profession involves remains mysterious for a while. Basically, however, it boils down to something that is of some relevance especially in times of banking crises, for Pardew deals in cheques and bills that are no longer worth anything; it is only later that the new owners of these bills find out that they are worthless and cannot be resold to anyone else. Money – in the form of cheques, bills, and with a little help from others – thus becomes a means of deceit, and the more educated characters are not as easily excused as naïve servants who never had the opportunity to gain the knowledge that might have hindered them from becoming ploys in immoral schemes.

Money may also serve to diminish the range of peoples' activities – physically as well as mentally. Dewar's lack of money has turned him into a puppet forced to act according to the wishes of whoever pulls his strings. In most cases, however, it is not that easy to determine just what is going on. The most interesting case in point is Pardew, who does not seem to need the money he gets by means of the spectacular robbery occurring at the end of the book. Nevertheless, in spite of the risk involved, he is unable to stop himself. For Pardew, the acquisition of money has become an end in itself; and the costs of his behavior to others fail to make it into any of his calculations.

Even more than the implications of the fraudulent use of money, the novel highlights its psychological significance. In some characters, money has a profound influence. The lack of money has robbed Dewar not only of his peace of mind, but also of his self-confidence. Quite the opposite is true with regard to Pardew, who is able to buy all the outer trappings of a gentleman and employs these self-confidently in order to access people "above his station." Money allows him a kind of self-fashioning that serves to convince – and impress – his mistress Jemima. However, the kind of profiling by way of money achieved by William, Pardew and Dewar is exposed as fraudulent and fragile: in most cases, it fails rather quickly.

It becomes clear, moreover, that this form of self-expression is not typical of the 1860s. There are instead two other factors just as important as money: reputation and one's social station. This is shown in Pardew's dealings with the seemingly respectable lawyer Crabbe, whom he needs for his crimes. Respectability and a good reputation can be turned to profit. While this seems to have some bearing even in the era of late capitalism, when buyers of shares sometimes pay more regard to promises by respectable brokers than to a plain understanding of what is going on, the second factor seems more remote today. In the novel, social station, especially titles above the rank of the baronet, still hold the same kind of power as money and reputation when it comes to the necessity of convincing others and making them act according to one's wishes. However, in the novel, reputation, money and social station are often divorced from one another: even Pardew fails when wanting to place a bill personally into the hand of a duke (194). When money is pitted against station, money fails dismally.

In spite of these examples, the novel mainly provides instances of non-egalitarian usages of money. The acquisition of money does not help any of the characters from the lower ranks; apart from Pardew, those who accumulate money 'above their station' fail with neither William nor Dunbar and Grace able to enjoy their illegally acquired capital. Large quantities of money would seem to help only those born with the 'right' to them. The novel thus points out an alternative system of values, in which money is closely related to social station and reputation, and thus invites us to consider different, more efficient or more just ways of ordering our world.

In a similar vein, the novel does not support the view of money's "power to move everywhere, to link everything to everything else, and to condition everything and everyone" (Laqué 2009: 184). The links provided by money (which are often only perpetuated because of mutual mistrust or physical force) are contrasted with other, more efficient, personal networks.

2 The depiction of alternatives to current attitudes towards money

In addition, Taylor's novel provides alternatives both to money-based self-fashioning and the deployment of money as an instrument which can "condition everything and everyone." There are at least three characters (or groups of characters) whose ways of living are not governed by the acquisition or the spending of money. John Carstairs and his family, for instance, live comfortably because they are in possession of enough money to maintain their life style; for them, money is not important. The same is true for Esther, though her financial means are far more modest. 'Living in' as a servant, her physical wants are – on a basic level – cared for, and she does not seem to need the twelve pounds that she earns in a year. The sole usage of her earnings that gets mentioned involves the buying of a new dress. When asked by Mrs. Ireton "'[w]hat should you do, Esther, if you could leave here & do exactly as you chose?',", her answer does not revolve around wealth or the acquisition of money: "'Why, ma'am [...] I should take a husband and have six children, & live in a cottage, & be happy I hope. Only I should take care that I wasn't poor'" (257). The lack of a means of subsistence is what she fears – but money plays a negligible role in her dream.

The most interesting case is perhaps Isabel Ireton, the widow pronounced "out of her mind" by the physician Dr. Connolly, and therefore placed under the care of a ward, Mr. Dixey. She is kept in an attic and only brought out when her ward wants to influence her. As the reader finds out in the end, this gentleman played some role in the murder of Mr. Ireton in order to gain access to his inheritance, Dixey even proposes marriage to Isabel. Ironically, Dixey couches his proposals in less than literally correct way in asking whether she wants to become "mistress of Easton Hall" (266) and everything in it – neglecting to mention the fact that with her signature under the marriage contract, she places all her money in his hands. However, Isabel does not seem aware of this; she simply takes up and echoes his words: "I would rather be mistress of myself." (267) Money plays no role in her desires – she wants freedom of movement and contact with others rather than gaining access to her capital.

These multilayered representations of money within the novel may serve as examples of the functions of money, for instance the extremes to which the want of – or merely the desire for – money may drive people. Thus far, I have tried to tease out the most important facts and their relationships within the novel – the consequences for the mental and physical well-being of characters as well as their (fraudulent) usage of money. It also becomes apparent that money serves as a means of structuring the cast of characters not only into 'haves' and 'have-nots', as an economic point of view might have it, but also into those who crave money and those for whom it is unimportant, into those that need it as a crucial facet to their self-fashioning and those that do not, or into groups distinguished by the various motives behind their desire for money, its legal and illegal usage, and related aspects.

One might even go one step further and ask what role the different attitudes towards and functions of money play in the system of values underlying the novel. Given that, as far as money is concerned, several characters embody contradictory attitudes and thereby endow money with a variety of meanings, how are these attitudes towards money positioned and evaluated within the novel? This, after all, might suggest how readers orient themselves with regard to money within the novel – and beyond.

3 Evaluating the perspectives on money

In order to gain insight into the implicit evaluation of the perspectives on money presented in the novel, two factors require consideration. On the one hand, we need to take into account the cultural knowledge at the time of the story production. On the other hand, the structure of the narrative and the narrative techniques contribute to our evaluation of events. With regard to cultural knowledge, we should remember that nowadays, for instance, we emphasize sustainability and the preservation of nature: a man like Dixey, who has rare animals hunted down and killed just in order to satisfy his own curiosity, is therefore suspect. Similarly, we are prone to pitying young people who have to spend their childhood working long hours away from home. These factors are culturally and historically variable, and with regard to *Kept*, there is an interesting tension between Victorian values, according to which these characters might be judged, and those of today.

The evaluation emerging from a consideration of narrative techniques is not as dependent on cultural change. One of the most obvious aspects regarding the set-up of a fictional work is, of course, the plot. In *Kept*, the old principle of poetic justice, which might indicate how attitudes are evaluated within the world of the story, is next to non-existent and we therefore have to rely on other aspects. Judging from the point of view of the plot, one might even think that the criminal Pardew is the 'best' character for he ends up the most successful. However, the wealth of character perspectives establishes a multilayered web of (partly contradictory) values that make several salient aspects towards money visible. Moreover, the meanings bestowed on money are placed in a context making judgments feasible on the meanings of money in a far more complex way than any mere economic perspective would allow. Looked at from a purely economic stance, Pardew is a 'winner', a new kind of entrepreneur. Should one take into account the values embodied in the novel, however, Pardew appears in a different and an ambivalent light.

On the one hand, he occupies the position of the 'hero' and protagonist, who is related to most other characters; he also displays many of the requisite character traits: courageous, adventurous, capable, and 'cool' even under pressure. On the other hand, he is presented in a less than favorable light. From his first mention in the novel, he is associated with unpleasant activities such as the reprinting of a few business letters demonstrating how Pardew makes recourse to blackmail to get hold of an important document. Even before Pardew makes his personal appearance, he has therefore been introduced as a negative character. This is complemented by a distance between the narrator and Pardew.

When readers first glimpse this gentleman in a chapter entitled "Singular History of Mr. Pardew," the first reference to him is from distance with the narrator stressing that neither he nor anyone else knows the most basic things about him: "There are some men whose lives are altogether mysterious. How do they come by their daily bread? No one knows, and yet they are always respectably dressed [...]. Their very wives, perhaps, are ignorant of the paths they tread in the course of their morning's business" (67). With the latter mere conjecture even though it is probably true as shown a few pages on, Pardew prefers to visit his mistress rather than his wife. Pardew thus seems an only outwardly respectable character. His physical description proves scarcely more favorable: at the age of about fifty, he seems to have dyed his hair and has "a hard grey eye that suggested its owner would brook no interference" (67).

Moreover, the reader is mostly denied access to Pardew's thoughts; even the omniscient narrator claims not to know what he is about. Sometimes, the character is even doubly removed from the reader, who is only presented with the impression of some people who happen to be on the spot: "A [man living in] Tooley-Street, a cabman [...] or one of the waggoners [...] who poked his head through the Black Dog's half-open door [...] would perhaps have remarked that the relation between Mr. Pardew and the landlord and his wife was rather peculiar" (292). This ominous introduction turns out to be quite true since the landlord seems afraid of Pardew, who manages to appear cruel even in his small talk about a sword the landlord owns: "'Feel that on your neck and you would know about it,' Mr. Pardew observed pleasantly" (293), with the application of the adverb indicating that Pardew is quite the opposite of a pleasant man.

Despite many indications that Pardew is a villain whom the reader should not identify with, we are not faced with what Roland Barthes would call a "readerly text" marked by redundancies. Although the distance the narrator assumes to this character is in accord with Pardew's illicit actions, he is not presented as a villain throughout. After all, he does display many of the trappings as well as the position of the hero. Most importantly, Pardew turns out the only character managing to fool everyone and escape even the very efficient police officer, who in the end remarks "that Mr. Pardew was a cool one and no mistake" (407). This might be put down as the opinion of just one – albeit positive – character were the omniscient narrator not to endorse this view with his final comment on this gentleman: "There are, perhaps, worse epitaphs." (407)

A similar ambivalence is discernible in the representation of Esther and Mrs. Ireton, who in many ways serve as counterparts to Pardew's attitudes. In contrast to the presentation of Pardew, the distance between the narrator (and, presumably, the reader) and these two characters is diminished by the use of narrative devices. Both are favored with several chapters featuring them as the sole focalizer or, in Isabel's case, even narrator of her own story. The first, called "Esther's Story," begins with her experience as a young girl travelling to a new position as a servant; the reader first meets Esther making her lonely way to Dixey's estate unaware of just how she will be exploited. From then on, she is portrayed as a meek, sensible, good-natured girl who wants to do good to everybody and willingly steps in when others are ill. Esther therefore embodies characteristics highly esteemed in Western cultures; moreover, she is shown in a vulnerable position; on her own in a house full of servants who have no reason to treat her kindly. In addition, her point of view is presented in a very immediate way: in contrast to all of the earlier chapters in which the narrator comments overtly on what is happening, Esther's view is given without any narrator intrusions.

However, even Esther displays negative traits and behaves in inexplicable ways. When living on ill-gotten money with William in a house in London, she does not treat her servant kindly – in fact, she seems to behave rather like the bad mistresses she herself experienced. Moreover, Esther has witnessed the predicament and unfair treatment of Isabel Ireton at first hand – but still refrains from helping her when having the opportunity to do so. It would therefore be difficult to support Esther's perspective whole-heartedly even though the text presents her in a more favorable light than nearly all other characters.

With Isabel Ireton, the impact of direct access to the character's thoughts is even more pronounced. Mrs. Ireton is first introduced as an attractive wife. At that stage, her faults are commented on; for her liveliness also results in witty remarks that hurt others who thus no longer wish to meet her again. Although she suffers from the death of her only child, her state of mind is presented from the point of view of her husband, who worries about her increasingly strange behavior. From being this object of worry, Isabel later on becomes the subject and narrator of her own sad story. We thus gain a perspective on the logic behind her actions, and share her plight, her loneliness and her attempts to occupy her mind when imprisoned in Dixey's attic without books or other diversions. Interestingly, she is the only character allowed to speak in her own voice. Her account comes across as pathetic in that she does not deny that there is something wrong with her: "I have been very ill. That is what they tell me, I daresay it must be true, for there is so much that has vanished from my mind that only sickness could have dragged it from me. It is not for want of thinking..." (167). She apparently cannot bear thinking about her lost husband and child and instead resorts back to the "golden times" when she lived with "Papa" and tried to be everything a good woman should be. She does not even know what she could do if she managed to flee; she admits to herself that where she should go "I have not the least idea in the world" (257). When Isabel – after two chapters as the narrator of her own story – is once again portrayed from the outside as a self-immersed, strange woman, the reader cannot but ask himself/herself whether the loneliness in Dixey's attic has contributed to an acceleration of her illness or whether the view from outside is merely inadequate. Whether Isabel is mad remains an open question even while it is clear that her concerns and attitudes form a foil against which the opinions of other can be measured.

4 Functions of literary works with regard to cognition

Should one consider to what extent novels might improve our understanding of attitudes towards and the functions of money, some tentative answers are feasible.[3] I hope to have already conveyed that a work of fiction achieves more than just an illustration of the workings of money as a means of exchange. One might certainly adopt this novel as an introduction to money markets – and the possibilities of deceit – in the 1860s; but the knowledge gathered in this way would have to be affirmed by other sources. This, however, does not represent the most important function of fiction in terms of cognition. There are, instead, several points I would now like to emphasize:

First, a novel not only presents the selected attitudes and actions of various characters, thereby making it easier to concentrate on salient properties; it also interrelates them with each other. In contrast to descriptions given in other discourses, this makes it possible to consider a host of factors that would not come to the fore if one were to choose an approach governed by, for instance, religion, finance or economics since these fields contain their own rules of selection, methodology and argumentation. Although one might not agree with Niklas Luhmann, who holds that money is the medium of communication in the economy, with the event being the payment (Luhmann 1988: 14, 52), it is quite obvious that an economic analysis of the quality of money would come up with different results and be limited to a more restricted focus. In spite of its own selectivity, literature integrates facts and data gleaned from several discourses, providing a

---

3 In this brief essay, I can only outline a few affordances of literature with regard to cognition. Some others I mention in V. Nünning, 2009, 145–168; but it is also important to take into account the characteristics of the narrative mode of thinking (*sensu* Jerome Bruner) and other aspects as well. Moreover, in a longer essay, the aspect of emotional engagement and the consequences of the de-pragmatization dominating the reception of literature would also have to be considered.

more integrative approach.[4] If we look for events connected with money in Taylor's novel, we find them not in references to money exchange and payment but rather in the steps leading up to transactions as well as in its consequences and in the subsequent usages of money.

Second, a novel such as *Kept* exemplifies the implications and consequences of different attitudes towards money. This concerns not just the relationships between different characters; it also involves showing the interrelations between attitudes towards money and other phenomena like physical and mental well-being, self-fashioning, and commanding the respect of others. As thought experiments, fictions serve to embody and exemplify abstract ideas, and to place these in densely described contexts. As far as a modern novel like *Kept* is concerned, this should not be confused with the eighteenth-century dictum that a novel should teach by way of example. When the dual goal of *prodesse et delectare* was once again brought to the fore in order to justify the 'new' genre of the novel, authors and critics presumed that works of fiction directly related to life and taught both proper sentiments and behavior by recourse to characters whose worth could be easily established. This rather simplistic view is contradicted by the density of signifying processes in most novels in which 'the meaning' of a character or event is always fraught with ambiguity.

Third, fictions present a dense description of selected events and characters. Several narrative features are involved in this intricate process. On the one hand, the complexity of the representation is due to the application of narrative means such as focalization (the importance of which has been shown with regard to the evaluation of Mrs. Ireton's behavior) and comments by the narrator.[5] Moreover, the order of the scenes plays an important role in that the impact of the plight of some characters becomes intensified when contrasted with the luxurious positions of others. On a more abstract level, the mode of narration always places

---

4 See Jürgen Link 1988, 284–307; esp. 285–287 as well as Jürgen Link & Ursula Link-Heer 1990: 88–99, esp. 92–96.

5 There are a host of features to be considered; *Kept*, for instance, makes ample use of intertextual references not only to classic works of contemporary fiction (such as John Fowles's *The French Lieutenant's Woman* (1969) and Antonia S. Byatt's *Possession* (1990)), but also with regard to Victorian literature. Most pronounced is Taylor's use of names which refer to fictional or historical characters, thus providing a further feature of relevance to our understanding of the characters. The woman who keeps Sarah as a prostitute, for instance, is called Mayhew, just like the famous Victorian reformer and observer of the London poor; the dean's daughter is called "Miss Marjoribanks," thus referring us to the ordered (and religious) world of Mrs. Oliphant's novels, and the brutal clerk Robert Grace shares part of his name with Grace Poole, who served as the keeper of the most famous Victorian woman in the attic, Bertha, in Charlotte Brontë's novel *Jane Eyre* (1847).

characters and events in a story with a specific beginning and end.[6] Novels show – in greater or lesser detail – the emergence of attitudes; they tell the story that led characters to perceive and act in specific ways in given situations. By providing significant roles in histories sometimes resulting in a very idiosyncratic and extreme situation, these enable us to adopt the characters' own perspectives and see some quality of a given, seemingly ordinary phenomenon that may otherwise have hitherto escaped our notice.[7] Even a desperate act such as murder may acquire very different meanings when one knows, for instance, that the victim has for years taunted and abused the murderer.

Fourth, fictions are embedded in a paradox in that they are, as Ian McEwan termed it, simultaneously both specific and universal (2005: 6). As a consequence of the usage of narrative techniques and the privileges of fiction, the events and characters in a text acquire a meaning specific to that work. We are confronted with a particular situation, with characters who are idiosyncratic, and sometimes persist in ideas and actions that a 'normal' human being would shun; plausibility does not always play a role in the make-up of events. Nonetheless, within the story's framework, the characters' motives have to be accepted. Even though we are confronted with extreme situations, we may recognize some salient factors which might enable us to understand fictional characters and, perhaps, some emotion or wish that we recognize in ourselves or others.

Fifth, the fictional rendering of selected events opens up the scope for readers to orient themselves in accordance with the characters and events. Most novels and even short stories contain highly selective and salient features the mutual relationships of which are easier to identify than in the unordered flux of 'real life.' In spite of the ambiguity of most fictional representations, discerning readers may recognize implicit criticism of some characters and actions, as well as the endorsement of others. By means of their selectivity, their fictional privileges and their narrative techniques, novels provide some reference points making it easier to grasp similarities with regard to situations in 'real life' and orient ourselves to others. In sum, they enlarge our understanding of the complexity of issues involved in the attitudes towards and functions of, for instance, money.

---

6 As Hayden White has stressed, the mere choosing of beginning and end and the integration of characters and events in a specific story is not a neutral device; instead, such a choice always exerts some influence on the meaning we ascribe to the parts of the story. Moreover, as Roland Barthes pointed out, in a narrative, *post hoc* is *propter hoc*; "the mainspring of narrative is precisely the confusion of consecution and consequence, what comes *after* being read in narrative as what is *caused by*" (Barthes 1977: 94).

7 I owe this insight to a lecture by Peter Bieri, which he held in the 2008 spring term in Heidelberg (as part of the *Heidelberger Poetik-Vorlesungen*).

However, this does not imply any ease in assigning precise meaning and evaluations to what we read. On the contrary, as a consequence of the complexity of the signifying processes, a work of fiction usually does not present us with simple models of behavior; as a rule, characters are neither 'good' nor 'evil.' In dense descriptions, there are too many issues involved, too many causes to be considered, too many different points of view and evaluations of the same instance. Though one can discern some guiding lines within texts, there are no simple messages even with regard to an apparently simple phenomenon such as monetary exchange. In spite of a number of redundancies, and in spite of the fact that some characters like Esther or Mrs. Ireton are treated more favorably than others, there is an excess of meaning generating the ambiguity and polyvalence that makes coming up with simple answers impossible.

Such a difficulty may well reflect one of the most important cognitive functions of literature. While as readers we may be given many indications that allow us to construct meaning in a specific way, and although we may discern salient facts and relations, these data usually do not add up to a coherent point of view encompassing the knowledge we get throughout the story. We are denied simple solutions. Instead, we have to deal with ambiguity and put up with the impossibility of assigning specific meanings and evaluations that would cover all important aspects. In contrast to (thought) experiments in the natural sciences, there are no conclusive deductions to be drawn. On the contrary, we gain a plethora of ways of evaluating and dealing with money as well as their human costs and consequences. On the one hand, we acquire an understanding of the importance of money in the lives of various characters, and may enhance our own ability to understand ourselves and others as well as orient ourselves in similar situations in real life. On the other hand, we have to accept the fact that there are no general answers even to a question as simple as the quality of money, and that any improvement in our understanding does not endow us with the means to pass simple judgments about either the attitudes of others or their lives.[8]

---

8 Literature can fulfil very different functions, such as taking stock of current attitudes towards money, drawing upon many spheres apart from the world of finance, and largely confirming existing attitudes. German scholar Hubert Zapf, who takes a more optimistic view on literature, distinguishes between three main functions of literature: the representation and critical balancing of deficits, contradictions and deformations, which he terms the "cultural-critical metadiscourse"; the confrontation of systems of power with a holistic-pluralistic approach, or "imaginative counter-discourse"; and the feeding back and reintegrating of the repressed into the whole system of cultural discourses, or "reintegrative inter-discourse" (Zapf 2005: 67–78).

Works cited

Barthes, Roland (1977) "Introduction to the Structural Analysis of Narratives" [1966], in *Image Music Text*, trans. S. Heath (NY: Hill and Wang), 79–124.

Eagleton, Terry (1990) *The Ideology of the Aesthetic* (Oxford: Blackwell).

Elgin, Catherine Z. (2007) "The Laboratory of the Mind," in *A Sense of the World: Essays on Fiction, Narrative, and Knowledge,* ed. John Gibson et al. (NY: Routledge), 43–54.

Ette, Ottmar (2007) "Literaturwissenschaft als Lebenswissenschaft: Eine Programmschrift im Jahr der Geisteswissenschaften." *Lendemains* 125, 7–32.

Jannidis, Fotis (2008) "Zuerst Collegium Logicum. Zu Tilmann Köppes Beitrag 'Vom Wissen *in* Literatur'," *Zeitschrift für Germanistik* XVII, 373–377.

Köppe, Tilmann (2007) "Vom Wissen *in* Literatur," *Zeitschrift für Germanistik* XVII, 398–410.

Laqué, Stephan (2009) *The Metaphysics of Isolation: Delimitation, Knowledge and Identity in Twentieth-Century Literature,* Habilitationsschrift (Munich), 183–195.

Link, Jürgen (1988) "Literaturanalyse als Interdiskursanalyse. Am Beispiel des Ursprungs literarischer Symbolik in der Kollektivsymbolik," in *Diskurstheorien und Literaturwissenschaft,* ed. Jürgen Fohrmann and Harro Müller (Frankfurt a.M.: Suhrkamp), 284–307

Link, Jürgen and Ursula Link-Heer (1990) "Diskurs/Interdiskurs und Literaturanalyse," *Zeitschrift für Literaturwissenschaft und Linguistik* 77 , 88–99.

Locatelli, Angela (ed) (2004) *La conoscenza della letteratura/The Knowledge of Literature,* (Bergamo: Sestante).

Luhmann, Niklas (1988) *Die Wirtschaft der Gesellschaft* (Frankfurt a.M.: Suhrkamp).

McEwan, Ian (2005) "Literature, Science and Human Nature," in *The Literary Animal: Evolution and the Nature of Narrative,* ed. Jonathan Gottschall and David Sloan Wilson (Evanston, Ill.: Northwestern University Press), 5–19.

Nünning, Vera (2009) "Literatur als Lebenswissen: Die Bedeutung von Literatur für menschliches Verstehen und Zusammenleben am Beispiel von Ian McEwans *Enduring Love,*" in *Literaturwissenschaft als Lebenswissenschaft. Programm – Projekte – Perspektiven,* ed. Wolfgang Asholt und Ottmar Ette (Tübingen: Narr), 145–168.

Ort, Claus-Michael (1992) "Vom Text zum Wissen. Die literarische Konstruktion sozio-kulturellen Wissens als Gegenstand einer nicht-reduktiven Sozialgeschichte der Literatur," in *Vom Umgang mit Literatur und Literaturgeschichte. Positionen und Perspektiven nach der "Theoriedebatte,"* ed. Lutz Danneberg und Friedrich Vollhardt (Stuttgart: Metzler), 409–441.
"

Taylor, D.J. (2006) *Kept. A Victorian Mystery.* (London: Chatto and Windus).

Zapf, Hubert (2005) "Das Funktionsmodell der Literatur als kultureller Ökologie: Imaginative Texte im Spannungsfeld von Dekonstruktion und Regeneration," in *Funktionen von Literatur: Theoretische Grundlagen und Modellinterpretationen,* ed. Marion Gymnich and Ansgar Nünning (Trier: WVT), 55–78.

Ana Margarida Abrantes
Cognitive Science and How We Think about Money

Most world societies adopt money for performing commercial exchanges and believe that money holds intrinsic value. Just how much and what influences this value in any specific conjuncture is probably best accounted for by economic theories. However, taking a step back and looking at this problem from a cognitive perspective, the question rather becomes: why do we believe that money has value? And we can formulate this still further: while the value of money is related to exchangeability, it is neither fixed by intentionality nor contingent upon the materiality of bills or coins (in this case, their pure reproduction would result in a proportional multiplication of value). In other words, the meaning of value and exchangeability is neither material nor embodied, nor generated by individual cognition but rather a representation established and maintained by social cognition. The belief in value required for a monetary transaction to occur is a phenomenon worth investigating from a cognitive angle. This proves particularly worthwhile at a time when transactions themselves are becoming increasingly virtual, i.e. conceptual, as happens in stock exchanges and in newer environments such as Second Life. Value is established in its conceptualization.

In recent years, findings from cognitive science and from cognitive neuroscience have contributed to enhancing our understanding of the mental processes that prove foundational to economic behaviors even while not exclusive to them: counterfactual thinking, decision making, and intersubjective representation are all examples of such processes. Furthermore, understanding where and how they unfold in the neurotypical brain informs on individual cognition processes. This research interest has given rise to the recent field of neuroeconomics, a field of study that combines economic theory with cutting-edge brain imaging and that aims at describing the neurobiological foundations of economic behavior. As often happens with these new areas of study, the "neuro" part of the designation, continuously enhanced at the speed of technological innovation, opens up new insights into the brain's biological processes. Nevertheless, when it comes to complex phenomena such as money, studying the brain on its own falls short of the objectives. Analyzing what we do with it, namely the mind, proves of equal importance. Moreover, this extends to what the mind does with other minds and how a collective cognitive synergy – which we may also name human culture – is capable of such intriguing and sophisticated creations as money.

Answering the question of how we think about money goes beyond the description of our behavioral interactions with it or any account of the observable brain activation supporting this interaction. We also need to situate both brain and behavioral facts within a larger framework that includes an account of the role money plays as an institutional symbol and a social phenomenon. These are the topics approached in this chapter.

1 What money is (for)

Money forms such an obvious part of our social existence that we hardly ever think about what it actually is. In all its forms – from coins and banknotes to credit cards or Linden Dollars – money is a representation of value and a means that can be exchanged for potentially anything else. First and foremost, money represents a commodity deployed in exchanges (of either goods or services), with the obvious advantage over barter as it does not remain contingent upon a symmetry of needs (also termed the "double coincidence of wants" in the jargon). Money enables the immediate acquisition of a product by the buyer, and ensures the seller the same potential of exchange, delayed to a future moment, and involving a different individual. The exchange thus established extends beyond the constraints of a one-on-one relationship. Money enables exchanges across dense social networks, ruled by norms other than personal acquaintance. In fact, we give most of our money to strangers.

The value of money arises from this potential for exchangeability and not from the actual materiality of its forms. A twenty Euro bill has no inherent value in the sense that, in and of itself, it remains a piece of paper unable to directly respond to any immediate need. Initial forms of money, in contrast, were actual commodities: precious metals, cereals or spices served as forms of currency and a trade-off for services or other goods. Their value was intrinsic as they could or would ultimately be used as materials: metals were melted down into new objects, such as weapons or jewelry while spices added an aesthetic flavor to the functional need for nourishment. In these forms of money, the value lies in the physical tokens exchanged. With the progress of history and the increased complexity of social organization, such forms of money were replaced by progressively virtual forms of representing value. Representative money had its value backed by gold or silver, and could ultimately be exchanged for these metals. One step further in the detachment of value from the token of money came with the introduction of *fiat* money. Here, exchangeable, backup metals no longer establish value of money, which instead, becomes normalized by a government order or fiat within the boundaries of a political region, typically a country. The value of money is thus established by an act of speech and is held in place by shared belief in the value of that linguistic act. Whereas one could take little pieces of commodity money for the value inherently held (and thus gradually and proportionally depreciate its initial value), this no longer applies to material symbols of value, such as banknotes: half a banknote does not count as half the value of the whole note; instead, it ceases to hold any value at all.[1]

The introduction of the fiat principle made clearer how the value of money lies in a shared belief, instead of the inherent value of a token or individual intentionality: were this the case, then a simple photocopy machine would solve all our money problems. Instead, this is not even regarded only as naivety, but as forgery, a form of deceit that society handles as a crime.

The shared belief in the representational value of money remains tacit in most cases. One is only led to consider this dimension when major changes occur, for example, when the Euro replaced many European national currencies. The value of banknotes and coins, which had thenceforth been used as currency, overnight retained only sentimental value (a value, nonetheless): those anchors no longer served as money. The default experience of money, though, is rather more transitive or dative than predicative: we tend to conceive of money in terms of what we can do or get in exchange for it, or how we can give it to others (either as a specific profiling within the former scenario, or as an exchange with the other as the ultimate point of arrival) rather than what it in the first place actually is.

2 Money matters – neuroeconomics

While money represents an abstraction, an idea with ever fewer material anchors and taking an increasingly virtual profile, in contrast, the behaviors it prompts are very concrete and manifold, ranging from individual transactions to phenomena such as the recent (or current) global economic crisis. Such large scale challenges to the world economy prompt the need to understand just what leads up to such crises so as to find a solution for the original problem and to prevent new crises from happening. Economic theories are born out of such needs. More recently, the spectacular boom in neuroscience has encouraged many fields of expertise and experience. The progress in imaging methods has enabled a view of the brain unthinkable just three decades ago, and the great investment in technological progress correlates with the great expectations as a new Grail for an-

---

1 Chipping away at material symbols for their value does prove possible in other cases. One needs only to think about the Berlin Wall, multiplied in infinite pieces that continue to proliferate. There is, however, one difference: the value of these pieces is not economic or prospective, but representational and historical. Thus, the metonymy works in this case.

swers to the many challenges and problems of social organization and, more generally, of human experience. Economics is just one of the fields looking at neuroscience with this same hope reflected in the emergence of the new field of neuroeconomics.[2] This area combines economics, psychology and neuroscience and seeks to describe how people reason and decide on economic matters. Neuroeconomics describes behaviors and correlates them to neurobiological evidence and ultimately strives to recognize patterns and make predictions about economic performance. By making generalizations from individual occurrences, this field of study attempts to describe both individual economic behavior and larger scale economic events and in this sense does prove informative as regards speculation and investment decisions at both the individual and macroscale levels. In any case, the ultimate goals of such studies remain quite pragmatic, in particular, improving levels of performance across both levels.

The challenging question asked by neuroeconomics is: how can observation of the individual brain at work generate insights into phenomena on such a social scale? This question is itself subject to further specification: just what kind of evidence is attained by such observations? Just what kind of information does it actually make available? Let us consider two examples of current neuroeconomics research topics: the impact of emotion on behavior, and the issue of trust.

Neuroscientist Brian Knutson has centered his research on the subcortical circuitry involved in anticipation and decision processes. His team's work has shown how the nucleus accumbens, a subcortical area of the brain involved in reward, pleasure and addiction, is activated when people anticipate making money (Knutson et al. 2001). The activation is proportional both to the amount of money people expect to make as well as to the individual degree of enthusiasm involved in that anticipation: the more money you expect and the more excited you are at the prospect, the more activated this brain area becomes.

Thus, there is a neural substrate mapping the expectation of value. That this activation can revert to self-stimulation may help explain why certain money associated risky behaviors (e. g. gambling) share features with certain compulsive conditions. Brain activation is therefore suggestive or predictive of financial behavior and choice.

In a later study, Knutson and his team found that when a subject is exposed to an alternative stimulus before performing an economic decision making task, priming occurs: when the stimulus is positive, the subject tends to take higher

---

2 The same tendency can be observed in other fields sharing the same prefix: neuroesthetics, neuroanthropology, neuroethics, neurolinguistics or neurotheology are just some examples of parallel research fields seeking to add the methodological insight of neuroscience to the study of their traditional objects.

risks in a subsequent gambling task. (Knutson et al. 2008). Therefore, reward cues unrelated to the task at hand influence risk behaviors, and the neurobiological process by which this occurs involves an activation of the nucleus accumbens, the reward center of the brain.

Paul J. Zak, another neuroeconomics pioneer, focuses his interest on the issue of trust and how this influences economic behavior (Zak 2008a, 2008b). Zak, who coined the term "neuroeconomics," studied the correlation between biology and behavior in decision-making processes involving risks and relationships with others, normally strangers. Intrigued by the variations in national levels of trust from different countries with respect to their overall economic well-being, Zak and his team set out to study the phenomenon from a neurobiological perspective on a smaller, more interpersonal scale. He used a simple behavioral trust game involving giving money to a stranger and correlating the degree of trust and trustworthiness subjects place on strangers with the release of oxytocin, a neurotransmitter associated with bonding and empathy.[3] Placing trust in others or feeling that others trust us causes the brain to release oxytocin. In turn, this physiological mechanism triggers generosity, thus influencing economic decisions: we tend to give more to strangers.[4]

In *Moral Markets: the Critical Role of Values in the Economy*, Zak edits the contributions of several scholars from various fields (e. g. anthropology, primatology, philosophy) to make the claim that the model Western economy is based on moral values and not just a set of cultural rules learned through reasoning and thought (i.e. the Kantian way), but instead values deeply ingrained in the biology of the species. This thesis in itself deserves a fairer formulation and even more a thorough discussion, which the limits of the present essay prevent. We can, however, make two points: the first deals with the relationship between innate values and social cognition. Human beings are highly social beings, not just because they depend on the group (and on strong kinship bonds) for survival through an unusually long period of maturation, from birth through to sexual maturity, but also because this period becomes even longer when considering the time taken for the cultural maturity of human beings.

---

3 Oxytocin, a mammalian hormone, is a neurotransmitter, i.e. a chemical substance involved in the transfer of the potential for action between neurons. The substance relates to female reproduction (released during labor and breastfeeding), and also to sexual arousal, bonding, and nurturing behavior. The release of this neurotransmitter is correlated with an inhibition of fear (thus suggesting a greater willingness to risk).

4 The experiment is described in Zak 2008a. The author also accounts for how he came to hypothesize the correlation between trust and oxytocin, especially through studies on animal behavior, particularly voles and their differences in mating and social behavior.

Human culture is very sophisticated and its cumulative learning and imparting requires a very elaborate social setting. Should we prove as much a result of our biology as of the environment that surrounds us, as Alva Noë claims (2009), it also holds true that the human environment is deeply social by nature. Evolutionarily, a question regarding two competing motivations arises. The evolutionary psychologist Jonathan Burns formulates this clearly:

> The individual experiences two contrasting motivations in attempting to negotiate the social world: on the one hand, there is an evolved drive to be part of a group (which brings security, companionship, mating opportunities and greater access to resources); while on the other hand, there is the drive to be more successful than others within the group (who compete for rank, food and mates). [...] Thus, the group-living or social individual needs to develop a finely tuned ability to detect, interpret and respond optimally to the motivations of others within that group. (Burns 2007: 87)

In other words, "character values such as honesty, trust, reliability and fairness," which is to say "our innate sense of fair play" (Zak 2008: xvii), which Zak maintains monitor economic processes and transactions, must be framed in this evolutionary context. Human empathy is hardly naively good (or moral); instead, it proves useful and advantageous to the individual.

This leads to the second point requiring consideration, the concept of "value," an inherently cultural concept (in the sense of human culture, not of different cultures). We will come back to this issue below. Here, we need to ask whether an "innate sense of values" (Zak 2008b: xii) is equivalent to the values themselves ("honesty, trust, reliability, and fairness," xvii): or whether the latter are the result of the cultural editing of the first.[5]

---

5 Zak further discusses the interweaving of emotion an reasoning in morality. An example from the introduction is particularly striking: "An important, consistent finding from neuroethics in the past ten years is that the Kantian notion of morality as being learned by rational deduction is generally incorrect" (Zak 2008b: xii). The author continues: "Many moral decisions have both cognitive and emotional components, including market decisions. For example, if your paycheck this month had an extra $10,000, you would likely feel joy ("extra money!"), and then perhaps fear ("I know they'll find me!"), and then maybe a cost-benefit *calculation* ("if I cash the check and play dumb, I can always return the money if they find out"). This might be followed by an emotionally weighted decision ("I didn't work for this money so I'm getting this unfairly, and *therefore* I should return it"). Not all of us would go through all these stages, but this example is meant to show that emotions and higher cognition are integrated and evolved to help us solve complex problems, including moral dilemmas" (Zak 2008b: xii–xiii, my emphasis). Zak proposes that decision making is *not* a purely rational process, but recruits emotions as well (an echo of Damasio's "somatic marker hypothesis" – Damasio 1995; see also Lehrer 2009). The example shows that the initial emotional response (happiness) is then modulated through reasoning

"So what?," the economists ask. What good is there in knowing what specific configuration of the brain lights up, or what hormone rush shapes a person's decision to give or to invest? For one, this may help understand the gap between the common sense perception that economic decisions are pondered and rational (after all, money matters), and the observation that these decisions are nevertheless often impulsive, risky and sometimes plain wrong. And even more interestingly, such decisions are sometimes just right even when we find no better words to describe our options other than a "hunch" or "gut feeling."

Moreover, the processes analyzed in neuroeconomics are not exclusive to economics but instead pertain to other domains of human experience. Knowing just what the brain does while making an economic decision, first and foremost constitutes knowing what the brain does in its own right. Nonetheless, the brain on its own hardly matters; it is what we do with it that counts. The mind is caused by the brain but is not ontologically the same as the brain. A rush of oxytocin or an activated nucleus accumbens actually tells us very little whenever we do not correlate these neurobiological processes with actual human experiences of taking chances, surviving recessions or helping out strangers. To this end, we need to inquire as to what it means to be a brained human being in a community of equally equipped humans; in other words, having a mind and being in a culture.

3 Some million-dollar-questions

"It's the economy, stupid!" This famous epilogue might well be adapted to describing the current enthusiasm about neuroscientific approaches to studying complex cognitive processes, such as consciousness, memory, reasoning and decision-making: "It's the brain..."

However, does the brain convey our epilogue? We have yet to ascertain how the brain generates the mind, how neurophysiological structures and the functions they perform give rise to ideas, to representations about reality, which while not being the same as those realities, nonetheless remain real. This represents a true million-dollar-question.

The brain is individual, and so is the mind. Nevertheless, our minds do not only generate ideas; they are engaged in communication, in sharing these ideas

---

("calculation", x "therefore" Y, in his own words), which produces a different outcome from that which one might expect as the result of that initial happiness. It is further relevant to note how important the anticipated evaluative perspective of the Other influences this decision process, throughout (*They*'ll find me", "I *should*"). Emotions certainly play a role in decisions, but so does thinking and intersubjectivity.

with equally equipped minds. This communication encapsulates a potential for exchange materialized in signs deployed for sharing what otherwise would remain as the individual's own mental life and thereby influencing and changing the mental life of others. Our minds have evolved to cooperate with other minds in this way, thus creating collective environments more amenable to an otherwise quite hopeless species; in other words, culture. Attuning to other minds proves of significant importance and hence we become deeply connected to them from our earliest days.[6] In this sense, human thought is shared by nature and is not the result of any individual mind thinking alone. Evolutionary psychologist Michael Tomasello puts forward a poignant example to illustrate this idea:

> If we imagine the forbidden experiment in which a human child grows up on a desert island, miraculously supplied with nutritional and emotional sustenance but in the total absence of contact with other human beings, this child would not invent a language or a complex technology or a complex social institution. [...] The reason that no single child or group of children could on their own in their own lifetimes create any version of a modern human culture and its material and symbolic artifacts is that human cultures are historical products built up over many generations (Tomasello 1999: 512).

A lonely human on a desert island might still hold the potential to learn a language, apply a numerical system or come up with a money system. An individual brain would allow for this potential, but these symbolic creations are only generated and sustained in social contexts. They all imply exchangeability, and this implies the Other.

Therefore, human thinking reaches beyond the individual brain. It consists of representations of things, situations, processes in the world (both external and experienced). The relationship between representation and the referent is based on some principle of authority[7] validating the correspondence. In the case of money, this authority is institutional in terms of ascertaining its value. However, the belief connecting the material anchor to the potential for value precedes this regulation. In the sense that it is not asserted, this may be viewed as tacit. This belief is shared, transcends the individual mind, and is epistemically relevant not by force of conventional agreement but by the recurrent continuity

---

6 This shows at very basic behavioral levels: newborns mirror their caregivers' facial expressions from the very beginning; strangers automatically replicate the menacing or the friendly expression of other strangers; infants attend intensely to the human voice or movement, while they boringly ignore similar stimuli from other sources once their initial curiosity is satisfied.

7 This idea is proposed and thoroughly elaborated in Per Aage Brandt's "semio-cognitive ontology" (in print).

of its practice resulting from a history of exchange. In this sense, money works like language with its usage regulated by institutional norms (government fiat vs. normative grammars or *Sprachgesellschaften*); but its representation, its semiotic potential (money stands for value; words stand for meanings) becomes a shared and assumed truth. The lonely child on Tomasello's island would not come up with either money or language on its own, because not only would the need to exchange value or meaning not arise (exchange being an inherently two-way path), but he would also lack the community of minds needed for such abstract concepts to arise in the first place.

However, where, if not in the brain, is this belief located? And how can it thus be shared? These are further million-dollar-questions. Beliefs are not material but they can materialize in processes or behaviors. Just like ideas, they can be shared and simultaneously thrive in different minds. These beliefs are in themselves not located in the mind and far less so in any individual mind. Money is not in the brain in that sense. However, they do exist as our economic transactions and our communicative exchanges daily reveal. Their recurrent updating in the practice of exchanges over time endows them with the epistemic force of being true: words have meaning (right or wrong), money has value (positive or negative). That this is the case is not merely the result of any tacit agreement between two parties, but also stems from the acknowledging observation of a third party, which recognizes the structured fulfillment of that value potential in the exchange. This observation, multiplied in practice and extended through time (and, as Tomasello claims, any single generation would not prove time enough to create the cumulative cultural environment for which humans develop genetic adaptations), materializes in the shared belief that words are exchangeable as representations for what they themselves are not; and that money is exchangeable whether for either immediate or potential objects. This belief represents a grounding condition for the exchanges edited by cultures (e.g. in different languages, texts; in different currencies, transactions), for which other cultures find equivalences.

Hence, when dealing with money, we begin with the belief that money has value. However before we set out to invest, speculate, give or buy, how do we conceptualize money? Another million-dollar-question. In order to account for why and how we conceive money, i.e. in order to understand how we make sense of money as a human conceptual and cultural creation, and moreover what we mentally perform when making money-related decisions, we need to situate money and economics within the network of concepts of human experience. The experience of dealing with money is a cultural experience, and therefore, by making cognitive insights into money, we are necessarily peeking into the brain/mind as much as we are peeking into culture. Moreover, as part of the economic system, money is a higher order concept (such as justice, for instance) and, in order to be grasped, needs to be correlated with the more basic domains of human experience as conceptualized and represented by the human mind.

We understand the world and ourselves in mutual interaction in terms of a network of related semantic domains, schematically structured and finite. In cognitive science, there have already been several attempts at describing this network, for instance, the theory of frame semantics by Charles Fillmore (1982) and the theory of basic and abstract semantic domains by Ronald Langacker (1987). One further account is that proposed by Per Aage Brandt (2004), who claims that we construe and make sense of our experience as naturally cultural beings in terms of a structured architecture of domains integrated at different levels of complexity. On a primary experiential level, we conceptualize experience in terms of a physical domain (of causal forces, objects and space, movement), a social domain (an intentional world of collective action, in which we participate), a mental world (a theater of the mind where imagined contents are performed and the interaction between ourselves and our external perceptions is enacted, of the memories and emotions involved in them), and a performative speech act domain (structured by dynamic schemas of intersubjective volition, permission and prohibition).

These basic semantic domains are integrated according to the principle of "maximally abstract notional meanings at minimal combinatory costs" (Brandt 2004: 52), instigating a second generation of anthropologically relevant domains: the domain of work, a social space where physical objects are manipulated and transformed and social identities are established; the domain of love, the integration of the social with the domain of the acts of speech, a private, domestic space where interaction and attunement are established with persons in collective constellations (from circles of friends to groups of colleagues and, more centrally, love, kinship and relative relations); and finally the domain of worship, in which causal phenomena interact with speech acts, so that physical causality becomes in a sense manipulable through performance.

From this second layer of domains – of practical actions – an integrated layer arises, based on the intersubjective exchanges established in the areas where the practical domains pair up. One of these is the domain of economic exchange: the objects produced in the domain of work (modeled in turn by the physical and the social domain) are acquired and stored in the domestic domain and eventually returned to the social domain, generating a market. The exchange of signs between the domestic and the worship domains generates the domain of beauty and aesthetics: the subjects offer goods to the sacred instance in exchange for magic signs, such as magic gestures and words, even names. Finally, the integration of the domains of work and worship gives rise to the domain of acts and their jurisdiction. These acts are compared and categorized by the binary opposition of right and wrong, and they entail a speech act value, such as obligations and prohibitions, while others, such as criminalization and punishment conform to a normative code, namely law, which inherits its deontic potential from the domain of worship.

These levels of exchange – markets, art, courts – constitute the foundations of the cultural life of a society, the socio-functional structures ensuring collective existence in a community. The domain of economy is thus one of the domains situated at the level of exchanges along with the level of jurisdiction and the domain of art. One notion proves common to these three domains, namely the notion of value, and the polysemy of this term may well represent an indicator of the same level at which these domains are situated: exchangeability value in the case of economics, moral values as regulators in jurisdiction and the order of life in a social community, and the aesthetic values, implied in the significance we assign to a work of art, which differs from the way we subjectively express our liking or disliking of it (for example, explaining how we can be elated by a sense of pleasure – not joy – when listening to a deeply sad piece of music – a difference drawing on Kant's distinction between beauty and the sublime).

In all these three levels of exchange, money circulates as a measure of value (economic, moral or aesthetic); this goes without saying for the economics domain. In the domain of jurisdiction, money may serve as a regulator of infraction, necessary to re-establishing the moral balance: fines and other monetary penalties work in this way. They are different from economic exchanges both given their deontic imprint and their reverse temporal sequence: you have to pay (back) for what you did wrong (as opposed to paying ahead for something you wish to acquire). The difference is linguistically marked in a significant way: even while the core syntactic structure remains the same (to pay X to Z for Y), both prepositions and modal verbs account for a significant difference: penance is not prophylactic; it is always remediatory.

In the case of aesthetics (and beyond the act of placing a price tag on a work of art, which would actually return us to the domain of economics), money assumes a dative profile, and is in this case either materially transformed into a gift (actual or potential, like a gift card), or mentally transformed, thus reconceptualized as a donation, an endowment, patronage, or philanthropy. The linguistic modulation in this case indicates the diverse aesthetic potential. Even if, in the end, these forms of exchange are economic (as they prompt a return – a thank you note, an act of public recognition), they are firstly considered in aesthetic terms. This differentiates them from functional, pragmatic transactions as they stand out from the "taking"-based norms of economic exchange.

4 Give or take? On excess, gift and philanthropy

The year 1950 saw the publication of an influential essay on the principles of gift-giving and obliged reciprocity as motors of exchange in archaic societies: *Essai sur le don. Forme et raison de l'échange dans les societies archaïques*. The author, French sociologist and anthropologist Marcel Mauss, described potlatch in indigenous tribes of Polynesia and the Northwestern Pacific, a ritual of gift exchange that sediments bonds in the community. This institution worked in these societies as a general theory of obligation, which ensured a balance of possessions that reaffirmed social position and the equilibrium of goods. This highly structured ritual of exchange created a juridical bond, as well as a spiritual link insofar as the gifts were regarded as extensions of the soul (Mauss 1990 [1950]: 13]. This complex exchange thus encompassed all three dimensions of economics, law and spirituality. Furthermore, given the plural value entailed in the objects exchanged, these were not viewed as inert but rather considered as parts in a dynamic circulation. Giving was in this sense as obligatory as taking (or accepting), which in turn required reciprocity.[8]

This transience, the eternal circulation of gifts (in which the souls and the objects were mixed, fused) ensured a balance in which even excess would be resolved in highly theatrical ceremonies of spending and giving.

Modern society regards these rituals and traditions as distant and foreign given the clear distinction between non-gratuitous giving and the gift instituted since the beginning of Western civilization. In fact, our contemporary perception is that we structure our society more by a principle of taking (highly structured and regulated) than by a principle of giving, and the exchange of gifts is regarded as an additional fact reinforcing the balance of social organization. Nonetheless, in his concluding essay on gifts, Marcel Mauss enumerates several examples of giving rituals as remainders, in Western societies, of the complexity of gift exchange in so-called primitive communities. Even the functional domain of work, institutionalized as we know it today from the eve of industrialization, saw such manifestations of giving: in the way businesses themselves established social benefits for their workers and by this "sacrifice" ensuring a morality with which early industrial law was in conflict. Such institutions were not established

---

8 "Et toutes ces institutions n'expriment uniquement qu'un fait, un régime social, une mentalité définie: c'est que tout, nourriture, femmes, enfants, biens, talismans, sol, travail, services, offices sacerdotaux et rangs, est matière à transmission et reddition. Tout va et vient comme s'il y avait échange constant d'une matière spirituelle comprenant choses et hommes, entre les clans et les individus, répartis entre les rangs, les sexes et les générations." (Mauss 2002 [1950]: 19)

on a principle of pure functionalism, but resulted from the need to balance juris-diction with morality.

In fact, even in what are considered the most selfish societies, where indi-vidualist citizens seem geared for taking, the principle of giving remains and still manifests itself in different ways. Even some commercial transactions reveal this dialectic of giving and reciprocating: bargaining, for instance, is based on the principle of refusing a fixed price, an act that would in this context be regard-ed as naivety or even offense: at the Bazaar, the predisposition for giving present-ed by the buyer, willing to give money to the seller in exchange for a certain good, is met by the latter in the compromise to decrease the price asked. Depriv-ing the seller of this opportunity to "give back" to the buyer (by lowering the price), can thus be regarded as offensive. This reciprocation can also be seen in certain contemporary consumer society contexts: the bargaining is here re-placed by the bargain or the special offer (a special gift?). In this sense, the *homo oeconomicus* mentioned by Mauss is a recent invention.[9]

Giving is resilient. One last question could be addressed: the place and role of money in the context of giving. The situations in which a material gift equates with money, with the actual pecuniary value expended on its acquisition by the giver, are culturally marked and regulated. Giving a present is not the same as giving the equivalent amount of money that such a present costs. The mere re-placement of the object by the equivalent in money is viewed as strange, inad-equate, even offensive. This is related with the exchangeability potential of money; money lives from its transience,[10] it is not kept for its own sake but as a potential something that may be acquired in the future (and which by default is chosen by the receiver, and no longer as an extension of the giver, i.e. of his/her intention of giving, or the care of his/her choice – something that might be regarded as a remainder of the "soul of the giver in the object" in the context of the potlatch). The object offered as a gift lives in the present moment of the ex-change and reaches its endpoint, its purpose as a gift in the act of giving: the object is the end in itself (even when inducing reciprocation).

---

9 "Ce sont nos sociétés d'Occident qui ont, très récemment, fait de l'homme un 'animal écon-omique'. Mais nous ne sommes pas encore tous des êtres de ce genre. Dans nos masses et dans nos élites, la dépense pure et irrationnelle est de pratique courante; elle est encore caractéris-tique des quelques fossiles de notre noblesse. L'*homo oeconomicus* n'est pas derrière nous, il est devant nous; comme l'homme de la morale et du devoir; comme l'homme de la science et de la raison. L'homme a été très longtemps autre chose ; et il n'y a pas bien longtemps qu'il est une machine, compliquée d'une machine à calculer." (Mauss 2002 [1950]: 100].

10 This transience is mentioned by Mauss in another essay on the origins of money: "La mon-naie [...] c'est aussi une valeur d'usage, [...] le moyen de se procurer d'autres valeurs fongibles, transitoires, des jouissances, des prestations." (Mauss 2001 [1914]: 7)

The same works in the reverse direction: alms are prototypically a money gift, as they entail the potential object, which will by default be chosen by the receiver at an opportune moment in the future. In contrast to the gift, which re-affirms the affective bond of the subjects, alms presuppose the likeliness that the two anonymous subjects will not meet again. Unlike the gift, which involves the self, the act of giving alms is a truly selfless act (and the epitome of generosity, in that sense).

In both cases – of gifts and alms – swapping the object and the equivalent money of its cost is possible: one can give money for a present, or any good (usu-ally food or a primary good) instead of alms. However, this replacement is not obvious and for this reason requires the explicit agreement by both parties, a verbal exchange, in which both take turns to legitimize and formalize it.

The prevalence of giving is deeply human and stable across the different ways in which cultures edit exchanges in different rituals of giving and reciproci-ty. In this prevalence, one can recognize the inherent cognitive foundation of human empathy, enabled by a social brain in a network of equally equipped brains, which have given rise to a contingent mental life foundationally ground-ed on a principle of exchange: of material goods as much as of knowledge. In evolutionary terms, this exchange is the basis of sharing, an adaptation of the species, which achieves evolutionary success through the learning of an accumu-lated cultural heritage. Human empathy is thus adaptive. Giving is one of its out-comes, and money is just one of its tools. It is a pervasive feature of human na-ture, to which culture lends expression.

Works cited

Brandt, Per Aage (2004) "The architecture of semantic domains," in *Spaces, Domains and Meaning* (Bern: Peter Lang), 33–67.

Brandt, Per Aage (forthcoming) "The world seen from within – A semio-cognitive ontology," paper presented at the Workshop organized by the Centre de Linguistique Anthropologique et Sociolinguistique (LIAS-IMM EHESS/CNRS), Semiotic Perspectives between Social Cognition and Practices (Paris, 7–8 June 2010).

Burns, Jonathan (2007) *The Descent of Madness. Evolutionary Origin of Psychosis and the Social Brain* (London, NY: Routledge).

Damasio, Antonio (1995) *Descartes' Error. Emotion, Reason and the Human Brain* (NY: Harper Perennial).

Fillmore, Charles (1982) "Frame semantics," in *Linguistics in the Morning Calm*, ed. Linguistic Society of Korea (Seoul: Hanshin), 111–138.

Glimcher, Paul W. et al (2009) *Neuroeconomics. Decision Making and the Brain* (London, San Diego, Burlington: Elsevier).

Knutson, Brian, Charles M. Adams, Grace W. Fong and Daniel Hommer (2001) "Anticipation of Increasing Monetary Reward Selectively Recruits Nucleus Accumbens," *The Journal of Neuroscience* 21, RC159.

Knutson, Brian, G. Elliott Wimmer, Camelia M. Kuhnen and Piotr Winkielman (2008) "Nucleus accumbens activation mediates the influence of reward cues on financial risk taking," *NeuroReport* 19, 509–513.

Langacker, Ronald (1987) *Foundations of Cognitive Grammar*, 1: *Theoretical Prerequisites*. (Stanford: Stanford University Press).

Lehrer, Jonah (2009) *The Decisive Moment. How the Brain Makes up Its Mind* (Edinburgh: Canongate Books).

Mauss, Marcel (1914) "Les origines de la notion de monnaie." Institut français d'anthropologie. Comptes-rendus des séances, II, tome I, supplément à *L'Anthropologie*, 1914, 25, 14–19. http://classiques.uqac.ca/classiques/mauss_marcel/oeuvres_2/oeu vres_2_02/origine_notion_monnaie.html (accessed 10 January 2014).

Mauss, Marcel (1950) *Essai sur le don. Forme et raison de l'échange dans les sociétés archaïques* (Paris: PUP). http://classiques.uqac.ca/classiques/mauss_marcel/socio_et_an thropo/2_essai_sur_le_don/essai_sur_le_don.pdf (accessed 10 January 2014).

Noë, Alva (2009) *Out of Our Heads. Why You Are Not Your Brain and Other Lessons from the Biology of Consciousness* (NY: Hill and Wang)

Sowell, Thomas (2007) *Basic Economics. A Common Sense Guide to Economics* (NY: Basic Books).

Smith, Barry and John Searle (2003) "The Construction of Social Reality: An Exchange," *American Journal of Economics and Sociology* 62.1, 285–309.

Tomasello, Michael (1999) "The Human Adaptation for Culture," *Annual Review of Anthropology* 28: 509–29.

Zak, Paul J. (June 2008a) "The Neurobiology of Trust," *Scientific American*, 88–95.

Zak, Paul J. (2008b) *Moral Markets: The Critical Role of Values in the Economy* (Princeton: Princeton University Press).

Cátia Ferreira
Second Life:
The Emergence of a New Moneyscape

> The modern consumer society turned the
> spending of money not only into a central
> economic practice, but into a dynamic, complex
> cultural and social activity.
>
> (Zelizer 2011: 137)

In *The Philosophy of Money* (1900), Georg Simmel conceptualized money as a
symbol and analyzed its effects upon people and society. Simmel proposes
that money has transformed real exchange into a symbolical act, with the abstraction of money leading to the rise of a new form of social interaction – economic exchange. Social development has been shaped by the money factor as
"with money in our pocket, we are free [...]" (Simmel 1991: 23). Money thereby
became one of the most prominent features of modern societies, but regardless
of the social evolution in the present era – an era characterized by the massifi-
cation of new communication technologies –, the OECD considers that the three
classical functions of money are unlikely to change in any near future. Yet new
digital forms of payment will continue to grow, thus making the economy increasingly more global. Nevertheless, money will continue to be a unit of account, a means of payment, and a storage of value (Miller et al. 2002).

In order to understand the new global cultural economy, Arjun Appadurai
suggests an alternative model to explore the relationship between the various
"scapes" of contemporary cultural global flows, which should certainly not be
perceived as homogenous as they only occur under specific conditions. Appadurai suggests that "they occur in and through the growing disjunctures among eth-
noscapes, technoscapes, financescapes, mediascapes, and ideoscapes" (Appadurai 1996: 37). The suffix "scapes" was chosen to represent the flows of late
capitalism: ethnoscape – the landscape of the persons populating a shifting
world; mediascape – the distribution of electronic capabilities to produce and
disseminate information as well as the world images created by these media;
technoscape – the global configuration of technology; financescape – the landscape of global and fluid capital; and ideoscape – a "scape" consisting of the
global master-narrative for understanding and representing the world (Appadurai 1996). Taking this conceptualization as a departure point, I propose a new
"scape," the virtual moneyscape. Moneyscapes are conceived of as complemen-
tary to "financescapes." Financescapes relate to a global capital structure that

becomes "a more mysterious, rapid and difficult landscape to follow than ever before" (Appadurai 1996: 34). Moneyscapes refer to the dimension of contemporary lives bound up with money whether as an economic factor or as a cultural factor. This chapter thus aims to contribute to strengthening the attention paid to the "cultural life of money" by presenting a proposal seeking to grasp the relevance of virtual environments, particularly of virtual worlds such as Second Life, to the emergence of this new virtual moneyscape because "the growth of the Internet, and of the shared virtual reality spaces within it, has enabled new choices in terms of what kind of physical beings we inhabit" (Castronova 2003: 7).

Second Life is a tridimensional social platform attracting a large number of users – with around 31 million registered users. Launched in 2003, developed by Linden Lab, the site assembles the main characteristics of virtual worlds: a tridimensional digital setting where users from all over the world run avatars to interact in real time and develop diversified social networks. One of Second Life's main components is produced content: within this digital environment residents are active contributors to in-world development, and only one per cent of the content available was actually created by Linden Lab (Ondrejka 2006: 163). Players not only contribute to constructing space – buildings, green spaces and general surroundings, but also to social development – institutions and groups that contribute to the in-world economy, culture, identity, and hierarchical organizations. Nowadays, within this virtual world, one may do almost everything one can do in first life: go for a walk in different tourist spots, practice sports, play games, go to the theatre, cinema or a concert, attend conferences or classes, talk with friends or meet new people, or even have a job. Another characteristic that makes this virtual world different is its economic system. The majority of massive multiplayer online role-playing games contain economic systems – players need "money" (usually designated as gold) to be able to buy the artifacts empowering their avatars. What makes Second Life different is not that it runs its own economic system or even its own currency, but the possibility of exchanging its virtual money for "real" money and vice versa.[1] This distinguishing feature makes its economy almost as complex as its first-life counterpart. To contribute to a better understanding of the role of Second Life in our "flowing global culture," the present chapter is organized into three sections: 1. Money and cultural identity; 2. Virtual lives, virtual economies; 3. Second Life: the emergence of a

---

1 The exchange process is similar to that for "real value currencies." Linden Lab operates an exchange platform – Lindex, enabling the exchange of first life currencies for Linden Dollars and vice versa. In the majority of virtual worlds (including immersive multiplayer game environments) the virtual currency is not exchanged but bought as an object; and we commonly find these currencies for sale on platforms like eBay.

new moneyscape. In the first section, we analyze the relationship between money and cultural identity while, in the second, we consider the impact of virtualization on our lives. In the final section we discuss Second Life's development and its potential as an alternative economic dimension. The last section also features economic statistical data released by Linden Lab between 2006 and 2011 and available at the platform's website – http://secondlife.com.

1 Money and cultural identity

Thus far, some research has focused only on money from the economic point of view and ignores its social facet. Bearing in mind the advent of common currencies like the Euro, understanding money's role as a feature of cultural identity proves especially pertinent. The Euro is considered a relevant example of the cultural dimension of money, whether as a currency around which a transnational community is currently being built, or as a key factor that is eroding the same community. Money represents part of daily capitalist interactions and plays a major role in shaping the everyday rituals of social interaction. The economic crisis experienced by some Eurozone member states has led to questioning the Euro's role as a factor fostering social cohesion. Nevertheless, as Kennedy proposed in 2012: "solidarity can certainly transform many parts of the [European Union's] cultural sense. Indeed, it may be the only thing to save the cultural integrity and social coherence of the EU." (Kennedy 2012: 34)

Most national currencies came to the fore in the nineteenth century. They resulted both from the establishment of nation-states, and from the need to strengthen identity bonds in order to consolidate "imagined communities" (Helleiner 2003). National currencies rapidly became part of daily life and money became "a medium through which social consensus, social integration and territorial borders are produced and reproduced" (Gilbert and Helleiner 1999: 40). The creation of currencies connected peoples and territories as well as nations and states while also contributing to the invention of tradition since money represents the most universal form of public imagery (Hobsbawm and Ranger 1983: 281). Besides this characteristic of territorial limitation, a currency is part of a community's cultural identity – national currencies reflect tangible symbols of a common identity.

With the Euro, a cultural change took place as several European countries replaced their national currencies for a common European one, symbolizing a collective European identity. The introduction of a common currency linking 19 of the 28 European countries represents the consolidation of the European Union (EU). Symbols are a key dimension of the EU's affirmation as a community. The flag, anthem, motto, currency and commemorative holiday are the signs chosen to represent the union between different states in the same continent. Should one add to this set of symbols the political meetings between EU members and the democratic rights of its citizens, we may realize that the EU is a broad imagined community (Anderson 1999). The common currency may thus be perceived as a daily remembrance of the bond between citizens and the state and as a factor reinforcing the sense of belonging to a common social entity despite the different cultural roots of its members.

The example of the Euro as a factor contributing for the establishment of a community helps grasp the impact that emerging virtual currencies, such as the Linden Dollar – Second Life's micro-currency, hold for the development of virtual economies leading up to the emergence of virtual moneyscapes.

2 Virtual lives, virtual economies

> Before the advent of the avatar, there was
> only one world to live in, Earth, and only one
> avatar to inhabit there, the Earthly body. The
> recent emergence of virtual worlds besides
> Earth has vastly expanded the range of choices
> regarding one's own physical being and the
> space which it inhabits. (Castronova 2003: 32)

The development of the Internet and the growth in the number of its users have proven very important in bringing reality closer to the fictional technological worlds and this has as well had fictional resonances, as a recurring theme in both literature and cinema since the beginning of the twenty-first century. The Internet's development alongside the rise of web 2.0, or the social web, led to the growth of social platforms. Recent years have seen the launch of several social applications. Their shared goal involves inducing interaction, collaboration and sharing among their users. Blogs, podcasts, wikis, social networking sites (Facebook, MySpace), content sharing networks (YouTube, Flickr) and massively multiplayer online social games (Second Life, Habbo Hotel) are among the most popular web 2.0 applications (Pascu 2008).

Social games, such as Second Life, are one of the characteristic applications of web 2.0. They are a sub-genre of massively multiplayer online games. These games have revolutionized not only the video games industry but the entertainment industry in general. The first online multiplayer games were remarkable in how they allowed players from all over the world to get together and play in a shared digital space. The virtualization of social space had a renowned impact on the entertainment industry and the number of networked players has grown rapidly. However, the goal of these games was similar to the majority of games – to win, to be the most powerful, and eventually the most feared.

The distinctiveness of massive multiplayer online social games within the scope of the genre rests on their ability to promote live experiences. The challenge is not to become the first to achieve the end and win the game but rather to live out an experience through an avatar,[2] a character created for this alternative space. This kind of game may take place in varied settings and offer different possibilities, but there is one factor in common – they recreate new worlds, new social spaces, second lives. One example of the new virtual experience economy fostered by this technology is a virtual space created to provide an alternative dimension for social interaction – Second Life. This platform – like other virtual worlds – is often called a metaverse, meaning a virtual world where humans represented by avatars interact in a tridimensional digital space.

Virtual spaces like Second Life open up the scope for virtual representation in a different dimension – the cyberspace. Through these web-based platforms, participants enter into an alternative sphere for the development of social lives, a sphere characterized by the de-materialization or the de-physicalization of social interaction (Knights et al. 2007: 750). Whilst the first multiplayer environments appeared in the 1970s, as soon as the Internet became available for personal computers the number of these platforms increased rapidly. Nowadays, there are more than 50 three-dimensional virtual environments. Edward Castronova terms such virtual spaces "synthetic worlds", i.e. "worlds that are created completely by design and live only within computers are synthetic, and the world of earth, air, fire, water and blood that we've inherited from our forebears is real" (Castronova 2007: 7). Second Life is one of the most complex synthetic worlds available with platform players called residents who actively participate in inworld's development – their world and their imagination.[3] Residents are represented by avatars, humanoid figures that may be totally personalized or may alternatively shed their original human look. Through these avatars, residents develop an active and complex social network: "The avatar mediates our self in the virtual world: we inhabit it, we drive it, we receive all of our sensory information

---

2 The etymology of avatar derives from the Sanskrit avatārah meaning the descending of a divinity from paradise to Earth. According to Boellstorff (2008) avatar means the incarnation of a Hindu deity (particularly Vishnu), nevertheless "while 'avatar' [...] historically referred to incarnation – a movement from virtual to actual – with respect to online worlds it connotes the opposite movement from actual to virtual, a decarnation or invirtualization" (Boellstorff 2008: 128).
3 This is in fact Second Life's slogan.

about the world from its standpoint" (Castronova 2003: 5). Avatars become the medium that enable virtual representation.

Second Life's development level has improved so much since its launch that residents may now do almost everything one can do in first life with ever greater exploration of the possibilities offered by this platform. The growth of resident interest in in-world activities has also encouraged economic development. Nonetheless, this interest was also promoted by Second Life's intellectual property rules, which define how everybody owns the intellectual property of whatever they create. This innovative right helped to stimulate the economy and residents began investing time and money in this virtual place. Linden Lab's business model then is based on the premise: residents pay for the land, they may build whatever they want, they may charge visitors for activities or products, and at the end take the Linden Dollars earned and change them back for "first-life" money.

The scope for exchanging Linden Dollars for material currencies represents one of the characteristics that made Second Life's economic activity so prominent – an average of US$30 million are traded monthly through LindeX.[4] This volume of transactions makes Second Life one of the largest user-generated virtual economies.

3 Second Life:
The emergence of a new moneyscape

Nowadays, Second Life is not the same platform as that launched in June 2003. It evolved and became an alternative social dimension. In order to understand how Linden Lab's policies for this virtual world influence the development of its economic dimension, I identify three key moments in Second Life's history for analysis: the launch of LindeX in 2006, the prohibition on gambling in 2007, and the Xstreet acquisition in 2009.

The LindeX is Linden Lab's currency exchange. Through this service, residents are able to buy and sell Linden Dollars available to residents on the platform's website[5] or in several in-world places.[6] This service allows Linden Lab to

---

4 Data available at <http://community.secondlife.com/t5/Featured-News/bg p/blog_feature_news/label-name/economy>. Amount of Linden Dollars exchanged in the third quarter of 2011.
5 This is only available to registered users.

control the micro-currency value and the Linden Dollar has been a stable currency since its launch. The prohibition on gambling also contributed to better control over the Linden Dollar. Until 2007, gambling was legal and had become an important activity to its economy. However, following the 2007 US gambling law, Linden Lab forbade all types of gambling games within Second Life:

> While Linden Lab does not offer an online gambling service, Linden Lab and Second Life Residents must comply with state and federal laws applicable to regulated online gambling, even when both operators and players of the games reside outside of the US. And, because there are a variety of conflicting gambling regulations around the world we have chosen to restrict gambling in Second Life as described in a revised policy which is posted in the Knowledge Base[7] under "Policy Regarding Wagering in Second Life."[8]

After this decision, economic development slowed, before recovering to previous levels just a few months later, – residents began to invest in land and traditional economic activity gained importance in this virtual space. At this time, the almost infinite Second Life capacity of creation began to be explored by residents. Nowadays, there are some very lucrative activities taking place within this virtual world; one involves the creation of objects and scripts enriching the virtual experience. Commerce became such a major activity that, in early 2009, Linden Lab bought one of the most important Second Life product shopping web sites, XStreet.[9] This acquisition made commercial transactions among residents much easier.

Through Second Life's development process, Linden Lab took efforts to present its synthetic world as appealing in order to compete for audiences with game worlds such as World of Warcraft or EverQuest. One of Second Life's major strengths has been its economic stability and solidity. Throughout the years – and because of the aforementioned adjustments – the Linden Dollar stabilized and became perceived as the official in-world currency. Users established close relationships with it and the monetary unit now gets used for all kind of transactions. Since the foundation of LindeX, Linden Lab has been able to guarantee its stability and the Linden Dollar's exchange value has since remained stable – at approximately L$250 to the US Dollar.[10] This constancy was understood as an

---

6 There are LindeX kiosks at several in-world locations, as well as ATM points. Both of them have the same purpose, but configuring them in different formats allows two different first life activities to be recognized – money exchange and cash withdrawals.

7 From <http://wiki.secondlife.com/wiki/Knowledge_Base>.

8 Announcement available at: <https://blogs.secondlife.com/community/features/blog/2007/07/26/wagering-in-second-life-new-policy>.

9 XStreet was replaced by Second Life Market Place in 2010.

10 Data available at LindeX (only accessible to registered users).

invitation to investment and I would suggest that residents are actually transforming the opportunity for a second life into a virtual representation of their
first life – while in-world they are in a synthetic world but still display 'real' economic behavior (Castronova 2005).

The number of hours and amount of money residents invest in Second Life reflect its level of development. For the period between 2006 and the first quarter of
2011, Linden Lab released statistical data on its in-world economy,[11] which allowed
residents to follow the evolution of the in-world economic system. In the second
quarter, 2006 users spent 10 million hours in-world. This number increased through
to the second quarter of 2009 and tailed away from the third quarter from 126 to 104
million hours in the first quarter of 2011 (see Chart 1):

Hours spent in-world

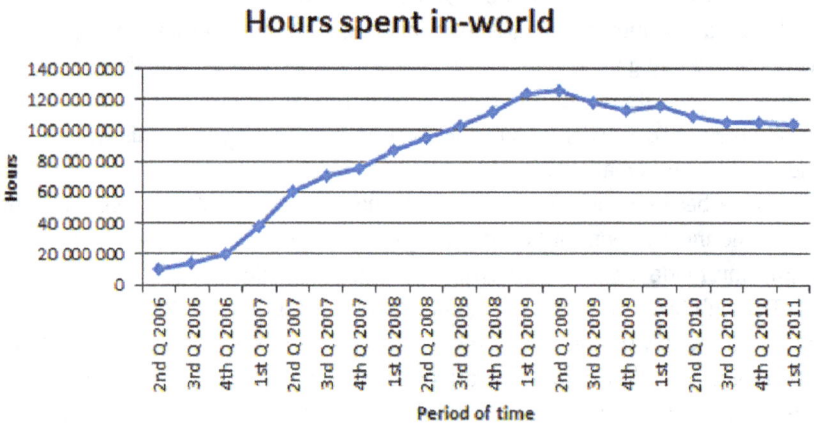

Chart 1: Hours spent in-world (2006 – 2009)

During the first three quarters of 2006, the number of users with repeated
logins stood at around 58,000, while in the same period of 2009 this number
had risen to approximately 731,000, before reaching 794,000 in the first quarter
of 2011 (see Chart 2):

When one compares the second quarter of 2006 to the same period of 2010,
we find that residents had transacted over 16 million Linden dollars between

---

11 From the second quarter of 2010, Linden Lab stopped publishing data concerning the land
auctions and transactions among residents before then ceasing the regular publication of detailed statistical data in 2011.

Logged in users

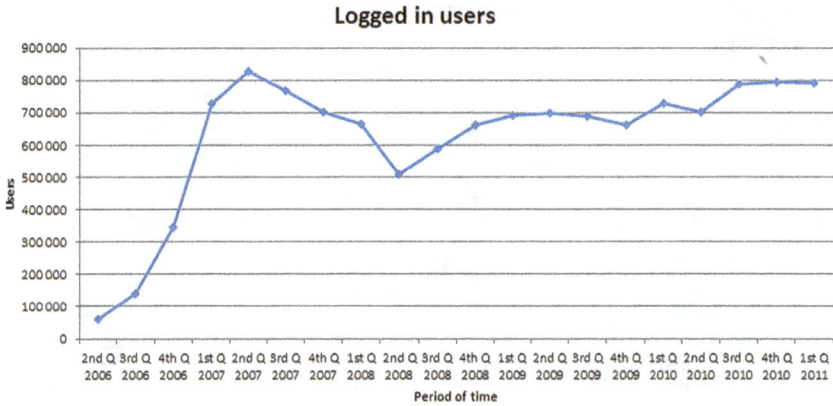

Chart 2: Average number of users with repeat logins

them, and that this number increased to over 100 million over the same period (see Chart 3).

Transactions among users

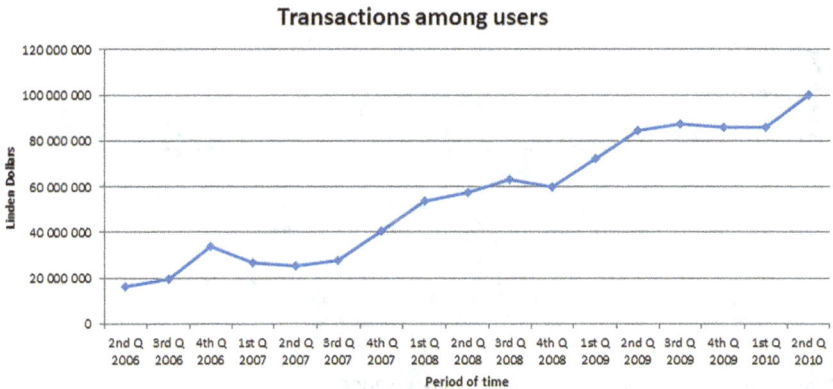

Chart 3: US$ transacted among users

The amount of virtual currency exchanged in LindeX increased from US$3 million in the second quarter of 2006 to US$31.5 million in the same period of 2011 (see Chart 4); and Second Life Market sales increased from L$28 million in 2006 (when it did not belong to Linden Lab) to L$956 million by the end of 2010 (see Chart 5).

Currency exchanged through LindeX

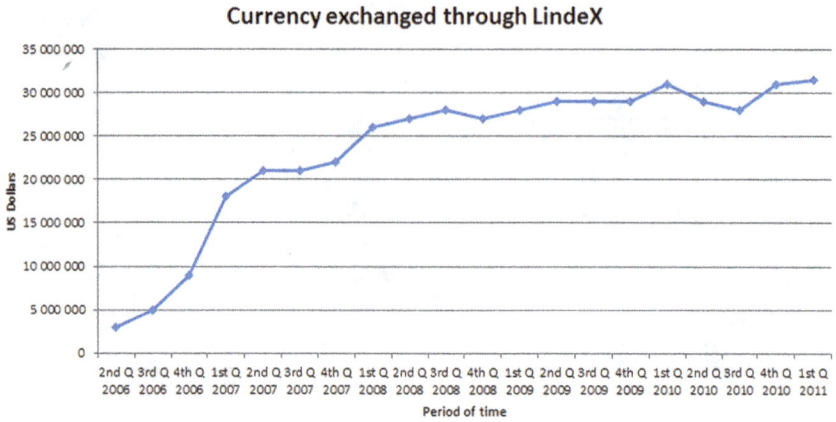

Chart 4: Volume of US$ exchanged through LindeX (2006 – 2009)

SL Market sales

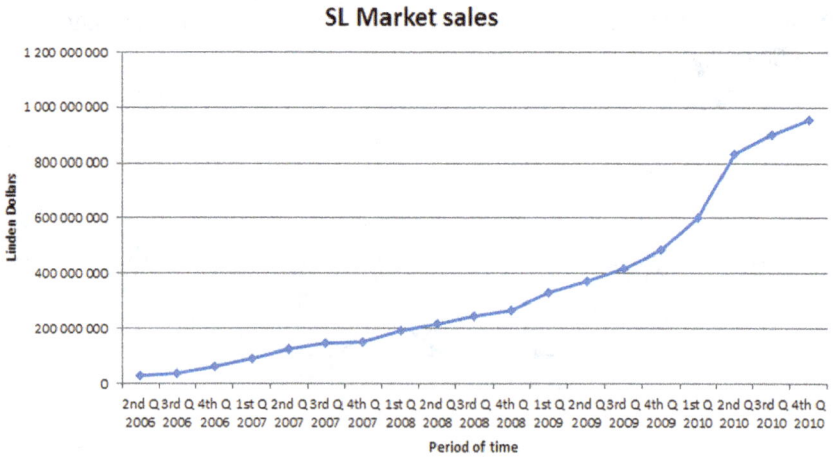

Chart 5: Volume of Xstreet sales (Linden Dollars) (2006 – 2009)

The investment in virtual land (see Chart 6), on the other hand, increased through to the third quarter of 2007 but fell away after the gambling prohibition. From the end of 2008 until the beginning of 2010, the acres of land auctioned remain stable but at lower rates. I consider that the decrease derives from the reduction of land plots made available by Linden Lab and as the acres auctioned decreased, land sales among residents increased – increasing from near 192 million square meters in the second quarter of 2006 to 366 million square meters in the same period of 2010. Land seems to represent a stable market among residents and may be a profitable business. However, in spite of being lucrative for residents, this still remains advantageous to Linden Lab as residents must upgrade their accounts to paid ones – known as Premium accounts – to be able to buy land.

Acres auctioned by Linden Lab

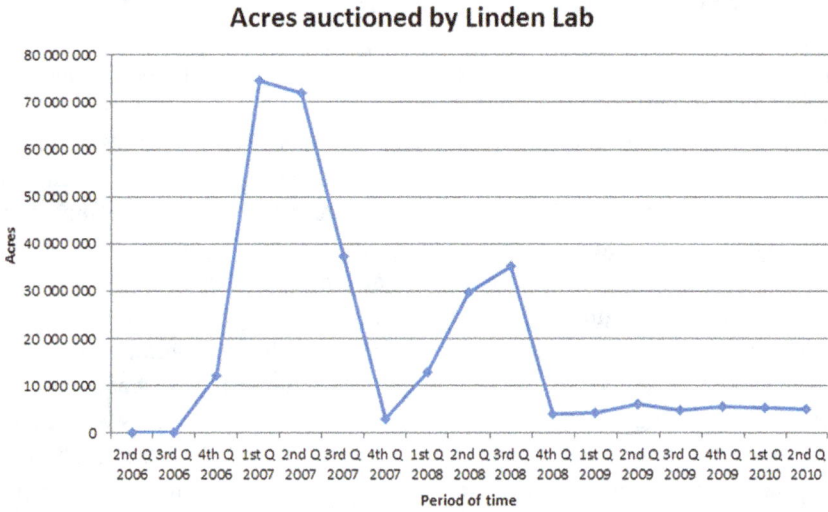

Chart 6: Land area owned by residents (m²) (2007 – 2009)[a)a)]For the analysis of the land area owned by residents we focused on data from 2007 to 2009 because this information is not available for 2006.

These data show that Second Life continues to grow but at a much slower pace than between 2006 and 2007. I propose that there are two main influences for this slow down: the 2008 financial crisis – still affecting the world economy, and the growth of social networking sites, particularly Twitter and Facebook, which provide different characteristics but are certainly easier to use – users do not have to learn to manage an avatar and these networks interconnect users mainly with people they already know from face-to-face interaction.[12] In fact, the stability of Second Life's economy since 2008 may be understood as re-

---

12 Another difference is the fact that these social networking sites do not contribute as much to connections between unknown people; while in Second Life people from all over the world get connected and interact for different reasons – whether just to socialize or to carry out common projects. In virtual worlds, there is a deeper sense of ownership and habitation.

sulting from the engagement of users with this digital environment. In fact, Second Life seems increasingly perceived as an alternative space for engaging in economic activities as it has none of the contingencies of first life and puts forward a new set of opportunities.[13]

Conclusion

Second Life's prominent economic development across different dimensions bears consequences at two levels of the economy: in-world and "out-world," meaning the second- and first-life economies, respectively. In terms of the in-world economy, an increase in monetary investment is observed, residents are exchanging more "real-value" money for virtual money, and thus stimulating transactions among them, which ends up influencing the *produsage* of digital content and services. On the other hand, at the level of the first life economy, residents are exchanging more Linden Dollars for currencies that have a "real" market value. This means that there is a higher volume of virtually produced money entering the "actual" economy and understanding the impact that this new economic dimension holds contains significant relevance. I would like to suggest that the economic capital produced inside virtual worlds results from the emergence of an alternative social dimension. People are cultivating new and existing social networks in cyberspace generating the rise of a new social-economic dimension constituting a "virtual mediascape."

Second Life's importance as a new moneyscape is growing and, despite the world economic crisis, residents and first life companies continue to invest in-world and to exchange significant amounts of first-life currencies for Linden dollars, and vice versa. This phenomenon might be understood as the growth of a parallel economic dimension running its own micro-currency and consequently its own economic system.

Despite the level of uncertainty still associated with virtual worlds, Second Life's economic data demonstrates how the level of trust in this alternative dimension is still growing. Hence, while this platform may not itself be the future of virtual moneyscapes, Second Life does help to understand what the future of the world economy might hold alongside the cultural life of de-materialized money.

---

13 There are research findings showing how tridimensional virtual social spaces are now used as alternative economic spheres (see Castronova 2002 and 2006, Dibbell 2007, Malaby 2006).

Works cited

Anderson, Benedict (1999 [1983]) *Imagined Communities* (London: Verso).

Appadurai, Arjun (1996) *Modernity at large: Cultural Dimensions of Globalization* (Minneapolis: University of Minnesota Press).

Boellstorff, Tom (2008) *Coming of Age in Second Life. An Anthropologist Explores the Virtually Human* (Princeton: Princeton University Press).

Castronova, Edward (2002) "On Virtual Economies," *CESifo Working Paper Series* 752. Available at <http://ssrn.com/abstract=338500> (accessed 10 June 2009).

Castronova, Edward (2003) "Theory of the Avatar," *CESifo Working Paper Series* 863. Available at <http://ssrn.com/abstract=385103> (accessed 10 June 2009).

Castronova, Edward (2006) *Synthetic Worlds: The Business and Culture of Online Games.* (Chicago: Chicago University Press).

Castronova, Edward (2007) *Exodus to the Virtual World: How Online Fun is Changing Reality* (NY: Palgrave Macmillan).

Dibbell, Julian (2007) *Play money. Or, How I Quit My Day Job and Made Millions Trading Virtual Loot (*NY: Basic Books).

Gilbert, Emily and Eric Helleiner (1999) *Nation-states and Money: The Past, Present and Future of National Currencies* (London & NY: Routledge).

Helleiner, Eric (2003) *The Making of National Money: Territorial Currencies in Historical Perspective* (Ithaca: Cornell University Press).

Hobsbawm, Eric and Terence O. Ranger (eds) (1983) *The Invention of Tradition* (Cambridge: Cambridge University Press).

Kennedy, Michael D. (2012) "Cultural formations of the European Union: Integration, enlargement, nation and crisis," in *European Identity and Culture: Narratives of Transnational Belonging*, ed. Rebecca Friedman and Markus Thiel (Aldershot: Ashgate), 17–51.

Knights, David, F. Noble, T. Vurdubakis, and H. Willmott (2007) "Electronic Cash and the Virtual Marketplace: Reflections on a Revolution Postponed," *Organization* 14.6, 747–768.

Malaby, Thomas M. (2006) "Parlaying Value: Capital in and beyond Virtual Worlds," *Games & Culture* 1.2, 141–162.

Miller, Riel, Wolfgang Michalski and Barrie Stevens (2002) "The Future of Money," in *The Future of Money* (Paris: OECD Books), 11–30.

Ondrejka, Cory (2006) "Escaping the Gilded Cage: User-Created Content and Building the Metaverse," in *The State of Play: Law, Games, and Virtual Worlds*, ed. Jack M. Balkin and Beth Simone Noveck (NY and London: New York University Press),158–179.

Pascu, Corina (2008) "An Empirical Analysis of the Creation, Use and Adoption of Social Computing Applications," *IPTS Exploratory Research on Social Computing.* Available <http://ftp.jrc.es/EURdoc/JRC46431.pdf> (accessed 28 July 2009).

Simmel, Georg (1982) *The Philosophy of Money* (Boston: Routledge & Kegan Paul)

Simmel, Georg (1991) "Money in Modern Culture," *Theory, Culture & Society* 8, 17–31.

Zelizer, Viviana A. (2011) *Economic Lives: How Culture Shapes the Economy* (Princeton: Princeton University Press).

Coda: **The Art of Giving**

Emílio Rui Vilar
Money and Philanthropy:
The Idea of Money

In illo tempore, when I was studying Law at Coimbra University, our text book on *Money and Credit* began with the following line: "Strange as it may seem, money has something in common with an umbrella as both are defined by their use". However, in the case of money – which ranges from a tool of exchange to a unit of account, or from greed to prodigality – such a wide range of usages renders its definition much more complex than that of an umbrella.

As money is the most common medium of exchange, giving it without expecting something in return might almost be seen as unnatural. Almsgiving and charity, however, have always been a permanent feature of our existence.

In 1201, Maimonides, the Jewish philosopher known as the doctor from Cordoba, codified the Eight Degrees of Charity, the highest being "And you will give strength to the resident alien, so he may live among you," meaning that we should empower the recipient of charity until he does not need to ask for help. This Eighth Degree already embodies the main challenge of modern philanthropy: helping to solve the causes of social problems rather than diluting their symptoms.

1 The idea of philanthropy

Around a century ago, in 1909, John D. Rockefeller, the founder of Standard Oil Company, wrote *The Difficult Art of Giving*, from which comes the following quotation: "The man will be most successful who confers the greatest service on the world."

Twenty years before, Andrew Carnegie, the founder of the Carnegie Steel Company, had written two articles in the *North American Review*, that later became known as The Gospel of Wealth, in which he states: "The man who dies thus rich dies disgraced." These two men had something in common; they had accumulated a gigantic amount of wealth, due to their entrepreneurial skills and were willing to spend it on behalf of humankind.

More than one century later, after these rather odd statements from two of the wealthiest men of their time, we could reasonably argue about their true underlying altruistic motivations or intentions. In any case, we can rightfully appoint Rockefeller and Carnegie as the fathers of modern philanthropy, as opposed to charity or almsgiving. Both helped shape American society during the twentieth century and continue to influence the generations of businessmen who decide to give their fortunes to philanthropic aims or institutions, either while living or after their death. The European counterpart, although American in origin, might be Henry Wellcome, who in his will stated that the pharmaceutical company dividends should be used for "the advancement of research work bearing upon medicine, surgery, chemistry, physiology, bacteriology, therapeutics, medical material, pharmacy and allied subjects." As one of Wellcome's biographers points out, Wellcome's will was "the first example in Britain of a bequest by which the profits from a great company are permanently dedicated to the advancement of knowledge for the benefit of mankind."

Microsoft's Bill Gates or Berkshire Hathaway's Warren Buffett, who together account for almost US$50 billion donated to philanthropy, are just two of the most recent examples of what we might call the not too Discreet Charm of Philanthropy or perhaps the appeal of Giving Back to Society. Former President Bill Clinton, with his annual Clinton Global Initiative (<www.clintonglobalinitiative. org>) and the billions of dollars of "Commitments for Action" represents the convening capital for the philanthropy of some individuals.

Carnegie, despite his controversial assertions, had an interesting view on his accumulated wealth, which he considered as belonging to the community, and saw himself only as an entitled temporary administrator for the common good. Yet, he advised against indiscriminate charity and believed that it was mandatory for wealthy men to carefully select the best philanthropic usages to the surplus of which they were mere trustees. Carnegie bequeathed 90 % of his fortune before his death "to promote the advancement and diffusion of knowledge and understanding" (mission of the Carnegie Corporation of New York).

Philanthropy, however, is not anything new. It is indeed a universal virtue, deeply rooted in western culture since ancient Greece, the term meaning, etymologically and literally, the love for mankind, the same love which unfairly bounded Aeschylus's Prometheus. Today's equivalent of modern foundations, one of the most privileged philanthropic arms, has existed in Europe for approximately 2,500 years in the form of long-lasting endowments established for educational, religious or other general interest purposes. As one American scholar noted, Plato set aside funds to sustain the Academy after his death, which lasted for more than 1,000 years; Epicurus wrote a will leaving properties that supported his school for some 600 years; and Theophrastus made a bequest to maintain the Lyceum of Aristotle. The medieval "monti di pietà," in Italy, or the Portuguese Houses of Mercy, are among these traditions of endowment establishments for philanthropic aims that survived through to the twenty-first century.

2 Several ways to achieve a goal

Large-gift philanthropy or the endowment of foundations, whether by individuals or by companies, is not, however, the only way to embrace our love for humankind. From giving time in voluntary actions to pro-bono activities, there are plenty of options to alleviate our philanthropic aspirations or altruistic desires.

In this regard, philanthropy, which we might simplistically translate as doing good, links directly to ethics, which we might, in turn, define as being good. Nevertheless, the relationship between philanthropy and ethics proves rather complex. We might state that philanthropy should not be neutral and may necessarily involve acts of self-denial and caring for others with evident generosity and altruism, which brings us again to the question of motivation and the underlying intentions.

When appraising the significance and impact of philanthropic activities of thoughtful agents, should we accept the raw consequences of the acts or should we assess the true *ex-ante* motivations? I do not wish to elaborate more on this speculative approach, but I do believe that as long as the philanthropic act has a positive outcome in someone's life we should disregard whatever triggered the individuals to behave philanthropically. Could we apply this rationale either to individual giving or to the more modern practices of corporate social responsibility?

3 The market value of virtue

The corporate citizenship concept, linked to the development of corporate governance and self-regulation, does raise some very interesting and different questions as opposed to individual responsibility towards society. In general terms, corporate social responsibility relates to how companies conduct themselves in terms of sustainability and in relation to their "stakeholders" (workers, consumers, suppliers, the community in which they operate or even future generations), as opposed to the main executive responsibilities towards the "shareholders," paying dividends and adding value.

Although corporate social responsibility could be seen by the majority as an axiomatic duty, this is far from the consensus and the current crisis has recently brought back some of the old fears and attacks from the most skeptical about these widespread practices of modern companies.

Milton Friedman, in an iconic article for *The New York Sunday Times* on 13 September 1970, stated: "The social responsibility of business is to increase profits," in a formula that still echoes nowadays when defining corporate social responsibility: "the business of business is business." The key to solving the dilemma between increasing company profits and its corporate social responsibility is that this must be directly assumed by its shareholders as the owners of the company and those entitled to define its strategy and goals.

4 The giving formula

In classical economic theory, the income of an entity or individual, within a specified time frame, equals consumption plus savings. My suggestion is that a third denominator should be included in this well-known formula: giving. I strongly believe that giving back to society in a philanthropic sense is not only a constant moral imperative but also signifies the full assumption of the responsibilities both corporations and citizens share in the present social contract. In the end, we should seek the "société de la fraternité," as proposed by Jacques Attali (Attali 2009) , in which each finds her/his pleasure in the happiness of the other and not in the market value of goods.

I would like to stress, however, that this new element of the income index should, as I mentioned earlier, demand a qualitative approach towards the eradication of the causes of social problems and not the alleviation of its symptoms.

5 The philanthropic arm

In the foundation world, when facing the complexity and dimension of today's problems, whether global or local, and the shortage of resources for addressing them, the question of impact and effectiveness in addressing social issues is taken very seriously. Furthermore, this also prompts foundations and civil society at large into immediate and creative action involving recourse to partnerships or the replication model.

In fact, foundations should concentrate their efforts on convening others and on testing new projects and programs that might then be replicated by other public and private agents. In addition, as learning organizations, foundations must be able to evaluate, monitor and correct their own mistakes while still trying out new approaches or solutions.

Philanthropy requires training and adequate professional skills and, in recent years, became a topic of academic research centers. New formula are constantly being coined to reflect different practices in the field, from Philanthrocapitalism to Catalytic Philanthropy or Philanthropic Terrain, which may represent new forms of intervention or simply be conceptualizations of old-school approaches. However, in order to avoid empty rhetoric, I believe that foundations must start by being fully aware of their stewardship responsibilities and by being capable of demonstrating that only on-going action can further their missions and overcome the intrinsic limitations of non-profit, public-good activities.

Philanthropy and foundations very modestly accept that they alone cannot solve the world's most pressing problems. Nevertheless, they certainly still do represent part of the solution and for this reason governments should recognize and encourage their work.

It is a common belief that money cannot buy happiness, but the money of a few, if well spent, can surely contribute to the happiness of many.

Works cited

Alliance Magazine 14 1, March 2009.

Attali, Jacques (ed) (2009) *Le sens des choses* (Paris: Robert Laffont).

Burlingame, Dwight F. (ed) (2004) *Philanthropy in America, A Comprehensive Historical Encyclopedia*, vol. II and III (Santa Barbara: ABC-Clio).

Edwards, Michael (2008) *Just Another Emperor, The Myths and Realities of Philanthrocapitalism* (London: Demos).

MacDonald, Norine and Luc Tayart de Borms (eds) (2008) *Philanthropy in Europe. A Rich Past, A Promising Future* (London: Alliance Publishing Trust).

Ribeiro, José Joaquim Teixeira (1949) *Introdução ao Estudo da Moeda* (Coimbra: Atlântida).

Rockefeller, John D. (1909) *Random Reminiscences of Men and Events* (NY: Doubleday). Project Gutenberg <http://www.gutenberg.org/files/17090/17090-h/17090-h.htm#CHAP TER_VI> (accessed 1 January 2014).

Smith, James Allen (2004) "European Foundations," in *Burlingame I*: 144–146.

Contributors

Editors

Isabel Capeloa Gil studied in Lisbon, Munich and Chicago and is Professor of Cultural Theory at the Catholic University of Portugal and Honorary Fellow at the Institute of Germanic and Romance Studies (U. London). Her main research areas include intermedia studies, gender studies as well as representations of war and conflict. Her work has been published in Portuguese, English, German, French and Spanish. She is the author of several books and collected editions of essays, amongst them *Landscapes of Memory. Envisaging the Past/Remembering the Future* (2004), *Fleeting, Floating, Flowing: Water Writing and Modernity* (2008) and *Visual Literacy. On the Disquiet of Images* (Lisbon, 2011). Her most recent book is *Hazardous Future: Disaster, Representation and the Assessment of Risk*(co-ed. With Christoph Wulf for De Gruyter). Isabel Gil is the director of The Lisbon Consortium, a doctoral collaborative network between UCP and the Lisbon creative industries cluster. She has been Vice-Rector for Research at UCP since 2012.

Helena Gonçalves Silva (PhD, University of London) is Associate Professor of German Literature and Cultural Theory at the University of Lisbon. She was also a visiting Professor at the University of Brasilia. Presently she is a Senior Member of the Research Centre for Communication and Culture at the Catholic University of Portugal. Her main research areas include European literature, cultural theory, as well as representations of the city and of memory. In addition, she is the author of *A Poética da Cidade* (2003), and co-editor of *Metrópoles na Pós-Modernidade* (2004), *Conflict Memory Transfers and the Reshaping of Europe* (2010) and *Intellectual Topographies and the Making of Citizenship* (2011).

Authors

Ana Margarida Abrantes studied English and German at the Universities of Aveiro, Essen and Innsbruck. She holds her MA Degree in Cognitive Linguistics and a PhD in German Language and Literature, which she completed in 2008 at the Catholic University of Portugal. Between 2006 and 2009 she was visiting scholar at the Center for Semiotics of Aarhus University and at the Department of Cognitive Science at Case Western Reserve University, (USA). In 2006 she joined the Research Center for Communication and Culture at the Catholic University of Portugal, where she is currently one of the senior researchers of the research line *Translating Europe across the Ages*. Her research fields include the study of cognition and culture, cognitive linguistics, cognitive poetics and German studies. She published *Meaning and Mind. A Cognitive Approach to Peter Weiss' Prose Work* (2010) and *Alemão: Uma Língua para a Europa?* (2004) and co-edited the volumes *Cognition and Culture. An Interdisciplinary Dialogue* (2011) and *Cognição Linguagem e Literatura. Contributos para uma Poética Cognitiva* (2005).

Cátia Ferreira, holds her PhD in Communication Sciences from the Catholic University of Portugal (UCP), with a thesis titled "*Second Life:* Representation and Remediation of Social Space." She is a researcher at CECC (Research Centre for Communication and Culture) at UCP and an external collaborator at the Centre for Research and Studies in Sociology (ISCTE). Cátia is also as adjunct faculty member at UCP. Her area of research is new media, particularly digital social platforms – virtual worlds and social networking sites, digital games and mobile phones. She is a member of the European research network COST – action 'Transforming Audiences, Transforming Societies'. She is also a member of a two-year research project on digital readership funded by the Calouste Gulbenkian Foundation.

Joyce Goggin is Senior Associate Professor of Literature, Film and New Media at the University of Amsterdam and a contributing member of Amsterdam University College where she served as Head of Studies for the Humanities from 2008 – 2010. Her research focuses on literature, film, painting and new media, approached from an economic perspective. She has recently co-edited a collection of essays entitled "Neo-Victorianism and Feminism: New Approaches" (http://www.neovictorianstudies.com/contents.htm) with Tara MacDonald; in 2010, she co-edited *The Rise and Reason of Comics and Graphic Literature: Critical Essays on the Form,* with Dan Hassler-Forest. Prof. Goggin is currently writing a book on the entertainment industries in Hollywood and Las Vegas.

Filomena Viana Guarda is Assistant Professor in the Department of German Studies at the University of Lisbon where she teaches German Literature and Culture, Literary Studies and Intercultural Communication. She studied at the Universities of Coimbra (Portugal) and Munich (Germany) and received her PhD from the University of Lisbon (Portugal) in 1998. She is also a member of the Research Centre for Communication and Culture (CECC) at the Portuguese Catholic University where she researches German post-unification and intercultural literature in the context of Culture and Conflict Studies. Her present research interests include the most recent German and Swiss Literatures (after 1990) and the study of History and Postmemory, focusing mainly on third-generation World War II narratives, on the portrayal of the former East Germany (GDR) in literature and film and on the reappearance of the family novel after the turn of the century.

Paulo de Medeiros is Professor of Modern and Contemporary World Literatures, and teaches on the English and Comparative Literary Studies program at the University of Warwick (UK). He was Associate Professor at Bryant College (USA) and Professor at Utrecht University (Netherlands) before moving to Warwick. In 2011–2012 he was Keeley Fellow at Wadham College, Oxford and is currently President of the American Portuguese Studies Association. Current projects include a study on Postimperial Europe.

João César das Neves is Full Professor of Economics at Universidade Católica Portuguesa (UCP). He holds a PhD and a BA in Economics (UCP), an MA in Economics (Universidade Nova of Lisbon, Portugal) and an MA in Operations, Research and System Engineering (Universidade Técnica of Lisbon, Portugal). Currently he is the President of the Scientific Council of Católica Lisbon School of Business and Economics. His research interests are poverty and development, business cycles, Portuguese economic development, medieval economic tought and ethics. He is the author of more than 40 books and a regular pundit in the Portuguese media.

Ansgar Nünning has been Professor of English and American Literature and Cultural Studies at the University of Giessen, Germany since 1996. He is the founding director of the Giessen Graduate School for the Humanities and of the International Graduate Centre for the Study of Culture (GCSC) as well as the academic director of the International PhD Program (IPP) "Literary and Cultural Studies" and a member of the Collaborative Research Centre "Memory Cultures."

Vera Nünning, is Professor of English Philology at Heidelberg University and Principal Investigator of the Cluster Asia and Europe. She has been since 2006 Vice-Rector for International Affairs of Heidelberg University. She has published widely on narratology, the English novel, cultural theory and memory practices. Amongst her publications are *Der Englische Roman des 19. Jahrhunderts* (2003); with Ansgar Nünning, she co-wrote *Konzepte der Kulturwissenschaften: Theoretische Grundlagen, Ansätze, Perspektiven* (2004) and *Erzähltheorie Transgenerisch, Intermedial, Interdisziplinär* (2002), amongst many others.

Alfred Opitz (1943–2014) studied Romance Studies in Mainz and Dijon and obtained his PhD from the University of Marburg in 1975. He lectured in Paris, Stockholm and Nancy and became Professor of German at the New University of Lisbon in 1982. He was an expert in the work of Heinrich Heine and published widely on travel literature, critical theory and intermediality. Prof. Opitz was also an artist and held several solo and collective exhibitions. From 1998 to 2000, he was the President of the Portuguese German Studies Association (APEG).

Vivaldo Andrade dos Santos is Associate Professor in the Department of Spanish and Portuguese at Georgetown University. He is currently the Director of the Portuguese program. He is an expert in Brazilian literature, Latin American avant-garde poetry, and Carlos Drummond de Andrade. He teaches courses in Portuguese language, Brazilian literature, Brazilian popular music and Brazilian cinema.

Márcio Seligmann-Silva is Professor of Literary Theory at UNICAMP in Brazil, as well as a translator and literary critic. He holds a PhD in Comparative Literature from the Freie Universität in Berlin and a Post-Doc from PUC-São Paulo and from the University of Yale. Prof. Seligmann has published extensively on Walter Benjamin, the theory of violence and critical theory.

Teresa Seruya is Full professor in the Department of Germanic Studies at the Arts Faculty of the University of Lisbon, teaching literature and culture in the German language. She also teaches History of Translation and Translation Theory. She is now directing the projects "Intercultural Literature in Portugal 1930 – 2000: a Critical Bibliography", and "Translation and Censorship in Portugal during the Estado Novo Regime" at CECC, UCP's Research Centre for Communication and Culture. Her current research areas include the history of translation in Portugal in the twentieth century and contemporary migration literature in German speaking countries. She has published on literature and culture in the German language, particularly from the twentieth century, the history of Germanic Studies in Portugal and the history of translation in Portugal. A literary translator from German, she translated works by Goethe, Kleist, Leopold von Sacher-Masoch, Döblin, Thomas Mann and Kafka.

Emílio Rui Vilar holds a Law Degree from the University of Coimbra and a Doctorate Honoris Causa from the University of Lisbon (2012). From 2002 to 2012 he was the President of the Board of Directors of the Calouste Gulbenkian Foundation and President of the nomination committee of the European Foundation Centre. Emílio Rui Vilar has a long history of service to the Portuguese State. He served as Minister of Transport and Communications of the 1st Constitutional Government (1976 – 1978) and as Vice-Governor of the Bank of Portugal (1975 – 1984). He has held numerous positions in banking and corporate finance as well as in cultural institutions such as the National S. Carlos Theatre (Lisbon), the Serralves Foundation (Oporto) and the Calouste Gulbenkian Foundation. Emílio Rui Vilar is currently the Chairman and CEO of the Portuguese energy company REN.

Samuel Weber (PhD) is an American philosopher and academic. Professor Weber is one of the leading American thinkers across the disciplines of literary theory, philosophy, and psychoanalysis. He is the Avalon Professor of Humanities at Northwestern University and the Paul de Man Chair at the European Graduate School (EGS). Weber was born in New York and obtained his doctorate from Cornell University in 1960, working with Paul de Man. He is also the Director of Northwestern University's Paris Program in Critical Theory.

Index